STUDY SECRETS COURSE!

Dear Customer,

Struggle with tests? Short on time? Not sure where to even start studying? We have partnered with Mometrix to offer you their Study Secrets Course. Mometrix designed the course to help every student, no matter what study scenario you are in.

This online course guides you through the full process, from study preparation to test day, so you'll be ready to ace your next exam. The Study Secrets Course contains **14 in-depth lessons** that break down top study strategies, **15+ video reviews** that walk you step by step through each topic, and **5 downloadable resources** to help you apply the strategies.

Online Study Secrets Course

Course Features:

- Techniques to Conquer Procrastination
- Steps to Building a Study Plan
- 7 Effective Note-Taking Methods
- Test-Taking Tips
- Memory Techniques and Mnemonics
- 50 Quick and Unusual Study Tips
- How to Create SMART Goals
- How to Study Math
- And much more!

Everyone learns differently, so they have tailored their Study Secrets Course to ensure every learner has what they need to prepare for their upcoming exam or semester.

To purchase this course and start studying, visit them at mometrix.com/university/studysecrets or simply scan this QR code with your smartphone.

If you have any questions or concerns, please contact them at support@mometrix.com.

Sincerely,

 in partnership with

Online Resources & Audiobook Access

Included with your purchase are multiple online resources. This includes all three practice tests in interactive format and this study guide in audiobook format. We also have a convenient study timer to help you manage your time.

Instructions for accessing these resources can be found on the last page of this book.

RBT Exam Study Guide 2025-2026
3 Practice Tests and Prep Book for the Registered Behavioral Technician Certification [Includes Detailed Answer Explanations]

Lydia Morrison

Copyright © 2025 by TPB Publishing

All rights reserved. No part of this publication may be reproduced, distributed, or transmitted in any form or by any means, including photocopying, recording, or other electronic or mechanical methods, without the prior written permission of the publisher, except in the case of brief quotations embodied in critical reviews and certain other noncommercial uses permitted by copyright law.

Written and edited by TPB Publishing.

TPB Publishing is not associated with or endorsed by any official testing organization. TPB Publishing is a publisher of unofficial educational products. All test and organization names are trademarks of their respective owners. Content in this book is included for utilitarian purposes only and does not constitute an endorsement by TPB Publishing of any particular point of view.

Interested in buying more than 10 copies of our product? Contact us about bulk discounts:
bulkorders@studyguideteam.com

ISBN 13: 9781637758946

Table of Contents

Welcome -- 1
Quick Overview --- 2
Test-Taking Strategies --- 3
Introduction --- 7
Study Prep Plan for the RBT Test --------------------------------------- 9
Measurement --- 12
   Practice Quiz --- 16
   Answer Explanations --- 17
Assessment -- 18
   Practice Quiz --- 22
   Answer Explanations --- 23
Skill Acquisition --- 24
   Practice Quiz --- 40
   Answer Explanations --- 41
Behavior Reduction -- 42
   Practice Quiz --- 50
   Answer Explanations --- 51
Documenting and Reporting --- 52
   Practice Quiz --- 62
   Answer Explanations --- 63
Professional Conduct and Scope of Practice ---------------------------- 64
   Practice Quiz --- 73
   Answer Explanations --- 74
RBT Practice Test #1 -- 75
Answer Explanations #1 -- 88
RBT Practice Test #2 --- 102

Answer Explanations #2 -- **116**
RBT Practice Test #3 -- **130**
Answer Explanations #3 -- **144**
Online Resources & Audiobook Access -------------------------------------- **159**

Welcome

Dear Reader,

Welcome to your new Test Prep Books study guide! We are pleased that you chose us to help you prepare for your exam. There are many study options to choose from, and we appreciate you choosing us. Studying can be a daunting task, but we have designed a smart, effective study guide to help prepare you for what lies ahead.

Whether you're a parent helping your child learn and grow, a high school student working hard to get into your dream college, or a nursing student studying for a complex exam, we want to help give you the tools you need to succeed. We hope this study guide gives you the skills and the confidence to thrive, and we can't thank you enough for allowing us to be part of your journey.

In an effort to continue to improve our products, we welcome feedback from our customers. We look forward to hearing from you. Suggestions, success stories, and criticisms can all be communicated by emailing us at info@studyguideteam.com.

Sincerely,
Test Prep Books Team

Quick Overview

As you draw closer to taking your exam, effective preparation becomes more and more important. Thankfully, you have this study guide to help you get ready. Use this guide to help keep your studying on track and refer to it often.

This study guide contains several key sections that will help you be successful on your exam. The guide contains tips for what you should do the night before and the day of the test. Also included are test-taking tips. Knowing the right information is not always enough. Many well-prepared test takers struggle with exams. These tips will help equip you to accurately read, assess, and answer test questions.

A large part of the guide is devoted to showing you what content to expect on the exam and to helping you better understand that content. In this guide are practice test questions so that you can see how well you have grasped the content. Then, answer explanations are provided so that you can understand why you missed certain questions.

Don't try to cram the night before you take your exam. This is not a wise strategy for a few reasons. First, your retention of the information will be low. Your time would be better used by reviewing information you already know rather than trying to learn a lot of new information. Second, you will likely become stressed as you try to gain a large amount of knowledge in a short amount of time. Third, you will be depriving yourself of sleep. So be sure to go to bed at a reasonable time the night before. Being well-rested helps you focus and remain calm.

Be sure to eat a substantial breakfast the morning of the exam. If you are taking the exam in the afternoon, be sure to have a good lunch as well. Being hungry is distracting and can make it difficult to focus. You have hopefully spent lots of time preparing for the exam. Don't let an empty stomach get in the way of success!

When travelling to the testing center, leave earlier than needed. That way, you have a buffer in case you experience any delays. This will help you remain calm and will keep you from missing your appointment time at the testing center.

Be sure to pace yourself during the exam. Don't try to rush through the exam. There is no need to risk performing poorly on the exam just so you can leave the testing center early. Allow yourself to use all of the allotted time if needed.

Remain positive while taking the exam even if you feel like you are performing poorly. Thinking about the content you should have mastered will not help you perform better on the exam.

Once the exam is complete, take some time to relax. Even if you feel that you need to take the exam again, you will be well served by some down time before you begin studying again. It's often easier to convince yourself to study if you know that it will come with a reward!

Test-Taking Strategies

1. Predicting the Answer

When you feel confident in your preparation for a multiple-choice test, try predicting the answer before reading the answer choices. This is especially useful on questions that test objective factual knowledge. By predicting the answer before reading the available choices, you eliminate the possibility that you will be distracted or led astray by an incorrect answer choice. You will feel more confident in your selection if you read the question, predict the answer, and then find your prediction among the answer choices. After using this strategy, be sure to still read all of the answer choices carefully and completely. If you feel unprepared, you should not attempt to predict the answers. This would be a waste of time and an opportunity for your mind to wander in the wrong direction.

2. Reading the Whole Question

Too often, test takers scan a multiple-choice question, recognize a few familiar words, and immediately jump to the answer choices. Test authors are aware of this common impatience, and they will sometimes prey upon it. For instance, a test author might subtly turn the question into a negative, or he or she might redirect the focus of the question right at the end. The only way to avoid falling into these traps is to read the entirety of the question carefully before reading the answer choices.

3. Looking for Wrong Answers

Long and complicated multiple-choice questions can be intimidating. One way to simplify a difficult multiple-choice question is to eliminate all of the answer choices that are clearly wrong. In most sets of answers, there will be at least one selection that can be dismissed right away. If the test is administered on paper, the test taker could draw a line through it to indicate that it may be ignored; otherwise, the test taker will have to perform this operation mentally or on scratch paper. In either case, once the obviously incorrect answers have been eliminated, the remaining choices may be considered. Sometimes identifying the clearly wrong answers will give the test taker some information about the correct answer. For instance, if one of the remaining answer choices is a direct opposite of one of the eliminated answer choices, it may well be the correct answer. The opposite of obviously wrong is obviously right! Of course, this is not always the case. Some answers are obviously incorrect simply because they are irrelevant to the question being asked. Still, identifying and eliminating some incorrect answer choices is a good way to simplify a multiple-choice question.

4. Don't Overanalyze

Anxious test takers often overanalyze questions. When you are nervous, your brain will often run wild, causing you to make associations and discover clues that don't actually exist. If you feel that this may be a problem for you, do whatever you can to slow down during the test. Try taking a deep breath or counting to ten. As you read and consider the question, restrict yourself to the particular words used by the author. Avoid thought tangents about what the author *really* meant, or what he or she was *trying* to say. The only things that matter on a multiple-choice test are the words that are actually in the question. You must avoid reading too much into a multiple-choice question, or supposing that the writer meant something other than what he or she wrote.

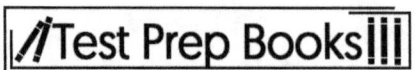

5. No Need for Panic

It is wise to learn as many strategies as possible before taking a multiple-choice test, but it is likely that you will come across a few questions for which you simply don't know the answer. In this situation, avoid panicking. Because most multiple-choice tests include dozens of questions, the relative value of a single wrong answer is small. As much as possible, you should compartmentalize each question on a multiple-choice test. In other words, you should not allow your feelings about one question to affect your success on the others. When you find a question that you either don't understand or don't know how to answer, just take a deep breath and do your best. Read the entire question slowly and carefully. Try rephrasing the question a couple of different ways. Then, read all of the answer choices carefully. After eliminating obviously wrong answers, make a selection and move on to the next question.

6. Confusing Answer Choices

When working on a difficult multiple-choice question, there may be a tendency to focus on the answer choices that are the easiest to understand. Many people, whether consciously or not, gravitate to the answer choices that require the least concentration, knowledge, and memory. This is a mistake. When you come across an answer choice that is confusing, you should give it extra attention. A question might be confusing because you do not know the subject matter to which it refers. If this is the case, don't

eliminate the answer before you have affirmatively settled on another. When you come across an answer choice of this type, set it aside as you look at the remaining choices. If you can confidently assert that one of the other choices is correct, you can leave the confusing answer aside. Otherwise, you will need to take a moment to try to better understand the confusing answer choice. Rephrasing is one way to tease out the sense of a confusing answer choice.

7. Your First Instinct

Many people struggle with multiple-choice tests because they overthink the questions. If you have studied sufficiently for the test, you should be prepared to trust your first instinct once you have carefully and completely read the question and all of the answer choices. There is a great deal of research suggesting that the mind can come to the correct conclusion very quickly once it has obtained all of the relevant information. At times, it may seem to you as if your intuition is working faster even than your reasoning mind. This may in fact be true. The knowledge you obtain while studying may be retrieved from your subconscious before you have a chance to work out the associations that support it. Verify your instinct by working out the reasons that it should be trusted.

8. Key Words

Many test takers struggle with multiple-choice questions because they have poor reading comprehension skills. Quickly reading and understanding a multiple-choice question requires a mixture of skill and experience. To help with this, try jotting down a few key words and phrases on a piece of scrap paper. Doing this concentrates the process of reading and forces the mind to weigh the relative importance of the question's parts. In selecting words and phrases to write down, the test taker thinks about the question more deeply and carefully. This is especially true for multiple-choice questions that are preceded by a long prompt.

9. Subtle Negatives

One of the oldest tricks in the multiple-choice test writer's book is to subtly reverse the meaning of a question with a word like *not* or *except*. If you are not paying attention to each word in the question, you can easily be led astray by this trick. For instance, a common question format is, "Which of the following is...?" Obviously, if the question instead is, "Which of the following is not...?," then the answer will be quite different. Even worse, the test makers are aware of the potential for this mistake and will include one answer choice that would be correct if the question were not negated or reversed. A test taker who misses the reversal will find what he or she believes to be a correct answer and will be so confident that he or she will fail to reread the question and discover the original error. The only way to avoid this is to practice a wide variety of multiple-choice questions and to pay close attention to each and every word.

10. Reading Every Answer Choice

It may seem obvious, but you should always read every one of the answer choices! Too many test takers fall into the habit of scanning the question and assuming that they understand the question because they recognize a few key words. From there, they pick the first answer choice that answers the question they believe they have read. Test takers who read all of the answer choices might discover that one of the latter answer choices is actually *more* correct. Moreover, reading all of the answer choices can remind you of facts related to the question that can help you arrive at the correct answer. Sometimes, a misstatement or incorrect detail in one of the latter answer choices will trigger your memory of the subject and will enable you to find the right answer. Failing to read all of the answer choices is like not reading all of the items on a restaurant menu: you might miss out on the perfect choice.

11. Spot the Hedges

One of the keys to success on multiple-choice tests is paying close attention to every word. This is never truer than with words like *almost*, *most*, *some*, and *sometimes*. These words are called "hedges" because they indicate that a statement is not totally true or not true in every place and time. An absolute statement will contain no hedges, but in many subjects, the answers are not always straightforward or absolute. There are always exceptions to the rules in these subjects. For this reason,

you should favor those multiple-choice questions that contain hedging language. The presence of qualifying words indicates that the author is taking special care with his or her words, which is certainly important when composing the right answer. After all, there are many ways to be wrong, but there is only one way to be right! For this reason, it is wise to avoid answers that are absolute when taking a multiple-choice test. An absolute answer is one that says things are either all one way or all another. They often include words like *every*, *always*, *best*, and *never*. If you are taking a multiple-choice test in a subject that doesn't lend itself to absolute answers, be on your guard if you see any of these words.

12. Long Answers

In many subject areas, the answers are not simple. As already mentioned, the right answer often requires hedges. Another common feature of the answers to a complex or subjective question are qualifying clauses, which are groups of words that subtly modify the meaning of the sentence. If the question or answer choice describes a rule to which there are exceptions or the subject matter is complicated, ambiguous, or confusing, the correct answer will require many words in order to be expressed clearly and accurately. In essence, you should not be deterred by answer choices that seem excessively long. Oftentimes, the author of the text will not be able to write the correct answer without offering some qualifications and modifications. Your job is to read the answer choices thoroughly and completely and to select the one that most accurately and precisely answers the question.

13. Restating to Understand

Sometimes, a question on a multiple-choice test is difficult not because of what it asks but because of how it is written. If this is the case, restate the question or answer choice in different words. This process serves a couple of important purposes. First, it forces you to concentrate on the core of the question. In order to rephrase the question accurately, you have to understand it well. Rephrasing the question will concentrate your mind on the key words and ideas. Second, it will present the information to your mind in a fresh way. This process may trigger your memory and render some useful scrap of information picked up while studying.

14. True Statements

Sometimes an answer choice will be true in itself, but it does not answer the question. This is one of the main reasons why it is essential to read the question carefully and completely before proceeding to the answer choices. Too often, test takers skip ahead to the answer choices and look for true statements. Having found one of these, they are content to select it without reference to the question above. The savvy test taker will always read the entire question before turning to the answer choices. Then, having settled on a correct answer choice, he or she will refer to the original question and ensure that the selected answer is relevant. The mistake of choosing a correct-but-irrelevant answer choice is especially common on questions related to specific pieces of objective knowledge.

15. No Patterns

One of the more dangerous ideas that circulates about multiple-choice tests is that the correct answers tend to fall into patterns. These erroneous ideas range from a belief that B and C are the most common right answers, to the idea that an unprepared test-taker should answer "A-B-A-C-A-D-A-B-A." It cannot be emphasized enough that pattern-seeking of this type is exactly the WRONG way to approach a multiple-choice test. To begin with, it is highly unlikely that the test maker will plot the correct answers according to some predetermined pattern. The questions are scrambled and delivered in a random order. Furthermore, even if the test maker was following a pattern in the assignation of correct answers, there is no reason why the test taker would know which pattern he or she was using. Any attempt to discern a pattern in the answer choices is a waste of time and a distraction from the real work of taking the test. A test taker would be much better served by extra preparation before the test than by reliance on a pattern in the answers.

Introduction

Function of the Test

The Registered Behavior Technician (RBT) examination is administered by the Behavior Analyst Certification Board (BACB), and tests a candidate's knowledge of the skills and tasks of an entry-level behavior technician.

Eligibility

Candidates must meet minimum requirements before applying for RBT certification. Candidates must be at least 18 years old, have a high school diploma (or equivalent education level), and must be able to pass a criminal background and abuse registry check. Applicants must also complete a 40-hour training course and an initial competency assessment. Once these steps are complete, candidates can apply for an RBT certification through their BACB account. The application processing fee is $50. If their application is approved, the applicant will be able to schedule their RBT exam.

Test Administration

RBT candidates have one year after their application is approved to schedule and take the exam, which is provided continuously throughout the year. Tests are available in-person at Pearson VUE testing sites across the United States. Exam appointments are $45, which must be paid when scheduling the exam. Accommodations are available for those who request them.

The RBT exam is administered via computer at a Pearson VUE testing center. Test takers should arrive at the testing center at least 30 minutes before their appointment so they can complete the check-in process. Those who arrive after a test has been going for 30 minutes will not be permitted into the testing room and must reschedule their exam. Candidates must provide two forms of valid identification to be allowed into the examination room. These identifying documents must be government-issued and include the test taker's name, photo, and signature.

Personal items are not allowed in the exam room, including cell phones, cameras, watches, purses, etc. Lockers are available at all testing centers for storing personal items. No scratch paper, food and beverages, or visitors are allowed in the exam area either.

Test takers are permitted to take breaks during the exam. They must raise their hand and tell the proctor, who will secure the workstation while they are gone. Candidates cannot leave their station without approval from the proctor. Access to food, drink, and medication is allowed during breaks, but not phones, electronics, or notes. Any use of electronic devices during an exam is grounds for ending the exam and invalidating the results.

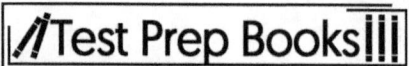

Test Format

RBT candidates are given 90 minutes to complete 85 multiple choice questions, 10 of which are unscored. A breakdown of the number of questions for each content area is below.

Content Area	Number of Questions	Percentage of Examination
A. Measurement	12	16%
B. Assessment	6	8%
C. Skill Acquisition	24	32%
D. Behavior Reduction	12	16%
E. Documentation and Reporting	10	13%
F. Professional Conduct and Scope of Practice	11	15%

Scoring

Each multiple-choice question only has one correct answer. Passing scores are determined by a panel of experts who review each exam question and establish the minimum level of competency a candidate must have in order to answer it correctly. This score ensures that each candidate has proven they have a sufficient level of knowledge and understanding to perform the duties of a behavioral technician.

Exam results will provided as soon as the exam is completed. Results will be confirmed via email, and will be posted in your BACB account within a week of completing the exam.

Those who don't pass the examination may take the examination again, but must wait seven days after their last examination attempt, as long as they are within one year of having their application approved. Candidates can retake the exam up to eight times in this one-year period. Once this one-year authorization ends, candidates need to reapply and meet the eligibility requirements

Study Prep Plan for the RBT Test

1 **Schedule** - Use one of our study schedules below or come up with one of your own.

2 **Relax** - Test anxiety can hurt even the best students. There are many ways to reduce stress. Find the one that works best for you.

3 **Execute** - Once you have a good plan in place, be sure to stick to it.

One Week Study Schedule

Day 1	Measurement
Day 2	Skill Acquisition
Day 3	Behavior Reduction
Day 4	Documenting and Reporting
Day 5	Professional Conduct and Scope of Practice
Day 6	Practice Test #1
Day 7	Take Your Exam!

Two Week Study Schedule

Day 1	Measurement	Day 8	Comply with applicable legal, regulatory...
Day 2	Assessment	Day 9	Professional Conduct and Scope of Practice
Day 3	Skill Acquisition	Day 10	F-4 Maintain professional boundaries...
Day 4	Implement Discrimination Training	Day 11	Practice Test #1
Day 5	Implement Shaping Procedures	Day 12	Practice Test #2
Day 6	Behavior Reduction	Day 13	Practice Test #3
Day 7	Documenting and Reporting	Day 14	Take Your Exam!

Build your own prep plan by visiting:

testprepbooks.com/prep

As you study for your test, we'd like to take the opportunity to remind you that you are capable of great things! With the right tools and dedication, you truly can do anything you set your mind to. The fact that you are holding this book right now shows how committed you are. In case no one has told you lately, you've got this! Our intention behind including this coloring page is to give you the chance to take some time to engage your creative side when you need a little brain-break from studying. As a company, we want to encourage people like you to achieve their dreams by providing good quality study materials for the tests and certifications that improve careers and change lives. As individuals, many of us have taken such tests in our careers, and we know how challenging this process can be. While we can't come alongside you and cheer you on personally, we can offer you the space to recall your purpose, reconnect with your passion, and refresh your brain through an artistic practice. We wish you every success, and happy studying!

Measurement

Preparing for Data Collection

Data is the foundation of the Registered Behavior Technician's (RBT's) work. It demonstrates whether a client is making progress or may require a different approach. RBTs must prepare for data collection intentionally and meticulously to ensure their work is accurate, meaningful, and reliable. An RBT should begin by reviewing the client's behavior plan to become familiar with the behaviors that need to be targeted and to identify the most appropriate interventions as well as the methods they should use to measure their effectiveness. Familiarizing themselves with the client's plan also means that they should be acutely aware of the client's current status, including preferences, motivations, and behavior history. Knowing what has or has not worked in the past, what the client's progress has been thus far, and what changes have been implemented in past trials can support the data collection process.

Next, the RBT should decide which measurement tools are most appropriate for the data collection. It's important to have materials that are accessible in the moment for tracking data consistently and often. Some RBTs prefer to use hard materials like physical data sheets and/or checklists, pencils, stopwatches, and timers. Other RBTs utilize real-time data collection software through a mobile app or through other platforms. Whichever methods the RBT uses, it's important to test all materials to ensure that they're functional prior to sessions. While software can be helpful, it also increases the opportunity for technical issues to arise at inopportune times. Testing data collection methods before working with the client decreases the chance that unanticipated problems will arise and increases the likelihood that the RBT will collect data that is uncompromised.

RBTs must ensure the environment they will be working in with the client is set up appropriately. Potential distractions to the client should be minimized, and materials like office supplies, electronic equipment, etc., or necessary resources like water/sustenance, restroom, etc. that the RBT or client may require during the course of the session should be accessible. Depending on the intervention in question, antecedent stimuli or reinforcers may be required to evoke the targeted behavior. This can include a toy, task, or activity. Whatever the stimuli may be, it should be consistently accessible within the environment so as not to disrupt data collection.

Implementing Continuous Measurement Procedures

In behavioral analyses, RBTs implement **continuous measurement procedures** in which they consistently collect data throughout a session or observational period. This sort of assessment allows the RBT to gain detailed and accurate insight into a targeted behavior or multiple targeted behaviors by measuring their patterns, frequency, duration, and latency.

Continuous measurement assessments require the RBT to gather data regarding every instance of behavior from start to finish. There are many types of measurement procedures that an RBT may utilize:

- **Frequency:** This refers to counting the number of times a behavior happens during an established time frame. This is most helpful to measure when targeting a behavior that has a clear beginning and end, such as hitting.

- **Inter-Response Time (IRT):** This refers to quantifying the amount of time between the end of one behavior event and the beginning of the next behavior event. This can be a helpful measurement when working to understand the rate of behavior over time in instances where one might want to increase or decrease the frequency of a behavior, such as self-injuring behavior.

- **Latency:** This measurement addresses the period of time between the presentation of a stimulus and the start of the target behavior. This is useful when attempting to understand responses to specific cues or instructions. For example, an RBT would want to measure latency if attempting to assess delays in behavior initiation, such as the client responding to instructions to transition to the next task.

- **Duration:** This refers to measuring how long a behavior lasts from beginning to end. This can be helpful when targeting behaviors that endure for notable periods of time, such as crying.

In some instances, an RBT may choose to record entire sessions, which can be helpful for collecting data about behaviors that fluctuate significantly throughout the session in an unpredictable fashion. Engaging in whole-session recording can support the RBT in establishing predictability through pattern identification. Because the RBT will be able to review the recording after the session, this data collection method can allow the RBT to be more present in the moment with the client, which can be important when trying to measure the client's overall engagement with the technician in the session.

Implementing Discontinuous Measurement Procedures

Although continuous measurement procedures are widely regarded as more detailed and accurate, it is not always practical or possible to collect data in this way. In these instances, the RBT would implement discontinuous measurement procedures. The ability to pivot and utilize different measurement procedures is indicative of a skilled RBT who is dedicated to supporting the client by meeting them where they are. Discontinuous measurement involves breaking down the length of a session into intervals of equal length and observing if the behavior occurs in those intervals. This enables the RBT to gain a snapshot of the behavior. Common tactics include:

- **Partial Interval Recording:** This involves recording whether a behavior occurs during a specified time interval regardless of the duration of the behavior or how many times it happens. This measurement method can be helpful for monitoring behaviors that occur frequently or are highly varied in their duration, such as self-injuring behaviors.

- **Whole Interval Recording:** This measurement tactic involves recording a behavior as having happened only if it lasts for the entire duration of an established interval. It is particularly helpful for measuring behaviors that the RBT is looking to encourage or that need to last a specific amount of time, such focusing on a given task.

- **Momentary Time Sampling:** This involves recording the behavior only if it is occurring at a specific moment in time, such as at the end of a predetermined time interval. This is a useful measurement procedure for behaviors that happen frequently or last a long time, such as staying seated.

Though there are established benefits to continuous measurement, discontinuous measurement is more practical in busy environments where continuous measurement procedures are difficult to implement. Furthermore, discontinuous measurement methods are less intensive as they don't require the observer

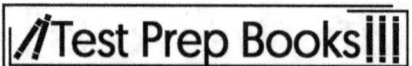

to track every instance of a behavior, which is useful if the behavior occurs too frequently to reasonably expect someone to record every instance.

Implementing Permanent-Product Recording Procedures

Permanent-product recording refers to a continuous measurement procedure in which the behavior is not observed in real time and the focus is on the outcome and/or result of the targeted behavior. This measurement is most helpful for cases where the intention is for there to be a tangible, lasting outcome. Examples of this could include a test or assessment score or a specific behavior reduction (e.g. the number of items destroyed at the end of the session).

This measurement technique is considered practical because it doesn't require continuous observation during the intervention or session and because it is applicable to a wide variety of circumstances and behaviors. The first steps in implementing a permanent-product recording procedure are to identify the behavior of interest and then define the outcome that will be measured. The idea is that the outcome would be a **permanent product**—something tangible that can be measured following the event.

After identifying the behavior of interest and defining the outcome to be measured, the RBT should then determine how the outcome should be measured. A benefit of this procedure is that the outcome can be quantified in any number of ways as long as the measurement is established and agreed upon ahead of time. If the permanent product is that the client has completed some reading, the outcome could be measured by the number of pages the client has read. If the outcome is that the client should have cleaned their play area, the measurement could be the number of items picked up or, simply, whether or not the room is considered clean (as defined by the lack of items on the floor or the presence of toys in their respective bins).

As the RBT puts their plan into practice, they should be reminded that they do not need to collect any data during the session if they are implementing a permanent-product recording procedure. They should collect the outcome data following their session and document it systematically and accurately. Ensuring reliable and accurate data collection allows for a clear and helpful analysis of the data, which will demonstrate whether the intervention is leading to consistent progress toward the established goal or needs to be changed.

Entering Data and Update Graphs

Data analysis is only as useful and meaningful as the consistency and accuracy of the data that is input. As previously mentioned, the RBT has the option of using either digital or manual (paper-based) data entry. If using paper-based recording, the data sheets and/or checklists should include the date of the session, the session number, and the exact behaviors that are to be tracked. RBTs will physically tally or check off behavior instances that they are tracking. It has become increasingly common for RBTs to utilize digital data collection methods such as software or mobile device applications, which have the benefit of providing data that is more readily accessible for graphing and analysis.

Describing Behavior and Environment

RBTs are responsible for recording data, including direct experiences with the client, in language that is clear, objective, and consistently understandable to the reader. When describing their data, RBTs must be careful to avoid excessive verbosity and unnecessary information while also ensuring that the wording is not so concise that the reader is unable to discern essential data points and the client's progress. Describing behavior and the environment is largely structured by three important elements: antecedent, behavior, and consequence.

There should be clear descriptions of what behavior or environmental element preceded the client's behavior. These detailed descriptions should not be subjective, as shown in, "The client didn't like that the teacher was giving them direction." Instead, "The teacher issued a verbal command to the client and his classmates," offers a description of the antecedent without offering an opinion or assumption.

Furthermore, it's important to offer context when describing the environment as this allows the reader to gain a full picture of why the targeted behavior may be occurring. If there are additional visual or auditory stimuli occurring, this can be helpful context for the reader to have.

The RBT should describe behavior in a concrete, detailed, and objective manner rather than using vague or subjective language to label or describe the individual themselves. For example, instead of simply saying, "The client is not engaging appropriately," an RBT should write, "The client is screaming, hitting their leg, and attempting to elope from the classroom." This offers specific, observable behaviors that one can address. It's also helpful to offer standard definitions for specific phrases to aid recognition and agreement on how to describe a behavior when it happens. For example, in the previous description, it might be helpful to define *elopement* as "leaving the designated area without permission."

RBTs should describe behavior in a way that can be measured. Sometimes there are multiple units of measurement necessary to record. For instance, instead of simply indicating, "The client was hitting themselves on the leg," the RBT may record, "The client hit themselves on the right leg with a closed fist three to four times following each directive given by the teacher."

The RBT should also describe what immediately follows the behavior, which is commonly described as the consequence. An example might be, "Following the attempted elopement, the client was given a 5-minute break in the sensory corner."

Practice Quiz

1. Jonah is working with a client who struggles with vocal outbursts. Today, he is seeking to count the total number of outbursts throughout their session. What is he measuring?
   a. Frequency
   b. Latency
   c. Duration
   d. Intensity

2. An example of something that could be measured using permanent-product recording is:
   a. The range of time between self-injurious behaviors
   b. How often a person raises their hand
   c. Whether a child has put away all their toys
   d. A client's emotional state following redirection from an instructor

3. You have a new client transitioning to your center following a cross-state move. During your case management meeting with their previous provider, the RBT mentions that they have been focused on measuring IRT during sessions. What does this entail?
   a. Recording the targeted behavior only if it occurs during an established interval
   b. Measuring the time intervals between the end of one instance of the behavior and the beginning of the next
   c. Counting the number of times the behavior occurs during a session
   d. Measuring how long the behavior lasts

4. You want to observe how well Samuel stays on-task. You instruct him to read for 30 minutes. At the end of every five-minute interval, you look at Samuel and note whether or not he is reading. What measurement procedure are you using?
   a. Momentary time sampling
   b. Partial interval recording
   c. Latency
   d. IRT

5. Gregory is writing a report about his most recent session with his client, Viktor, and is describing the latency of a behavior. Which sentence best meets this requirement?
   a. Viktor hid under the table seven times during a 40-minute time frame.
   b. Viktor hid under the desk every 7-8 minutes.
   c. Viktor hid under the desk for 2 minutes.
   d. Viktor hid under the desk 45 seconds after an unknown person entered the room.

See answers on the next page.

Answer Explanations

1. A: Counting the total number of times something occurs is measuring its frequency. Choice *B* is incorrect as latency refers to measuring the time between the presentation of the stimulus and the onset of the target behavior. Choice *C* is incorrect as duration measures how long a behavior lasts. Choice *D* refers to the measurement of the magnitude of a behavior.

2. C: The child putting away their toys offers a tangible, lasting result that can be directly measured after the established time frame has passed. Choice *A* is incorrect as it refers to measuring latency. Choice *B* is incorrect as it refers to measuring frequency. Choice *D* is incorrect as an emotional state is variable and doesn't offer something lasting that can be measured as a permanent product.

3. B: IRT, or inter-response time, refers to the measurement of time between behavior occurrences. Choice *A* is incorrect as it refers to partial interval recording. Choice *C* is incorrect as it refers to frequency. Choice *D* is incorrect as it refers to duration.

4. A: You are using momentary time sampling as you are only recording the behavior if it happens at the end of the activity. Choice *B* is incorrect as this refers to recording the frequency of a behavior during a specified amount of time. Choice *C* is incorrect as this refers to measuring the amount of time between the presentation of a stimulus and the occurrence of the targeted behavior. Choice *D* is incorrect as this measures the amount of time between behavior occurrences.

5. D: This sentence describes the time between the stimulus and the behavior, which is latency. Choice *A* is incorrect as this describes the rate of occurrence. Choice *B* is incorrect as this describes frequency. Choice *C* is incorrect as this describes duration.

Assessment

Conducting Preference Assessments

An essential part of a Registered Behavior Technician's role is to develop a deep understanding of their client. They must not simply become familiar with the behaviors that need to be targeted for support but must also become aware of the client's motivations, preferences, and reinforcers.

Preferences can include a wide range of things, such as items (toys, stuffed animals, games), activities (eating a snack, playing), or social interactions (visiting a friend, conversation about a preferred topic).

Reinforcers are stimuli (usually identified as a preference) that can be coupled with a behavior to make it more likely that the behavior will be replicated in the future. For example, Sunny loves stickers. Each time Sunny follows the teacher's instructions instead of walking away, they receive a gold star sticker on their sheet. The gold star is considered the reinforcer.

The quality of the preference assessment can either help or hinder interventions with a client. Gathering a caregiver report prior to conducting a formal preferences assessment is recommended as caregivers can give useful insight into the client's behavior. Though the RBT cannot rely primarily on this information, it can help lay a foundation for understanding a client's intrinsic and extrinsic motivators.

There are a variety of preference assessments an RBT can conduct to garner the most helpful and accurate data surrounding their clients' preferences.

Multi-Stimulus Without Replacement (MSWO)

The assessor presents the client with several options, each placed at an equal distance from the client, who is given 30 seconds to select one. The selected item is removed from the lot, and the process begins again with the remaining items. It is helpful to allow clients to interact with the items prior to the assessment to allow them to become familiar with the items.

Given that the structure of this procedure limits the client to a narrow set of actions, it can be useful when data needs to be gathered quickly and effectively due to time constraints. This assessment provides a hierarchical ranking of items, which can be useful in determining the client's preferences. If the client has developmental delays, however, offering several choices can be an added and undesirable stressor. Additionally, the MSWO is only appropriate if the client has the ability to scan items and make choices.

Multi-Stimulus With Replacement (MSW)

The assessor presents the client with several options, each placed at an equal distance from the client, and the client is given 30 seconds to select one. Instead of removing that item for the next round (as in MSWO), the item is placed back into the lineup. This can sometimes lead to the client re-selecting the item during the next round.

Similar to the MSWO, the time-structured nature of the MSW makes it a useful tool if time with the client is limited, and the assessment is only appropriate as long as the client has the ability to scan items and make choices. Because the item is replaced rather than removed, the MSW can give the RBT useful insight into whether there is an item that is highly preferred above all others. On the other hand, if the client *continues to select* the same item repeatedly, it would not allow the RBT to gather an order of preference.

Paired Choice

The assessor has several items but only presents two at a time to the client, who is given a specified amount of time to pick one item. This process continues until every potential combination of items has been presented. There should be a predetermined sequence of item combinations to be presented.

Because being presented with only two options at a time is less overwhelming for most clients, this can be a helpful tool to use with clients who have difficulty scanning. It also offers a significant quantity of data as several trials are conducted within the assessment. This method, however, can be time consuming due to the number of trials required to present all possible combinations to the client.

Free Operant

This assessment is less structured in that the client is permitted to freely engage with a multitude of items over a specified time frame. Observations are recorded, usually pertaining to frequency and duration of engagement with each item.

This method is particularly helpful if a client responds well to less structure—for example, if structured assessments cause significant anxiety or distress. This approach is more natural and not as intrusive as a structured assessment. However, the lack of structure can lead to less thorough data sets, including a lack of ranked preferences.

Assisting with Individualized Assessment Procedures

An RBT assists the treatment team with conducting individualized assessments. Assessments are conducted by a variety of professionals, including teachers, licensed psychologists, Board-Certified Behavior Analysts (BCBAs), Speech and Language Pathologists (SLPs), and more. These assessments are conducted to establish the client's baseline functioning and skills and to offer valuable insight into their strengths and areas identified for growth.

The RBT's role in these assessments is primarily twofold. They serve as an advocate for the client, offering immediate information to the assessor about the client's current progress, and they serve as on-the-ground support during the assessment, both managing behavior that may arise as well as offering motivation and encouragement for the client to engage fully in the assessment.

The most common types of assessments are curriculum-based assessments, developmental assessments, and social skills assessments.

Curriculum-based assessments evaluate whether a student is making progress within a specific curriculum. This can speak to both the curriculum's effectiveness and the student's potential need for changes to their learning environment, approach to learning, or curriculum content. A few common curriculum-based assessments include:

- **Verbal Behavior Milestones Assessment and Placement Program (VB-MAPP):** This assessment focuses on communication skills (primarily verbal behavior) for individuals with autism or another developmental disability.

- **Assessment of Basic Language and Learning Skills (ABLLS-R):** This assessment measures the client's skills as they relate to independent functioning. These include academic skills, self-help skills, social skills, and receptive and expressive communication skills.

- **Assessment of Functional Living Skills (AFLS):** This assessment evaluates basic life skills like personal hygiene and meal preparation.

Social skills assessments measure the progress a client has made in developing age-appropriate social skills. While formal social skills assessments are helpful, it's important to note that direct observation can sometimes be the most helpful tool in determining how well developed a client's social skills are. This observation could be conducted naturally (in everyday interactions with the client, in public settings, during mealtimes, etc.) or in structured social settings (classrooms, group activities, community centers, etc.). It's helpful for the assessor to establish which social skills they are looking to measure, such as initiating conversation or making eye contact, and then to establish how they might want to track their measurements, such as by frequency, duration, or quality. When a formal assessment is needed, a few common social skills assessments include:

- **Vineland Adaptive Behavior Scales, 2nd Edition (VABS-II):** This assessment offers insight into the client's adaptive skills as they pertain to communication, activities of daily living, social skills, and motor skills.

- **Social Behavior Assessment Inventory (SBAI):** This assessment measures a child's social behavior within the classroom and is typically used with students who have experienced trauma, including witnessing interpersonal violence within the home.

- **Social Skills Improvement System Rating Scale (SSIS):** This assessment is conducted with children and measures skills such as sharing, responding to social cues, and listening to instructions.

Developmental assessments focus on measuring a client's developmental level as compared to typical same-age peers. Developmental skills can include a wide variety of skillsets including fine motor skills (smaller, more precise movements such as writing or dressing), gross motor skills (large movements like sitting or walking), social-emotional skills (self-awareness, decisional making), expressive and receptive language skills, and more. A few common developmental assessments include:

- **Brigance assessment tools:** These tools are far reaching and offer assessments for both children and adults. The most common assessments include Early Childhood Screens (younger children), Brigance Diagnostic Inventory (older children and adults), and Brigance Inventory of Basic Skills (general skills). These tools measure skills such as communication, academic progress, activities of daily living, gross and fine motor skills, and emotional development.

- **Battelle Development Inventory II (BDI-2):** This assessment gathers data from a variety of sources: observations of the client, interviews with caregivers, providers, and/or teachers, and participation in structured tasks.

- **Bayley Scale of Infant Development III (Bayley-III):** This assessment is used with infants and toddlers and measures all aspects of development, including motor, language, social-emotional, and adaptive behavior.

Assisting with Functional Assessment Procedures

A **functional behavioral assessment** (FBA) is an important facet of behavior analysis that supports identifying the antecedents, functions, and consequences of targeted behaviors. An FBA posits that every behavior serves a purpose, has a pattern that can be identified, and can be modified. The FBA provides a significant amount of information that is critical for providing services to the client, including:

- Which strategies and interventions have previously been implemented

- What typically occurs before the behavior (the antecedent), including environmental factors that contribute to the behavior's occurrence

- A description of the targeted behavior in specific, measurable terms (i.e. where, when, and with whom the behavior occurs)

- What typically occurs after the behavior (consequences that contribute to reinforcing or maintaining the behavior)

A BCBA typically spearheads the functional behavior analysis while the RBT assists by supporting behavior management of and advocacy for the client, data collection (including observational data), and the implementation of procedures to elicit behaviors. FBAs involve establishing a hypothesis regarding the function of the behavior being exhibited by the client. There are three main strategies to conducting a functional behavior assessment:

- **Direct Assessment:** This strategy is the most comprehensive. It includes direct, systematic observation and recording of the client's behavior(s). This gives the RBT a first-hand account of what the client's behavior looks like, as well as its triggers and consequences.

- **Indirect Assessment:** This typically includes short interviews with involved parties who can help define the challenging behavior(s)—such as teachers or caretakers—and reviewing the client's records and reports to understand their behavioral, educational, and psychological background. Indirect assessments should be used alongside direct assessment to get a comprehensive look at the client's behavior.

- **Functional Analysis (FA):** This is conducted to test a hypothesis regarding circumstances around a behavior—such as its purpose or cause—and can help identify an effective intervention for the behavior. This involves manipulating the environment around a client so that the specific antecedent to the behavior can be isolated along with the events that follow (behavior, reinforcers, consequence, etc.).

Practice Quiz

1. Sandy presents Elizabeth with seven toys. Elizabeth picks the rubber ducky, which Sandy then removes from the lineup. The process is repeated. Which type of preference assessment is being conducted?
    a. Paired choice
    b. MSWO
    c. MSW
    d. Free operant

2. A child is displaying new aggressive behavior to the other children in class. The RBT learns that a grandparent was recently incarcerated following a violent encounter in the home with one of the child's parents. Which assessment might be most appropriate to conduct in this instance?
    a. SBAI
    b. AFLS
    c. Bayley-III
    d. VB-MAPP

3. A teacher tells the group they'll be packing up the craft supplies in 5 minutes to move on to lunchtime. Mary begins to cry. The teacher tells her that she can spend a few more minutes working on her crafts. The next day, when the teacher announces her 5-minute warning, Mary begins to cry. What is the reinforcer in this example?
    a. The crafts
    b. The teacher announcing the activity change
    c. Mary crying
    d. The teacher allowing extra time for Mary to do crafts

4. Teagan sets up her client, Amanda, in a room with several toys and lets Amanda know she is free to spend the next 30 minutes doing what she'd like until their formal meeting. What type of preference assessment is this?
    a. Functional analysis
    b. MSW
    c. Free operant
    d. MSWO

5. Which procedure helps identify the antecedent, reinforcer, and consequences surrounding a targeted behavior by observing the client in their natural environment?
    a. MSWO
    b. Descriptive FA
    c. Brief FBA
    d. Experimental FA

See answers on the next page.

Answer Explanations

1. B: MSWO, or multi-stimulus without replacement, involves removing the item from the lineup after it has been chosen. Choice A is incorrect as paired choice involves the presentation of only two items at a time to the client. Choice C is incorrect as MSW, or multi-stimulus with replacement, involves the item being placed back into the lineup. Choice D is incorrect as free operant involves unstructured engagement with a variety of items during an observed session.

2. A: The SBAI appears appropriate for this case given that it measures social behavior, particularly in cases where a child has experienced trauma. B is incorrect as AFLS focuses mainly on a client's ability to conduct activities of daily living. Choice C is incorrect as the Bayley-III is conducted with infants and toddlers. Choice D is incorrect as the VB-MAPP focuses on communication skills in children with developmental delays, and there is not enough information in this example to suggest that this is an appropriate assessment for this situation.

3. D: The reinforcer here is the teacher allowing a few extra minutes of craft time in response to Mary's crying. Choice A is incorrect as being allowed to continue doing crafts is the reinforcer, not simply the crafts. Choice B is incorrect as announcing the activity change is the antecedent. Choice C is incorrect as crying is the behavior.

4. C: This is a free operant assessment because Teagan is allowing Amanda to freely interact with the toys without creating additional structure. Choice A is incorrect as a functional analysis is not a preference assessment. Choices B and D are incorrect as MSW and MSWO refer to highly structured assessment options that do not allow the client to freely interact with the items.

5. B: A descriptive FA is the process by which the assessor observes the client in their natural environment to help identify what leads up to the behavior and what could be occurring after the behavior to reinforce its occurrence. Choice A is incorrect as MSWO is a preference assessment. Choice C is incorrect as a brief FBA typically focuses on short interviews with involved parties. Choice D is incorrect as an experimental FA is a more structured functional analysis that requires a systematic approach to testing a hypothesis.

Skill Acquisition

Skill Acquisition Plans

A **skill acquisition plan** (SAP) is a document used to track a client's progress toward achieving specified goals as part of the behavioral therapy process. The SAP is created by a certified behavior analyst in collaboration with the client and other stakeholders in the client's care team (such as parents and social workers). Goals are determined based on the client's needs and wants. While all SAPs ought to utilize person-focused treatment goals, dimensions of a client's capacities can make this challenging. For example, clients who are very young or present with communication difficulties may struggle to express their own goals at the beginning of therapy.

Behavioral therapy focuses on **building skills to help clients adapt to their environment.** The ultimate goal is that, as the client's skills improve, they will begin to use those skills without assistance, and eventually those skills will become habit. The registered behavior technician (RBT) supports this process by following the SAP's written teaching strategies and interventions. They are the member of the care team most responsible for recording a client's ongoing progress after each therapy session.

Particular skills are selected for the SAP based upon the client's identified goals. A skill-based goal must be both **objective** and **measurable**.

For example, one of a client's overall goals in therapy might be improved ability to socialize and make friends. A specific skill with which they may need assistance is using appropriate greetings in social situations (like waving and saying "Hello"). Giving an appropriate greeting exemplifies an *objective* goal because it is an external behavior the RBT can record without assuming subjective information about the client. Further, it is also a *measurable* goal because the RBT can record how frequently the client uses this skill.

Frequency is commonly used to measure a client's progress on the SAP because it reflects the client's increasing ability to use that skill without assistance from the RBT or other supportive persons. Other dimensions a behavior analyst will use when designing the skill goal include accuracy and consistency. For example, a client who waves and says "Hello" every time they enter a grocery store may not be accurately using this skill to socialize—they might instead be using it because they have entered a grocery store.

Over the course of treatment, an SAP will change and adapt to better suit the client's growing skills. Even with a familiar client, it's important to review their SAP regularly and ensure the RBT is helping the client grow in the dimensions specified by the plan.

The RBT's session-by-session role when providing services to a client is also specified by the SAP's description of **teaching strategies**, **reinforcements**, and **prompting**.

Teaching strategies vary from a high-level description of effective person-centric approaches to working with the client—similar to their overall goals—to specific requirements for teaching a single skill. For example, a behavior analyst might specify that the RBT should implement shaping procedures to help a client "break down" a skill into its components. Using the SAP's teaching strategies for overall approaches as well as specific skills improves client outcomes through consistency of care.

Methods of *reinforcement* are used to help connect the use of a skill to a positive experience or outcome. The SAP specifies which types of reinforcement ought to be used when a client uses a skill as specified in the plan. Using the written method of reinforcement reduces the risk that reinforcement will have unintended consequences (for example, as sometimes occurs when using token economies).

Finally, the SAP also specifies the *prompts* the RBT should use while working with a client. Prompting a client to use the skills they're practicing is an important element of behavioral therapy. Using the correct type of prompt—such as a verbal reminder or a nonverbal gesture—helps grow the client's ability to use skills independently. It can also avoid unintentional negative reinforcement, such as social embarrassment due to being verbally prompted in public.

Beyond specifying how the RBT ought to provide services to a client, the SAP also describes **communication methods** to be used between team members and briefly describes the decisions made when designing the plan. These decisions help providers implement the described therapeutic interventions by understanding the **behavior analyst's rationale.** Likewise, a written plan of how to record and communicate the client's progress ensures stakeholders can track the client's progress and provide effective support through collaboration.

Preparing for Sessions

The RBT should always review their client's objectives prior to a therapy session. Even when working with a long-term client, it's important to avoid complacency. Consistent preparation habits improve session results by helping the RBT keep the client's goals and learning tools firmly in mind. In addition to reviewing the SAP, it's also important to review the documentation from recent sessions. Even if the RBT was the provider who wrote this documentation, refreshing information helps establish continuity of care from one session to the next.

The first step in session preparation is reviewing the client's SAP. A therapy session's activities should provide opportunities for the client to practice skills specified in their plan's skill-based goals. While a client's larger goals are important—and are often a useful source of motivation—structuring a session around the skill-based goals helps ensure the behavior therapy process remains measurable. The RBT should ensure the client's opportunities to practice their skills are both formal and informal. For example, waving and saying "Hello" offers an *informal* opportunity for the client to practice a social greeting but is not an "activity" taking place during therapy.

The RBT should review the SAP's specified learning tools and behavioral interventions. Using the listed tools improves a client's ability to learn by providing consistent reinforcement for their behaviors. Reviewing these tools is important because they may vary widely from client to client. An unspecified reinforcement may appear effective during a session, but its use can hinder a client's overall growth since such inconsistency weakens the connection between behavior and outcome.

Changes in a client's SAP often do not change their *generalized* learning strategies but may change the *specific* learning strategy used for a skill-based goal. For example, nonverbal prompting may be identified as one of a client's preferred learning tools. However, a specific goal may be revised to measure the client's use of that skill without prompting, due to the client's growth during therapy.

The second step in session preparation is to review documentation of the client's recent sessions. This helps the RBT identify ongoing patterns during therapy sessions and adjust their implementation of the

SAP to best fit the client's needs. Remember that the RBT must continue to follow the SAP as specified by the client's behavioral therapist.

After reviewing all relevant documentation, the RBT should prepare the physical environment for the therapy session. A clean, orderly environment is desirable for all clients. Individual adjustments to the environment help prepare the RBT to provide therapy and can also help build rapport. For example, when working with a 6-year-old child on social skills, setting out building blocks is an age-appropriate preparation for practicing sharing the toys.

Using Contingencies of Reinforcement

When a client performs a behavior correctly, the use of **reinforcement** strengthens their connection between the behavior and a particular outcome. In most circumstances, positive reinforcement is used to support desired behavior by connecting it to a positive stimulus from the provider. This reinforcement is **contingent** because the positive stimulus is only provided when the client uses their skills correctly. Consistent use of contingent reinforcement helps the client understand a direct cause and effect between using their skills and positive outcomes, encouraging them to perform the behavior more frequently.

A *negative* reinforcement is the removal of stimulus in response to the use of a desired behavior. This remains reinforcement because removing the stimulus is intended to make the behavior more likely to occur in the future. For example, in physical therapy, performing an exercise regimen is negatively reinforced by the client experiencing reduced pain in day-to-day activities. The stimulus (the pain) has been removed by the behavior (the exercises).

Reinforcement is contrasted with **punishment**, the use or removal of a stimulus to decrease the frequency of a behavior. Positive and negative punishment are generally not used in modern behavioral therapy because the use of reinforcement is more effective at helping a client establish the requisite cause and effect in their behaviors.

One notable exception is the concept of a natural punishment (or consequence), which is not implemented directly by the RBT or provider. For example, if a child frequently reaches for a lit candle, the parent may eventually let them touch it. The hot candle is a positive punishment—a stimulus is added that makes the behavior less likely in the future, namely the pain of the hot flame. While it is never acceptable for an RBT to allow a client to risk injuring themselves, this is a good example of a natural consequence for undesirable behavior.

In a therapeutic setting, allowing a client to experience the unpleasant consequences of their own choices is acceptable so long as they're capable of understanding the causal connection. For example, a natural consequence of a child refusing to clean their room might be difficulty finding their toys in the clutter.

Conditioned/Unconditioned Reinforcement

All reinforcement methods can be separated into one of the following categories: unconditioned reinforcement and conditioned reinforcement.

Unconditioned reinforcement is the use of a stimulus that any person would enjoy or value, usually due to biological needs—for example, offering a piece of candy for using a skill successfully. In behavioral therapy, unconditioned reinforcement typically only uses the biological drive for food as a motivating factor. Other unconditioned reinforcers—like water, sleep, or using the restroom—are not appropriate to make contingent upon a client's behavior.

Conditioned reinforcement is the use of a stimulus that requires some amount of learning (conditioning) to enjoy or value—for example, giving a teenager permission to drive the family car to a friend's house. Most reinforcements RBTs use are *conditioned* reinforcements. Effective conditioned reinforcements are targeted not just to general learned stimuli but also to a client's individual interests and motives for participating in therapy.

For example, social praise and acceptance is a conditioned reinforcement that is broadly effective. Most individuals desire approval, which the RBT can easily provide in both formal and informal ways. Giving a client a cheerful greeting at the beginning of each session exemplifies an informal use of social approval to reinforce their behavior (in this case, attending the session).

While social approval is a broad and effective reinforcer, it isn't as effective as methods targeted for an individual client. For example, teenagers don't necessarily want approval from parents, teachers, or therapists—teenagers are most interested in the approval of their peers. A better conditioned reinforcement is engagement with the client's interests, such as playing a game with them or discussing an activity that excites them.

Continuous/Intermittent Schedules

The frequency with which the RBT provides reinforcement is its schedule. This does not refer to an external time-based schedule but instead describes the connection between a client's use of a behavior and how often the RBT ought to provide reinforcement. A reinforcement's schedule is either continuous or intermittent.

A **continuous schedule** is one in which the RBT reinforces the client's behavior every time they demonstrate it. One common use of a continuous schedule is verbal affirmation or praise. For example, when a student correctly answers a question in the classroom, the teacher always provides verbal approval to indicate that the answer was accurate. This example also demonstrates how a schedule need not always be formalized.

When using an **intermittent schedule** of reinforcement, the RBT does not reinforce the desired behavior after every time the client performs it. Instead, there is an interval between each use of reinforcement, which is either fixed or variable. A *fixed* intermittent schedule uses a consistent pattern of reinforcement, such as every third time a client uses the behavior. A *variable* intermittent schedule avoids overt consistency but is typically designed to provide a consistent average ratio of behavior to reinforcement.

For example, the RBT's positive response to a client waving and saying "Hello" at the start of a session demonstrates a fixed schedule of reinforcement. If the client seeks verbal praise by using the behavior later in the session, the RBT will withhold the desired stimulus. This reinforcement is scheduled for once per session, at the beginning of the session.

A variable schedule is demonstrated by occasionally thanking a child for passing a game piece during a board game. This schedule is effective because maintaining an average use of praise encourages the behavior to continue, while the variability helps the child practice using their sharing skills without an immediate reward.

It's important for the RBT to implement these schedules as specified in the client's SAP. New skills often begin with continuous schedules of reinforcement. As the client's abilities improve, reinforcement is provided less frequently until they're capable of using the skill independently with minimal formal reinforcement. Often, a skill's best reinforcement is the positive consequences from using it in daily life.

Implementing Discrete-Trial Teaching Procedures

Discrete-trial teaching is an educational method primarily used when providing behavioral therapy to children with autism spectrum disorder (ASD). It is closely related to the concept of *shaping* a client's behavior by breaking it down into its smallest components. Discrete-trial teaching is not used exclusively with children, nor is it only used as a teaching method for clients with ASD. This distinction is important to remember so that the RBT does not assume discrete-trial teaching should only be used when providing services to people with autism.

When using discrete-trial teaching methods, the RBT instructs the client to perform the smallest possible element of a larger task or skill. Correct implementation of the task is reinforced, and a different, related, element of the target skill is then tested. This process breaks down complex skills into a simpler pattern of **stimulus, behavior, and reinforcement**. Discrete-trial teaching is effective for clients with autism—especially children—because this disorder often causes difficulties in recognizing stimuli and learning to respond to them "naturally" in day-to-day social settings.

The goal of implementing discrete-trial teaching is for the client to generalize the practiced behaviors for use in day-to-day life. **Generalization** in this context is a person's ability to identify a specific stimulus and provide the appropriate response across a wide variety of situations and settings. Children with ASD frequently struggle to generalize a behavior across different physical environments or social relationships. For example, someone might have mastered that "Hello" is used as a greeting but fail to generalize this skill for use outside their home or school (such as while shopping at the mall with a parent).

Breaking down a skill into its elements during discrete-trial teaching allows the RBT to vary the stimuli in a controlled manner. Changing how a question is asked, the conditions in which the discrete-trial is practiced, and so on helps the client internalize the behavior and become better prepared to generalize it outside of the therapeutic environment.

For example, a child with autism is practicing language skills using parts of the body. The RBT begins using discrete-trial training by asking the child to touch the part of their own body that the RBT names. Each time the child performs the task correctly, the RBT reinforces the behavior. Later, the situation is changed by having the child touch part of a doll's body, or part of the picture of a person. As the child's skill improves, the RBT further alters the situation by pointing at a diagram and tasking the child with *naming* that part of the body. All three of these discrete trials occur in the same location, but varying the element of the same task helps the client generalize that the names of body parts—and eventually, words at large—have the same meaning in different contexts. This skill can support various aspects of the child's day-to-day living—for example, if they're feeling ill and need to communicate what body part hurts to their school nurse.

When utilizing discrete-trial teaching, it's important to make the structure of tasks and reinforcements as consistent as possible. This is especially true when beginning a new skill or when implementing discrete trials for a new variation on a skill. Predictability supports learning in general but is especially important when working with individuals with ASD since they generally have more difficulty distinguishing between meaningful and irrelevant variations in stimuli. Using the prior example, during the first trials, the RBT should instruct the child in the same way each time—for example, asking, "Please touch your nose," and then later asking, "Please touch your foot." A consistent sentence helps the client identify the varying information. This principle further extends to the therapy session's physical environment. Taking the same seat, with the same arrangement of furniture, provides stability and consistency, which supports early stages of discrete-trial teaching.

Variation in stimuli and environment is a necessary step for clients to master generalization. However, consistency is also necessary for discrete-trial teaching to succeed. Recognizing when to remain consistent and when to provide controlled differentiation varies from one client to the next. Since no two clients have identical capacities or skills, it's important for the RBT to adjust standard session methods to best fit their client within the guidance provided in their SAP.

Implementing Naturalistic Teaching Procedures

In contrast with the formal teaching methods used in a classroom, **naturalistic teaching** uses behavioral therapy to educate clients and shape their behavior during example or actual day-to-day activities. When working with children, naturalistic teaching is sometimes called *play teaching,* or play therapy, because children regularly learn social skills through games and play. Adult clients benefit from naturalistic teaching as a way to practice daily living skills, such as telling time or making their own purchases.

The RBT implements naturalistic teaching by structuring their therapy session around an activity that the client might engage in (or might *want* to engage in) outside of a formal setting. For example, instead of practicing greetings and responses in the RBT's office or classroom, the RBT would provide prompting and reinforcement while a client visits a store and greets the employees. The advantage of naturalistic teaching methods is that they **support a client's motivation** to be engaged in behavioral therapy. Even if a client struggles with using their skills independently, naturalistic teaching provides support while practicing those skills in their actual context. This encourages clients to improve their skills by striving to achieve independent use in day-to-day life.

This rather "adult" logic applies to children as well. For example, a child may *want* to enjoy playing with other children but struggle with the emotional regulation skills needed to avoid conflict. While children do not seek independence in the same way as adults who require assistance with day-to-day activities, most children also experience an age-appropriate desire to act independently.

Consequently, implementing naturalistic teaching with children typically engages them in games or other play activities. Taking turns playing a video game or sharing toy blocks to build a fort exemplify ways to practice social skills that most children learn spontaneously (or with occasional parental intervention). These teaching methods can be more effective than formal methods due to the child's motivation and interest in the play activities.

Naturalistic teaching is most effective when used to strengthen and improve a client's skills. Formal methods like discrete-trial training are often necessary when beginning to teach a new skill. As the skill improves, the client's behavioral therapist will update their SAP to provide the RBT with guidance on when and how to best implement a more naturalistic approach.

When using naturalistic teaching within a more formal environment, like the RBT's office or classroom, it's important to prepare the environment to better engage the client. For example, when working with

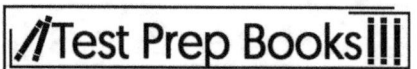

a new child, the RBT might make three or four different toys readily available for them to investigate. If the RBT already has established a therapeutic relationship with the child, they instead ought to prepare the environment with toys that both engage the client's interests and facilitate the skills the RBT intends to practice during that session.

Incidental Teaching

Naturalistic teaching does not need to be implemented only through intentional, structured activities. **Incidental teaching** applies to "seizing the moment" to use a naturalistic approach during specific opportunities that arise while providing education to a client. Incidental teaching is effective because it takes advantage of moments during which a client is attempting to use a skill in a day-to-day context while the RBT is present and providing educational support. It's also effective because it engages with a client's expressed needs or wants. If the client has initiated the moment during which it's possible to provide incidental teaching, it's likely they're motivated to interact with the RBT and achieve their goal.

Imagine a client typically points and makes a nonverbal noise when requesting an object. One of the SAP's goals is to begin using verbal requests so that the client's requests are fulfilled more accurately. During a session practicing a different skill, the client points and requests their water bottle. This is an opportunity for incidental teaching to practice making verbal requests, such as "water" or "please." Thus, the RBT seizes this moment and prompts the client to specify what they want. Although verbal requests weren't the session's focus, the client's desire to be handed the water bottle encourages them to practice the skill in a "real-life" way rather than a structured and "artificial" way.

Implementing Task-Analyzed Chaining Procedures

The process of breaking down a target skill into its smallest elements is **task analysis.** This is a life skill used by people of all ages and abilities that's formalized as part of behavioral therapy. For example, when learning to play a new board game, people might break down "taking a turn" into the different steps used in that process (drawing a card, rolling dice, moving game pieces, etc.). Each of these small steps is a single *task* that must be mastered to use the skill effectively.

Mastering task analysis simplifies the learning process for clients and helps the RBT understand how to spontaneously use task analysis to simplify teaching during therapy sessions, classes, and so on. The client's SAP will not always include a task analysis of their skill goals, and some skills they struggle with may not be included in those goals at all. Thus, analyzing the discrete tasks a skill involves improves an RBT's ability to support a client in the moment.

Breaking down a skill into its discrete tasks requires considering the steps in using the skill as simply as possible. For example, when teaching a child to brush their teeth, the first task is to pick up their toothbrush. While "pick up the toothbrush" might seem an obvious requirement for brushing one's teeth, explicitly including this simple task helps individuals with learning disabilities or other disorders fully understand how to use the target skill.

These tasks should be tailored to the environment in which they will be using the skill. For example, if in the client's home toothbrushes are stored in a cabinet, then the first task ought to be "open the cabinet door." Even if a cabinet is not conveniently available in the teaching environment, practicing this task will strengthen the client's ability to use it in their own home.

The RBT should also be aware of a client's personal preferences in how they want to perform a task or skill. Often, there is room for variation in executing a skill that does not impact the skill's overall effectiveness. For example, there's no meaningful difference in whether one uses the right or left hand to brush one's teeth. If the client wants to use their nondominant hand, it's most appropriate for the RBT to accommodate their preference. Likewise, the RBT must also account for their client's age and developmental progress during task analysis. An adolescent client may require assistance mastering hygiene skills but feel that specific tasks are condescending. Considering the client's current abilities during analysis improves their ability to learn by providing more appropriate instruction.

A skill's discrete tasks are **chained together** during sessions as the client improves their mastery of each task. Each task is linked to the next needed to perform the skill in sequential order. When implementing chaining, the RBT doesn't necessarily need to begin with the first task and end with the last. If the client has mastered a task in the middle of the chain, that competence often provides a good foundation for connecting the task to subsequent elements. For example, a client may struggle to brush their teeth but be good at washing their toothbrush. Chaining can be used to link washing the toothbrush to the tasks required to put it away.

Chaining in ordinary sequential order is called *forward* chaining. In contrast, *backward* chaining practices the tasks in reverse order. This is effective because the client is still learning to perform these tasks and that the tasks belong in a particular sequence. The RBT should avoid jumping nonsequentially from task to task. The goal of chaining is to connect a sequence of tasks—if the client is directed to perform the tasks independent of their chain, they are not likely to improve their competence with the target skill.

As a client's ability to use chained sequences of tasks improves, these individual tasks or chained sequences continue to be linked together during therapy sessions with the RBT. The final goal is for the client to be able to perform the complete skill independently and in their own environment. After chaining is used to teach the target skill, behavioral therapy shifts to using the skill consistently and in its intended context, as described in the client's SAP.

Implementing Discrimination Training

The ability to tell the difference between types of stimuli is **discrimination.** In the context of behavior analysis and behavioral therapy, *discrimination* does not refer to civil rights or social injustices. Rather, the RBT provides this training to clients to help them *discriminate* one stimulus from among others.

The ability to identify and navigate different stimuli is essential to people's ability to understand the world around them. This capacity can be as simple as distinguishing between different colors or as complex as understanding unfamiliar words based on the speaker's tone and body language. Persons with disabilities may struggle to navigate the various stimuli around them. Failure to discriminate causes confusion, distress, and frustration. In turn, these emotions may result in a client's use of problematic behaviors to express themselves. Discrimination training targets the root cause of these emotions by improving the person's ability to understand their environment. Although discrimination training is provided with the goal of reducing problematic behavior, this teaching method does not itself improve a client's emotional regulation skills.

Discrimination training is implemented by encouraging a client to pick between two or more options. The RBT then provides reinforcement if the client chooses correctly. A **stimulus** is an option that the client can choose—usually, a physical object with distinct perceptual properties that the client is asked to identify. For example, a small child might be asked to select a red object from a collection of red and green objects. The stimulus for which the client receives reinforcement is called the *discriminative stimulus*.

The complexity of discrimination training depends on the client's abilities. Simple discrimination tasks are often presented to small children in both formal and informal contexts—for example, making animal noises while a parent reads a picture book. The RBT must ascertain the appropriate complexity for discrimination training based upon their familiarity with the client and the available information about the client's abilities in their SAP. Training that is too simple doesn't help the client's skills improve and may also harm the RBT's therapeutic relationship with the client if they appear condescending.

As a client's skills improve, discrimination training becomes more complex. Asking a client to use multiple perceptual skills or perform familiar exercises in more chaotic environments requires them to discern the correct response from among a larger group of incorrect options. These methods of complication assist the client in learning to discriminate against the "noise" of other stimuli and focus only on the task at hand, which can be especially helpful for clients who express feeling overwhelmed by their environment. An improved ability to focus on the discriminative stimulus and ignore other stimuli helps the client avoid feeling overwhelmed by the variety of perceptions they're exposed to outside of controlled environments.

Once basic discrimination is mastered, discrimination training methods can be used to teach clients to discriminate for (or against) less obvious stimuli. Depending on the client's abilities, this can include learning to recognize causes of distress or to discriminate in the use of alternative behaviors when distressed. During this process, the RBT must avoid reinforcing the problematic behavior, even if in the moment doing so increases the difficulty of the session or class. This must be balanced with the RBT's professional concern for a client's well-being. For example, if a client smacks themselves in the forehead with a rolled-up paper when distressed, they are not likely to harm themselves. In contrast, a client who strikes their head against their desk is engaged in a more unsafe behavior. When in doubt, the RBT should prioritize the client's safety over avoiding reinforcing the problematic behavior. Allowing a mild problematic behavior to continue until the client discriminates against it and chooses an alternative behavior to receive the desired reinforcement (such as leaving a noisy classroom) improves the client's ability to discriminate against problematic behavior in the future.

With older or higher-functioning clients, discrimination training is often most effective when combined with a naturalistic approach. Identifying the produce section's fruits in a grocery store, or practicing discrimination by using crosswalks, provides additional reinforcement to discrimination training by supporting the client's participation in their community. These examples also demonstrate practicing discrimination in a more chaotic environment, where the task may be more difficult. By providing support in a complex environment, the RBT trains the client to be better able to manage other environments with abundant stimulation.

Implementing Stimulus Control Transfer Procedures

In applied behavior analysis (ABA), all behavior is conceived as following three steps:

1. Antecedent
2. Behavior
3. Consequence

A person performs a behavior in response to various stimuli. These antecedents range from a personal desire to being asked a question, or simply being in a different environment. When an antecedent consistently results in performing a behavior, that stimulus is said to *control* the behavior. For example,

Skill Acquisition

when a person feels thirsty, they engage in the behavior of getting a drink of water. The specific behavior might be standing up to refill their water bottle, asking someone to bring them a glass of water, and so on. The *consequence* of the behavior is that the person's thirst is quenched. Drinking water thus reinforces the use of that behavior when the individual experiences thirst.

When a client is able to use a skill effectively in formal settings, like therapy, but struggles to do so in day-to-day life, the skill may not be associated with the correct stimulus. **Stimulus control transfer** is the process by which an RBT helps their client change the relationship between an antecedent and a behavior. While this teaching procedure does utilize consequences (such as reinforcement) to help shape behavior, stimulus control transfer prioritizes the behavior's relationship with the antecedent rather than the consequence.

Stimulus control transfer is effective as long as one variable—antecedent or behavior—is intended to remain consistent. This process is used to transfer a mastered skill to a different stimulus, or to teach a client that the consistent stimulus should control a different behavior. A *transfer* in which only one variable is changing is necessary for this teaching method to succeed. Likewise, stimulus control transfer is only effective if the client's response to the antecedent is already consistent. Once a reliable connection between stimulus and behavior has been established, stimulus control transfer can then transfer either variable to a more beneficial antecedent or behavior.

This teaching method is often used when clients present problematic behavior. Such behavior is often a habitual response to particular antecedents and occurs consistently because the client has found that using the behavior consistently meets their needs. Transferring the antecedent's control of this behavior to a different behavior consequently reduces or eliminates the problematic behavior. An appropriate behavior can become problematic if it is controlled by an inappropriate antecedent. In this circumstance, stimulus control transfer seeks to retain the behavior and change the stimuli by which it is controlled.

For example, a client consistently punches the wall when feeling overwhelmed. This is a problematic behavior that risks self-harm. The antecedents are both the feeling of being overwhelmed and the events that caused the client to feel overwhelmed. The behavior is punching the wall. In this example, it is likely that the client's problematic behavior has been reinforced due to people giving them time to "cool off" after expressing anger by punching the wall. The client's *consequence* was that they got to take a break until the stimulus—feeling overwhelmed—ended.

Stimulus control transfer is an effective teaching method in this scenario because the client's behavior is consistent. It's unlikely that the antecedent can be transferred easily, since it is an internal emotion, so stimulus control is best used to exchange a more appropriate behavior for the problematic behavior. Further, stimulus control transfer is effective in this example because the consequence—the client's need for a break when overwhelmed—is appropriate.

The direct implementation of stimulus control transfer during therapy sessions is executed using other techniques common to behavioral therapy. Discrimination training might be used to help a client make distinctions between the correct and incorrect antecedents when using a behavior. Prompting is usually effective as well, providing a client with support to use the desired behavior instead of the behavior typically controlled by the antecedent.

After initially establishing a new connection between the antecedent and the behavior, the RBT completes this transfer by *fading* the teaching method. Fading reduces the frequency or nature of the support while continuing to provide consistent reinforcement for use of the correct behavior. A verbal prompt might instead become a tactile prompt, or a full-color picture used as the practice stimulus might instead become a black-and-white drawing. Continuing to provide consistent reinforcement during the fading process supports the client's ability to transfer the new antecedent or behavior with the old. Receiving the same consequence strengthens the new connection between antecedent and behavior by ensuring the client gets the reinforcement they desire.

Implementing Prompting Procedures

One of the most diverse and widely used teaching tools in behavioral therapy is prompting. **Prompting** is the act of reminding a client to perform a desired behavior in response to a previous antecedent. This type of stimulus is used as a teaching tool—like training wheels on a bicycle—to support the client's learning process.

There are six general types of prompts an RBT might use while providing services to a client:

- **Verbal:** Spoken encouragement, reminders, or directions

- **Gestures:** Nonverbal cues using hands, head, facial expressions, or other parts of the body

- **Modeling:** Performing the behavior themselves to encourage the client to mimic the RBT

- **Physical:** Providing direct support with physical contact, such as hand-over-hand assistance in performing a skill

- **Visual:** Showing the client an image or text as a nonverbal stimulus

- **Positional:** Adjusting the environment to encourage a particular response (such as moving a correct object nearer)

Prompting is not itself a teaching method; it is a tool implemented by the RBT to provide instruction while following a particular teaching method. Prompts are widely used in behavioral therapy to encourage clients to perform a particular behavior, to remind clients of appropriate behaviors, and to help clients recognize the correct response to a stimulus. For example, a prompt might be used to help a client recognize their need to use a skill to regulate their emotions, or it might be used to give a client a "hint" to the correct response during discrimination training.

There is no single "best" type of prompt for an RBT to use. Instead, the best prompt is typically contingent on the situation. For example, a gesture is often less obvious than a verbal prompt and may be a better fit when in public with a client because it may avoid embarrassment. Using prompts effectively also relies upon the RBT's familiarity with the client. Following a client's preferred method(s) of prompting demonstrates that the RBT is listening to the client and respecting their choices. Clients are consequently more likely to engage with the prompts. This improves both their motivation to participate in therapy and their rapport with the RBT.

Often, a client's skill acquisition plan (SAP) will specify preferential prompts. This information can be based upon the client's expressed preferences or upon the experience of the parents, behavior analyst, and other stakeholders while providing support to the individual. When specific prompting methods are specified by the SAP, it's important for the RBT to use them accordingly. Doing so ensures the RBT's sessions comply with the overall goals and methods of the client's care team. Recording the frequency of prompts and regulating their use provides the behavior analyst with measurable data by which to evaluate a client's progress with the SAP. If the RBT's use of prompts does not follow the SAP, that inconsistency may make it more difficult for the client to continue improving their skills.

Prompt Fading

As a client's ability to perform a skill improves, they should be prompted to use it less frequently. The process of reducing the use of prompts is called **prompt fading.** Fading is an important step in the teaching process because it helps the client become able to generalize the behavior to other situations. It's important to fade prompts because a support professional often isn't available to assist the client outside of the therapeutic environment. Ultimately, when the use of prompts has faded entirely, the client ought to be able to perform the skill independently in response to stimuli in their environment.

For example, a teacher might use a modeling prompt to help a student remember to raise their hand in class. Initially, the teacher uses this prompt plus a verbal prompt every time the student asks a question without raising their hand. As the student's skill improves, the teacher begins only modeling the desired behavior. By increasing the number of seconds the teacher waits between the student asking a question and modeling the prompt, the teacher fades the prompt. The result is that the student associates raising their hand with getting their question answered and does not require an external prompt to use that skill.

If prompts are not faded, the client may become reliant upon the prompt's stimulus to perform the skill. While fading a prompt too quickly can result in client frustration, overuse of a prompt risks replacing the desired stimulus with the prompt instead. For example, a child might say "cat" whenever they see a picture of an animal due to misunderstanding the visual prompt used in language-learning behavioral therapy.

Implementing Generalization and Maintenance Procedures

The final goal of applied behavior analysis is for clients to utilize learned behaviors and skills on their own in day-to-day life. This outcome promotes a client's independence by strengthening their ability to care for themselves and meet their own needs, thereby building up their self-esteem and allowing them to continue striving to grow. **Generalization** is the client's ability to use a skill in a variety of circumstances. Teaching generalization supports the client's skill use outside of familiar and structured environments, such as at home or in a therapy session.

Differing environments are the type of variation most widely considered when generalizing the use of a skill. Naturally, it's important that a client not only use their skills during behavioral therapy but practice generalizing skills with alternative variables as well. True mastery of a skill is demonstrated when a person is able to use it appropriately in response to a wide variety of stimuli. Common stimuli include using the skill with different objects or in response to a different person. The varying circumstances can also be internal, such as generalizing a skill for use in different emotional states. For example, if a client has learned a skill for self-regulation when feeling frustrated, they might also generalize it to self-regulate when feeling sad.

Generalization is taught by providing the client with stimuli to use the skill while in different environments. For example, a parent might help their child practice generalization by giving them a new toothbrush and then providing the usual reinforcement for brushing their teeth. Exercising the ability to generalize is also an advantage of naturalistic and incidental teaching methods. Spontaneous opportunities to use a skill often overlap with chances to practice generalizing, since these opportunities typically occur when outside of a structured therapy session, classroom, etc. Modeling prompts and shaping procedures often assist in generalizing a skill by allowing the client to see the skill's use while in an unfamiliar context.

Once a skill has been generalized, it may require occasional **maintenance** by practicing the behavior with the RBT or another support professional. Even if an individual demonstrates excellence at a task, it's not unusual for them to struggle to retain that excellence if they don't utilize their ability to perform the task. However, a person is not likely to lose their ability to do the skill entirely. If a person learns to ride a bicycle and then doesn't use the skill consistently, years later they'll likely retain *some* ability to ride a bicycle.

The goal of maintenance exercises is to retain most or all of a client's ability with the practiced skill. The frequency of maintenance will vary, depending on the client's abilities. For example, some clients may require monthly practice and education to retain a skill, while others may only require maintenance when they directly request assistance from the RBT. Understanding a client's need for assistance as well as their ability to ask for assistance are two reasons the therapeutic relationship and continuity of care are important.

Implementing maintenance exercises requires practicing the use of the skill with the client. Keeping these exercises similar to the teaching methods used when the client first learned the skill helps the client continue to associate the appropriate antecedents and consequences with their behavior. If a client has mastered some skills but continues to receive services from the RBT focusing on other skills, it's best to integrate maintenance exercises into the RBT's regular sessions. Practicing a known skill both helps the client retain their ability to use and generalize the skill and bolsters their confidence. This can be especially helpful if the client is finding their current goals frustrating. For example, a musician often begins their practice session with familiar scales before continuing to work on a more complex piece of music. This allows the individual to maintain competence and bolster confidence in their abilities prior to the more challenging work.

Maintaining a client's skills offers a good opportunity to integrate parents or other stakeholders into behavioral therapy. Educating a parent on how to support their child in the home often presents challenges, especially if the client is struggling to use or generalize a particular skill. Skill retention is often easier for parents to engage in, since the client has already learned the skill being practiced. Further, teaching maintenance exercises to the client's stakeholders also reduces the risk of backsliding when the client is no longer receiving services. Consistent maintenance helps clients retain their ability to use and generalize skills, thereby retaining their ability to meet their own needs.

Implementing Shaping Procedures

Shaping is a teaching method in which a client learns to use a new skill through reinforcement of skills and behaviors they're already able to perform. By reinforcing the new use of an existing ability, the client's behavior is *shaped* toward being able to perform the target skill.

For example, a client demonstrates the ability to lift and move their arm but struggles a bit with full motor control. When trying to teach that client to raise their hand before asking questions, the RBT would shape this skill by reinforcing any use of arm movement prior to asking the question. As the client demonstrates improved ability to move their arm prior to asking a question, the RBT increases

Skill Acquisition

reinforcement for when the client lifts their arm higher up. This use of shaping results in a transition over time along the following stages:

- The client interrupts class when they need to ask a question.
- The client performs any arm motion prior to asking a question.
- The client raises their arm upward prior to asking a question.
- The client fully raises their hand prior to asking a question.

Further use of shaping in this example might then involve continued reinforcement to help the client learn patience and to recognize that the correct time to ask the question is when a teacher says the client's name.

Shaping is a fundamental tool used in behavioral therapy. By beginning with reinforcement of the client's current abilities, shaping strengthens the client's ability to learn new behaviors and skills to meet their needs. Although shaping can be slower than other teaching methods, its gradual progress is often more successful. This is especially true when shaping is used to support persons with learning and developmental disabilities. Using shaping helps keep the therapy process focused on the person's abilities and goals. It also boosts self-esteem and avoids frustration by asking the client to perform tasks of which they're already capable—not difficult or unfamiliar tasks.

When implementing shaping, the RBT should also implement task analysis to break down the target skill into its elements. Shaping and task analysis overlap but are *not* identical. Directly teaching the discrete tasks required to perform a skill is not shaping because the teaching process has not begun from the client's current abilities. For example, task analysis of the skill "ask the teacher a question" includes the discrete task of "raise your hand." However, if a client lacks sufficient motor control to do so, educating the client to perform this task will not be successful. Instead, the RBT should use shaping to help the client grow from using their current abilities to being able to independently perform the elements identified in the task analysis. Although both procedures involve incremental learning and a gradual change in behaviors, the functions of shaping and task analysis are complementary, not identical.

Using reinforcement methods effectively is critical to shaping behaviors. The client may associate previous use of a behavior or skill with particular positive or negative consequences. The RBT should account for the client's past experiences with reinforcing or punishing behavior when deciding how to reinforce a behavior so that it is shaped toward performing the target skill.

One particularly effective reinforcement technique for shaping a client's behaviors is differential reinforcement. This method is suitable when implementing shaping because it relies on the client's choice of what behavior to use and what reinforcement to receive as a consequence. **Differential reinforcement** uses variation in the consequence for behavior to incentivize the desired behavior through a consequence that the client prefers to other consequences. This type of reinforcement always differentiates between alternative *positive* reinforcements. Providing options for the type of reinforcement the client will receive encourages the client to continue participating in therapy. Offering a less desirable reinforcement when the client uses their current skills also helps maintain their ability to use those skills.

For example, when teaching a small child to walk, offering the child a toy is an appropriate reinforcement for their behavior. After working with the child for some time, the RBT likely knows what toys the child prefers. They place a desirable toy on a shelf the child can reach while crawling and place the child's favorite toy on a shelf that requires standing to reach. This use of differential reinforcement allows the child to choose which reinforcement they prefer, with a more desirable reward offered for use of the skill being practiced. This example also demonstrates the use of shaping, since the child is not expected to walk over and reach the toy—they are able to crawl over and then stand up, practicing a step in the walking skill that they're currently able to perform.

Implementing Token Economy Procedures

One of the most broadly used reinforcement methods is the token economy. **Token economies** reinforce behavior by exchanging symbols or objects for an individual's desired reinforcer. Not only a tool used in applied behavior analysis, token economies are also used in homes, classrooms, and even professional settings.

For the RBT, implementing a token economy is an effective way to help parents, teachers, and other stakeholders reinforce a client's behavior outside of therapy sessions. A token economy is designed using three basic components:

- **Tokens:** The symbols, objects, etc., that the client receives
- **Target behaviors:** The behavior(s) the client must exhibit to receive tokens
- **Reinforcers:** The reinforcement method(s) the client desires and can receive when they earn sufficient tokens

An adult's job is a large-scale demonstration of a token economy in action. In exchange for the target behavior (working), adults receive tokens (money) that can then be exchanged for a wide variety of reinforcers (food, shelter, entertainment, etc.).

Token economies are most effective when tailored for use with a client. While the RBT or their organization might maintain a "standardized" example token economy for ease of implementation, all three components ought to be evaluated and adjusted to be most effective for use with the client. For example, one client might be motivated to receive and keep a collection of plastic coins, while another might be motivated by a paper chart with star stickers displayed on their household's fridge. In both cases, the token used has been adapted to best suit the client's personality and wishes. By working together with the client in designing the token economy, the RBT bolsters the client's motivation to participate by giving them a sense of "ownership" over the reinforcement method.

When designing the token economy, the RBT needs to consider all three components. Doing so improves the token economy's ability to incentivize the client's behavior because each component has been tailored to engage the client. Further, a token economy is often used by other stakeholders as well, not only the RBT. Careful design improves the token economy's success by easing the reinforcement method's use by other providers.

First, the RBT should determine the target behaviors in consultation with the client and their stakeholders (such as parents and the behavior analyst). Often, target behaviors will be specified by the client's SAP. The selected behaviors must be objective and measurable. This ensures it is clear when someone should give the client a token and makes it easy for the client to understand how to earn a token.

Second, the RBT should determine the reinforcers provided in exchange for a particular number of tokens. This can be as simple as a single method of reinforcement or as complex as a variety of options from which the client can choose to "spend" their tokens. Collaboration with the client is most important for this component because the reinforcers must truly be desirable to the client. While a client may be reluctant to engage in the token economy's target behaviors, if the reinforcers are ineffective, the entire method will not be successful. When agreeing upon the reinforcers, it's also important for the RBT to consider the ease or difficulty of providing the reinforcer. For example, exchanging tokens for a toy or a piece of candy is a quick interaction that does not interrupt day-to-day routine. On the other hand, a reward like going to a zoo or going to see a movie may not be a reinforcer the provider can immediately deliver. Such privileges are an effective reinforcement but may be less effective with some clients (for example, those who struggle with patience).

Finally, the tokens and their method of distribution must be selected. A classic example is the chart of stickers often used in elementary schools. This method adds social reward when a student earns a sticker but can also lead to social punishment by implicitly comparing student behavior. The RBT must determine if the tokens are retained by the client, recorded by the provider, and so on. These methods can be combined. For example, the token economy might be a sticker chart kept by the client's teacher. However, receiving a sticker might come with the additional reinforcement of the client having the *privilege* of selecting the sticker and putting it on themselves.

Practice Quiz

1. Which of the following is true of skill goals on a client's skill acquisition plan?
    a. There must be between five and ten goals on the plan.
    b. Each goal must be measurable by a specified metric.
    c. The plan's goals must always specify a positive reinforcement method.
    d. All goals must include at least one prompting method for the behavior.

2. Each of the following sentences is a verbal direction given by the RBT to a client. Which sentence best exemplifies the use of discrete-trial teaching?
    a. Please clean up the building blocks on the floor.
    b. Would you like to walk to the store with me?
    c. If you feel thirsty, tell me by raising your hand.
    d. Pull the paper outward from the paper towel roll.

3. A client is afraid of dogs and runs away when they are near. Afterward, the client's parent hugs them. Which of the following is the "control" when analyzing this behavior?
    a. Seeing or hearing a dog
    b. Running in the opposite direction
    c. No longer being near a dog
    d. Being hugged to soothe fear

4. Physical prompts are most effective when
    a. changing the environment will help the client recognize the desired behavior.
    b. providing support in public to avoid socially embarrassing the client.
    c. the client attempts the skill but struggles to perform it independently.
    d. the RBT wants to provide positive reinforcement to the client.

5. The reinforcer given to a client as part of a token economy is best exemplified by which of the following?
    a. Receiving a piece of candy
    b. Adding a sticker to a sheet
    c. Verbally praising the client's behavior
    d. The client using the toilet independently

See answers on the next page.

Answer Explanations

1. B: Choice *B* is correct because the primary criteria for goals on the SAP are that they are objective and measurable. This ensures that the client's progress can be analyzed without subjectivity. Choice *A* is incorrect because the number of goals depends on the client's needs and overall goals—it is not an arbitrary number. Choices *C* and *D* are incorrect because, while the SAP often includes methods of prompting or reinforcement, a skill goal does not *always* specify how these teaching methods should be used.

2. D: Discrete-trial teaching uses very small steps to help a client prepare to use a skill and then chains these discrete steps together. Choice *D* is correct because the sentence exemplifies a small step in the process of using paper towels to wipe up a spill (in this case, pulling the paper outward prior to tearing off a sheet). Choices *A* and *C* are incorrect because these sentences do not provide directions that break down the skill into its simplest parts. Choice *B* is incorrect for the same reason and also because this leading question demonstrates *naturalistic* teaching by encouraging the client to participate in an activity based on their own interest.

3. A: In applied behavior analysis, the *control* is the antecedent stimulus (or stimuli) to which behavior is a response. A dog's presence causes the client to run away; thus, seeing or hearing a dog is the control. Choice *B* is incorrect because this is the behavior, not the control. Choices *C* and *D* are incorrect because both answers demonstrate different *consequences* that reinforce the client's behavior—in this case, the negative reinforcement that the dog is no longer nearby and the positive reinforcement of the parent's affection.

4. C: When the RBT uses a physical prompt, they physically touch the client and guide their hands, arms, etc., to perform the skill correctly. Choice *A* is incorrect because physically changing the environment to prompt the client is a *positional* prompt. Choice *B* is incorrect because making a physical motion to give a nonverbal prompt to a client (and thus reduce embarrassment) is a *gesture* prompt. Choice *D* is incorrect because reinforcement is not a prompting method—it is a consequence for the behavior a client performs.

5. A: The three components of a token economy are the tokens, the target behavior, and the reinforcers. Choice *A* is correct because the piece of candy best exemplifies a reinforcer, which is given in exchange for tokens. Choice *B* is incorrect because the sticker is a token, which can be exchanged for a reinforcer. The sticker itself, however, does not exemplify reinforcement. Choice *C* is incorrect because, while verbal praise does indeed reinforce a client's behavior, it is not generally used as the reinforcer in a token economy. It's more likely that verbal praise is a reinforcement provided *in addition to* giving the client a token. Choice *D* is incorrect because this answer exemplifies a target behavior (using the toilet), not a reinforcement of behavior.

Behavior Reduction

Written Behavior Reduction Plans

A written behavior reduction plan, also known as a behavior intervention plan (BIP), is created by a board-certified behavior analyst (BCBA) and implemented by those working with the client, such as registered behavior technicians (RBTs) and other caretakers. These plans are created to reduce harmful behaviors for any clients who require behavior reduction goals. Clients in this category exhibit harmful or maladaptive behaviors that interfere with activities of daily life, such learning or interacting with others. These maladaptive behaviors are referred to as "target behaviors." A behavior reduction plan should clearly outline the planned interventions and strategies that will be used to both prevent and respond to problematic target behaviors. These plans seek to teach new healthy behaviors in addition to reducing the occurrence of the unhealthy target behaviors.

A list of target behaviors and an operational definition for each behavior are the first components to include in any behavior reduction plan. These definitions should specify what the behavior looks like to help identify it clearly. It should also establish specific criteria that can be used to measure and assess the behavior or behaviors. Use clear, objective language to avoid ambiguity or confusion when carrying out a written behavior reduction plan. For example, the behavior "self-harm" should not be written by itself with no further explanation. The definition should include objective observations of the target behavior, such as punching oneself or banging one's own head. The specific criteria of measurement for this could be listed as frequency per hour or frequency per day.

Additionally, the plan should include the target behavior's function—its purpose—that explains what the client is seeking by acting this way. All functions of behavior will be categorized into one of four main categories: automatic reinforcement, avoidance or escape, attention, and access to tangibles. Understanding a client's behavior and its function will help an RBT provide the best care possible.

To ensure clarity and transparency, any written behavior reduction plan should identify the individuals responsible for carrying out the plan. This includes anyone who will help implement care, such as RBTs, parents, and other workers or caregivers.

Another key component of a written behavior reduction plan is preventative strategies. These strategies, also known as antecedent manipulations or antecedent strategies, are implemented to reduce the likelihood that the problematic target behavior will occur in the first place. As such, preventative strategies are meant to be implemented before the target behavior occurs. Common examples of antecedent strategies used in applied behavior analysis (ABA) therapy include using visual aids, providing clear choices to help set the client up for success, and modifying the environment to reduce disruptions and promote positive behaviors.

It is also important to include planned replacement behaviors. Replacement behaviors are socially acceptable behaviors that replace unwanted target behaviors through ABA therapy. Common replacement behaviors include breathing exercises, sensory equipment that is accessed independently, or visual cues that aid in processing and regulating emotions.

The behavior reduction plan should include consequence modifications. Consequence modifications are planned responses that should be implemented if a target behavior occurs to try to reduce the likelihood of it happening again. Types of consequence modifications include positive and negative reinforcement, differential reinforcement, positive punishment, extinction, behavior contracting, and token economy. Examples of consequence modifications include ignoring the behavior or redirecting the client to another activity.

Finally, a written behavior reduction plan should always include crisis interventions for any target behaviors that could possibly result in harm to the client or others. This is important to ensure the safety of the client as well as those providing care. It should include de-escalation techniques to help calm situations that may arise and safety protocols to ensure the security of everyone involved.

If a client begins to engage in a new maladaptive target behavior not previously included in the written behavior reduction plan, the RBT should record it and report to the board-certified behavior analyst so the new behavior can be added to the plan and addressed as necessary.

Common Functions of Behavior

When a person engages in a particular behavior, there is always a cause for that action; the person is attempting to meet a need, whether that need is straightforward or more difficult to understand. The causes that drive people toward certain behaviors are known as functions. Behavior analysts can determine the function or functions of a client's target behavior by conducting functional behavior assessments. The functions of a person's behavior must be understood to effectively implement strategies to change the target behavior.

Behavioral functions are organized into four main categories: automatic reinforcement, avoidance/escape, attention, and access to tangibles.

Automatic Reinforcement
The first function of behavior is automatic reinforcement. This type of reinforcement does not involve external factors or people beyond the client themself. Instead, reward and reinforcement are driven entirely by the person's internal stimuli. When they engage in a seemingly random behavior because it feels good to them, that behavior usually falls under this category. Examples include repeatedly tapping one's foot or biting one's nails. These are self-soothing behaviors that do not seek anything tangible or from anyone else; the satisfaction gained from performing the behavior comes from the person themself.

Avoidance/Escape
The second function of behavior is avoidance or escape. This occurs when a person engages in a certain behavior to avoid an unpleasant task, situation, or demand. It involves the removal of a stimulus that is perceived as negative, which usually applies to activities that a person associates with feelings of discomfort, anxiety, or being challenged to the point of stress. An example would be a child tossing away their school supplies because they do not want to do an assignment, but avoidance/escape could also apply to a more complex situation, such as a high schooler not attending a school dance because they want to avoid the anxiety that they associate with social events. One way to address avoidance behaviors is to implement noncontingent escape (NCE), which involves placing a client on a set schedule where they stop doing a task at certain times for planned breaks and set periods of activity, instead of stopping activities as a direct result of negative behaviors.

Attention
The third function of behavior is attention—when a person engages in a behavior to gain attention from others. One example of this is a child throwing a tantrum whenever their parent attempts to take a

phone call. This behavior occurs because the child does not like that the parent's attention is directed elsewhere, and the point of the behavior is to redirect attention back onto the child, even if the attention is not necessarily positive. However, it is important to note that this function of behavior can apply to both positive and negative attention-seeking behaviors. It does not only apply to unhealthy coping mechanisms. For instance, if a child studies hard for a test because they want to impress their parents with a good grade to win their approval, that behavior would still fall under this category.

Access to Tangibles

The fourth function of behavior is access to tangibles. The point of this behavior is to gain access to a specific, tangible thing that they desire. This could refer to a certain physical item such as a snack or toy, or it could apply to a person wanting to gain access to a certain experience or activity. For example, a child might scream or cry because they want cupcakes for dessert, but the function of behavior would also fall into this category if a person had a melt down because they really wanted to go on vacation or play a game of basketball. Access to tangibles can apply to a wide range of things, so when considering this function, remember to associate it with wanting a certain physical object or experience.

It's important to note that these functions apply to all behaviors, whether they are maladaptive or not. The healthy actions most people perform on a regular basis still fall under one of these categories. Knowing the functions of a client's target behaviors is key to knowing how to address those behaviors. You cannot fix a problem if you do not understand why it is happening in the first place.

Implementing Antecedent-Modifying Interventions

An antecedent is anything that occurs right before a target behavior. The point of modifying antecedents is to change a client's environment with the intention of preventing certain behaviors. Common examples of antecedent modifications include using timers, offering choices, priming, or providing visual aids.

Motivating Operations (Cycles of Motivating Behavior Through Reinforcers)

Motivating operations (MOs) temporarily decrease or increase the effectiveness of a given stimulus as the driving reinforcer in a situation. A reinforcer is something that drives a certain action; it's a reward that drives a person to follow through with a behavior associated with a thought that occurs to them. When a certain stimulus is the driving reinforcer, that means it is the driving force in a situation.

The easiest example of this is food, which is a common and necessary stimulus for any human being. The need for food drives us to act out certain behaviors to achieve the means to eat so that we may physically provide for ourselves. Those behaviors might include hunting animals in the wild or working at a store to earn the money to buy food. However, your level of hunger changes. It waxes and wanes over time depending on how long it has been since you last ate, as well as the quality and satisfaction gained from the food you consume. Food in this case is the stimulus, which serves as the driving reinforcer for certain target behaviors.

Motivating operations affect the overall intensity of a certain stimulus. These operations are broken down into two general categories: abolishing operations (AOs) and establishing operations (EOs).

Establishing operations aim to increase the likelihood that a behavior will occur by increasing the effectiveness of one or more reinforcers. In essence, if a person is deprived of something they want very much for a long time, that person will begin to want that thing more and more over time. The thought of having that thing will become more of a motivating factor over time as their desire for it continues to increase. This deprivation over time is the establishing operation.

Abolishing operations decrease the effectiveness of reinforcers, which in turn decreases the overall likelihood that a behavior will occur. The more often a person has had something that they want, the more their desire for it is satisfied. This is referred to as satiation. When a person's desire for a particular thing is satiated, the idea of having that thing becomes less of a driving force for them. The satiety is the abolishing operation.

The best, and possibly most common, example of establishing and abolishing operations is hunger versus fullness, with food as the reinforcer. If a person has not eaten anything recently and they are hungry, food will be a strong reinforcer for that person. Hunger is the establishing operation. However, if a person has just eaten a large meal and they are feeling full, food will be much less of a reinforcer for them. The feeling of fullness, or satiety, is the abolishing operation.

Discriminative Stimuli (External Cues)

The term discriminative stimulus (DS) refers to environmental cues that indicate or signal whether a particular reinforcer is available, or whether a certain action should be taken. Discriminative stimuli are used as prompts for teaching new behaviors or for reinforcing positive existing behaviors. These form a process of behavior modification through cues and reinforcements. Signs or cues help show the client what actions can or should be taken in a given context to help set them up for success from the start.

A discriminative stimulus can fall into any of the following categories: visual, verbal, tactile, or environmental. Visual discriminative stimuli include symbols or pictures that are designed to represent a particular desired behavior. One example of this would be a picture of a toothbrush designed to prompt a person to remember to brush their teeth. Verbal discriminative stimuli include spoken phrases or words that are meant to signal a particular behavior. For example, a parent or caretaker might say, "cleanup time" to signal that it is time for a person to clean up and put their things away. Tactile discriminative stimuli involve the use of physical touch to prompt the desired behavior, which is particularly helpful for kinesthetic learners; for example, tapping a person's hand to let them know not to touch something that they shouldn't. Environmental discriminative stimuli use the presence of certain nearby people or objects to signal a behavior, which can be a useful tool when working with clients who are contextual learners. One example of this would be keeping a bookshelf in a reading area to signal to a person that it is time to read when they see it.

Implementing Differential Reinforcement Procedures

The aim of differential reinforcement is to increase the likelihood of a positive behavior that is being reinforced, while decreasing the likelihood of a negative behavior put on extinction. Differential reinforcement is commonly used to facilitate the behavior modification process. Both extinction and reinforcement are combined to form the process of differential reinforcement, which involves selectively reinforcing certain desired behaviors while also selectively withholding reinforcement for negative or maladaptive behaviors.

Reinforcement can be either positive or negative. Positive reinforcement is the process of providing something positive when a certain behavior occurs, while negative reinforcement is the process of removing a negative or unpleasant stimulus after the desired behavior has occurred. Regardless of which type of reinforcement one chooses to use, it ultimately involves producing or removing a stimulus in response to a given action to promote that behavior.

Extinction, on the other hand, is the process of withholding reinforcement after a particular behavior has occurred. This is done to reduce the occurrence of a negative action, and it is neither reinforcement nor punishment. It is simply a lack of reward that can be used as a tool in ABA therapy.

There are five types of differential reinforcement procedures. These include differential reinforcement of alternative behavior (DRA), differential reinforcement of incompatible behavior (DRI), differential reinforcement of other behavior (DRO), differential reinforcement of higher rates (DRH), and differential reinforcement of lower rates (DRL). However, for this section it is important to understand two of those procedures: differential reinforcement of alternative behavior and differential reinforcement of other behavior.

Differential Reinforcement of Alternative Behavior

Differential reinforcement of alternative behavior (DRA) works by reinforcing a positive action that is meant to serve as a more functional alternative to the undesirable target behavior while still fulfilling the same function of behavior. This is a widely acceptable intervention for reducing a multitude of negative or maladaptive behaviors. Before beginning behavior reduction therapy, it is important to identify the function of the target behavior to successfully identify healthy alternative behaviors that will fulfill the same function and help set the client up for success.

One common form of DRA procedure is functional communication training (FCT). FCT directly focuses on improving the client's communication skills that pertain to activities of daily living. It serves to improve their communication with others by reducing problematic target behaviors that pertain to communication and replace them with more desirable or more socially appropriate behaviors. This form of DRA is often used when providing therapy for people with autism spectrum disorder (ASD) who are having an especially difficult time communicating with others.

Consider the following example of DRA: If a teenager develops an unhealthy habit of cursing in regular conversation and it is determined that the function of the behavior is attention because they want their peers to notice them more, a healthy alternative behavior that could be reinforced is telling jokes. DRA can be used to reinforce this healthy change to transition from swearing to telling jokes when the person providing the therapy is able to identify the teenager's desire for attention from their peers.

Differential Reinforcement of Other Behavior

Differential reinforcement of other behavior (DRO) involves reinforcing the absence of a negative target behavior. This method is particularly useful in teaching clients who require the reduction of maladaptive behaviors that are especially challenging to address or actions that are potentially harmful or dangerous.

DRO is generally considered an easier method of differential reinforcement to implement because it does not require the identification of specific functions of behavior or the reinforcement of alternative behaviors. It simply involves reinforcing the client after a specified increment of time has passed if the negative target behavior did not occur. Therefore, if care providers have been unsuccessful in determining the function of a particular action in the past and previous attempts at intervention have failed, this method of differential reinforcement can be a helpful way to manage the difficult target behavior. The main downside of DRO is that it does not teach the client appropriate alternative actions to take; however, research has consistently shown that it is highly effective in reducing problem behaviors.

One example of DRO being put to good use is if a client has frequent, seemingly random outbursts of aggression. Say the client attempts to hit or scratch people around them multiple times per hour, and the function of the behavior cannot be identified because it keeps happening no matter what the situation is. DRO could be implemented by setting a timer for a set increment, such as twenty minutes at a time, and rewarding the client each time they make it the full twenty minutes without scratching or hitting anyone. If they do engage in the aggressive behavior, the timer is reset with no reward (the client engaging in the negative target behavior is the only time the timer should be reset in this way). Over time, the absence of the aggressive behavior is reinforced, which in turn leads to a reduction in the outbursts of hitting and scratching.

Implementing Extinction Procedures

As previously introduced, the term *extinction* refers to a behavior reduction process that withholds reinforcement for target behaviors that have already been reinforced in the past at some point. It is generally recommended for low-intensity target behaviors to prevent them from worsening. It is rarely recommended for severe behaviors that involve danger or serious risk of harm. Extinction can only be implemented if the target behavior has been previously reinforced to some extent. This method cannot be effectively used if the action has never been rewarded because the process relies on unlearning a learned negative behavior.

The goal of extinction procedures is to make the undesirable target behavior extinct, which means that the action no longer occurs. This term is easier to remember if you make a mental comparison to dinosaurs, which are now extinct: They once existed, and they no longer do. This is exactly what we want for the disruptive target behavior when implementing extinction procedures.

One important thing to remember when it comes to extinction procedures is that when this process is implemented it often leads to what is known as an "extinction burst." This is a temporary spike or increase in the occurrence of a target behavior or related negative actions when the reinforcement for that behavior is initially removed. Extinction bursts tend to happen because, in the past, the behavior led the client to receive a certain reinforcement. Now the association of the reinforcement with the behavior must be unlearned, which takes time. The amount of time this can take varies widely; a major contributing factor is the length of time a client was exposed to reinforcement for the target behavior. An extinction burst is to be expected in most cases, and anyone responsible for providing care should be made aware of this and of the plan for managing it to help ease the process.

Managing extinction bursts can be a challenge because its behavioral manifestations vary widely in frequency, intensity, and duration. Sometimes the outbursts are frequent occurrences of the original target behavior. However, sometimes they result in new, related behaviors that serve the same function of the original target behavior. The goal for the client is to achieve the reinforcement they have previously learned that they would receive, so now their frustration leads them to try harder to get the reinforcement, often in the form of aggression or other undesirable behavior. Patience and persistence are the two most important qualities when managing extinction bursts. Keep in mind that as long as consistency is maintained and the extinction procedures are continuously applied, the negative behavior will eventually subside.

In ABA therapy, extinction procedures fall into two main categories: "denying access to reinforcers" and "planned ignoring." Both involve a process of reducing an unwanted target behavior by cutting off access to reinforcers, but they are different in the details of how they are implemented.

When denying access to reinforcers, the aim is to prevent access to certain activities or items that act as reinforcers for unwanted target behaviors. One example of this would be if a child repeatedly tries to

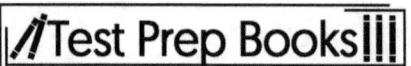

run outside for recess at school before lining up with the other kids like they are supposed to. You could deny access to reinforcers by not allowing the child to leave the room to participate in recess until they calmly line up with their peers and wait their turn. This method can be helpful in encouraging desirable replacement behaviors.

Planned ignoring, on the other hand, involves cutting off any access to the driving reinforcer for the unwanted target behavior. For example, if a child is having an issue with throwing tantrums because they want attention, traditional methods of punishment may not work because negative attention still provides the child with the reward they were looking for (attention). You could implement planned ignoring by not paying attention to the tantrums and not feeding into the behavior anymore. Eventually, the tantrums are likely to subside because the child no longer gets the attention they were seeking from the behavior.

When using any extinction procedure, regardless of the details of its implementation or what category the procedures fall under, it is vital to combine it with positive approaches and the teaching of desirable replacement behaviors. Always take into consideration the individual needs of the client and maintain a respectful commitment to learning better skills for managing behavior. The process should always involve thoughtful, individualized planning and a constant, ongoing reflection on outcomes from start to finish.

Crisis and Emergency Procedures

While a crisis intervention plan is not considered necessary for all clients, one should be put in place for any person who may reasonably be expected to inflict any type of harm, whether that is due to high-risk behaviors or other circumstances such as potentially serious medical conditions. A crisis intervention plan should always lay out individualized step-by-step instructions for the behavioral technician and any other people responsible for providing care to follow if an emergency situation takes place.

In addition to ensuring physical safety, good management of crisis and emergency situations through proper protocol reduces anxiety for everyone involved. Staff, caregivers, and clients can all benefit from knowing that there are clear, carefully planned procedures to follow if an emergency situation arises. Effective crisis management also helps to maintain the overall treatment integrity by reducing or minimizing disruptions so that therapy interventions can continue as planned.

A crisis intervention plan is vital for anyone who poses a risk to themselves or others due to dangerous target behaviors. The goal of these plans is to help ensure the safety of the client, as well as caregivers and anyone else involved. There are four main categories of crisis or emergency procedures. The first three categories all pertain to harmful behaviors on behalf of the client: elopement, self-injurious behavior, and physical aggression. The final category, medical emergencies, pertains to clients with medical conditions that make it necessary to plan for emergencies that may arise as a result of those conditions. These crisis plans are meant to handle medical emergencies and do not reflect the client's actual behavior.

Behavior Related Crisis Intervention Plans

A crisis intervention plan that falls under **elopement** is put in place because the client is considered at risk for attempting to leave a safe area without permission. For example, if a child were to repeatedly try to run away from home, it might be necessary to create a crisis intervention plan that lays out necessary steps to follow if they either run away or attempt to leave the home without permission.

The **self-injurious behavior** category refers to crisis plans that are put in place for a client who exhibits specific, known behaviors that could result in them causing harm to themselves. For instance, a client may repeatedly bang their head or attempt to cut themselves, so step-by-step instructions may be laid out to effectively respond to this behavior and prevent as much harm to the client as possible.

A crisis intervention plan that falls under the category of **physical aggression** is put in place for a client who has displayed behaviors that put them at risk for causing physical harm to the people around them. The goal of emergency protocols in this case would be to de-escalate the aggression before any physically harmful action is inflicted on the behavioral technician, other caregivers, or anyone else involved in the situation.

Non-Behavior Related Crisis Intervention Plans

Finally, crisis plans should always be prepared for clients who suffer from medical conditions that may require emergency medical treatment or intervention. Plans in this case may involve the implementation of interventions such as providing necessary medications. For example, if a person suffers from a condition such as asthma, the care plan would likely include the administration of the client's inhaler. Similarly, if a client has a disorder such as epilepsy, a care plan may lay out the steps to follow in the event that a client has a seizure.

Strategies for Successfully Implementing Crisis / Emergency Procedures

Effectively carrying out crisis emergency procedures involves five key strategies. The first is to identify the crisis, which may seem like a simple concept, but it also means recognizing the warning signs that a crisis is coming before it occurs so that you can intervene as early as possible. The second is to keep open communication throughout the situation with any other caregivers, staff, or first responders if necessary. It is also important to communicate and discuss a crisis event with supervisors.

The third strategy is to prioritize safety above all else by using any necessary protective equipment, de-escalation techniques, or other interventions such as securing the area to prevent more people from becoming involved in the situation or to prevent the client from leaving a safe, controlled environment. The fourth strategy is to always follow protocol. Go through the steps provided in the plan and enact it as smoothly as possible. The interventions were planned out for a reason, and deviating from the plan does not usually help anyone involved. The fifth and final strategy is to debrief and document the incident after it has been resolved, as well as to report it to any necessary parties such as parents or caretakers.

Practice Quiz

1. Which of the following is NOT one of the essential components of a written behavior reduction plan?
    a. The function of the target behavior
    b. Any emergency protocols related to a client's care plan
    c. A list of maladaptive behaviors that have not occurred but are likely to
    d. Antecedent strategies

2. A client begins crying and throwing things whenever they see a certain peer arrive for group activities, so the RBT provides a schedule that can be used as a visual reminder of when the client will have to be around that peer. What is the visual schedule an example of?
    a. An antecedent manipulation
    b. A crisis protocol
    c. A reinforcer
    d. A method of differential reinforcement

3. A client is in the cycle of hunger and satiety. They become more motivated by hunger and the desire for food the longer they have gone without eating, and less motivated by food the more recently they have eaten. What is the abolishing operation?
    a. Food
    b. Hunger
    c. Satiety (feeling full)
    d. None of the above

4. A client regularly gets up out of their seat during mealtimes and demands dessert, refusing to eat the healthier parts of their meals. The RBT responds by not allowing the client to eat any dessert until the client sits down calmly and eats their healthier foods first. Which method of behavior reduction is this?
    a. Negative reinforcement
    b. Punishment
    c. Planned ignoring
    d. Denying access to reinforcers

5. A client regularly refuses to engage in social situations because they do not want to experience the anxiety they associate with interacting with new people. The function of this behavior would fall under what category?
    a. Attention
    b. Escape/Avoidance
    c. Automatic Reinforcement
    d. Access to tangibles

See answers on the next page.

Answer Explanations

1. C: A list of maladaptive behaviors that have not occurred would not be necessary. A written behavior reduction plan focuses in detail on actions and behaviors that have occurred and how to manage them, rather than actions that haven't taken place. The functions of behavior, emergency protocols, and antecedent strategies are all vital components of any behavior reduction plan.

2. A: A visual sign or cue that is meant to aid in the modification of behavior is considered an antecedent modification. More specifically, it is an example of a visual discriminative stimulus, which is one form of antecedent modification. These types of visual aids are helpful in behavior modification because they provide clear, reliable cues that make it easier for clients to adjust to learning new behaviors. Choice B is incorrect because a crisis protocol refers to a specific plan for an emergency situation, which has nothing to do with this scenario. Choice C is incorrect because the schedule is a tool to help the client learn, rather than a reward to motivate their behavior, which is the definition of a reinforcer. Finally, Choice D is incorrect because differential reinforcement is a process of motivating one behavior while discouraging another through the use of a combination of reinforcement and extinction, which is not happening in this example.

3. C: An abolishing operation is a motivating operation that reduces the effect of a reinforcer. The abolishing operation in this case is satiety because the feeling of fullness reduces the effectiveness of food as the reinforcer. The fuller you are, the less likely you are to be motivated by a drive to get food. Choice A, food, is the driving reinforcer. Choice B, hunger, is the establishing operation.

4. D: The RBT is cutting off access to the driving reinforcer (dessert) of the negative target behavior (getting up and refusing to eat the rest of their food) until the client ceases the maladaptive action (the target behavior) and exhibits the proper behavior (sitting and eating their meal) instead. This is called denying access to reinforcers, a type of extinction procedure that should never be considered a form of punishment. Choice A is not the right answer because negative reinforcement is the removal of an unpleasant stimulus when a desired behavior occurs, which is not happening in this example. Choice B is incorrect because extinction procedures, when properly implemented, should never be looked at or used as a form of punishment. Choice C is incorrect because the behavior is not being ignored. Instead, access to dessert is being denied until the client corrects their behavior.

5. B: The aim of the client's behavior is to avoid the negative feelings associated with anxiety that they connect with the idea of interacting with new people. Choice A is incorrect because the client is doing the opposite of trying to get attention by avoiding social activity. Choice C is incorrect because they are not engaging in internal self-soothing behavior, and Choice D is incorrect because their actions have nothing to do with trying to access a specific physical item or experience.

Documenting and Reporting

Ongoing Communication with Supervisors

Cultivating a collaborative, supportive working relationship with a supervisor is integral to the success of a Registered Behavior Technician (RBT). A supervisor's duty is to support the RBT in their efforts to provide the highest-quality service to their client. They should be considered the subject matter expert who is there to listen, guide, and offer feedback as the RBT works with the client. The supervisor helps nurture and grow the RBT's skills and experience. The foundation of effective communication between a supervisor and supervisee is a strong rapport built on understanding, respect, and a common working goal.

Method and Frequency of Communication

RBTs should understand the preferred method with which to connect with their supervisor to ensure effective and timely communication. Some supervisors may prefer emails and texts for informal, routine check-ins, like if the RBT has a minor question or wants to offer a small client update. Alternatively, meeting in person or via video might be preferable for discussing more complex topics, like a major shift in client behavior, struggles with implementing an intervention within the behavior plan, or debriefing a particularly challenging session. Once the supervisor and RBT agree on preferences for communication procedures, they are more likely to be able to engage in productive, effective conversations.

The RBT and supervisor must establish an expectation for how often they should be in contact so that they are each able to rely on predictable intervals of communication with each other. A new RBT may require a higher frequency of communication with their supervisor in order to ensure that their work meets expectations, since they're still learning the nuances of the role. It may be helpful to reengage in a discussion around communication frequency expectations at regular intervals to ensure that both parties' needs are being met and there are not any gaps in communication. As an RBT gains more skill and experience, their supervision may become less frequent. However, supervisors need to meet a minimum requirement for monthly supervision as outlined by the Behavior Analyst Certification Board (BACB). The BACB requires that supervision occur at least monthly, and the length of supervision should be equal to at least 5 percent of the RBT's direct client contact hours.

Feedback

RBTs should be receptive to both giving and receiving feedback. Feedback is essential to learning and growing, and supervision is the best place to support that growth. The RBT should be willing to provide feedback to the supervisor about their own learning style, questions and concerns that arise, and when they need more support. Frequent feedback has been demonstrated to lead to higher rates of motivation and performance. Supervision should be a safe place to both give and receive feedback about the important work that is being performed. Some RBTs prefer very direct and frequent feedback, while others benefit from a softer, more nuanced approach. On the other hand, supervisors themselves can excel at providing feedback in a specific way, based on their own training, disposition, and prior supervisory experience. Discussion at the beginning of a supervisory relationship can set helpful expectations around communication and feedback style. It can take some effort and intentionality on the part of both the supervisor and supervisee to ensure that they are in alignment. Furthermore, the supervisor should open the door to receiving feedback themselves, as this can offer an opportunity to deepen the supervisory relationship and grow professionally.

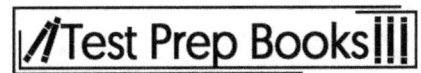

Documenting and Reporting

Objectivity and Cultural Responsiveness in Consulting

Presenting information to the supervisor from a place of fact and objective assessment, rather than opinion and emotional evaluation, is vital for effective discussion. This includes sharing observable behaviors and concrete data to support valuable discussions. An RBT should offer regular updates to the supervisor as well as informing them of any irregularities in serving the client. It can be helpful for the RBT to disclose when they feel that their own personal interpretation may be getting in the way of serving a client with objective professionalism.

No matter how experienced they are, any RBT can be susceptible to experiencing transference and countertransference. Transference is the subconscious association of a present person with someone in their past. For example, the client might remind the RBT of a family member, which could subconsciously alter the RBT's perception of or behavior toward the client. Countertransference is defined as responding to someone in the present with the feelings/reactions that were attached to a previous relationship. For instance, a client's aggressive behavior may remind the RBT of a past relationship in which they experienced a violent partner. This can lead the RBT to react strongly to that behavior in session, limiting their objectivity and perhaps leading them to behave unprofessionally. While it is normal for this issue to arise when serving other people, the only way to combat it and ensure it does not interfere professionally is having awareness of it and addressing it regularly in supervision.

In order for a client to feel safe enough to engage in treatment, their identity must be honored and given space to thrive. This means that the RBT must be extremely conscious of their own approach to providing treatment, including their own bias, in order to provide equitable services. Supervision should serve as a safe place for the RBT to engage in self-evaluation, reflecting on how their own experiences and beliefs might intersect with their clients. Supervision should offer not only a place for that self-evaluation and discussion but also a place to identify what extra training might be appropriate to enhance the RBT's scope of knowledge and practice.

Contingency Planning

Establishing a contingency plan that identifies alternate supervisors in an emergency helps save time in potential crisis situations. The RBT and their supervisor should create safety and contingency plans and regularly check in about these plans, as this will increase the RBT's confidence in managing direct client contact and lessen the likelihood of a mismanaged crisis situation. Additionally, should issues or concerns arise with the supervisor's conduct, the RBT should have an appropriate avenue laid out through which to seek support.

Seeking Clinical Direction from Supervisors

RBTs should be able to recognize when to seek clinical oversight and direction from their supervisor. The RBT could require supervisory guidance for situations that can range from routine concerns to urgent matters. The RBT and supervisor should agree on what constitutes a routine versus urgent concern to reduce potential for misunderstanding, increase prompt response time, and contribute to a productive partnership. Clinical consultation strengthens the RBT's skill set and ensures they are using an intervention that is ethical, effective, and appropriate for the situation.

A frequent topic of discussion in supervision is client behavior plans. Because RBTs are responsible for implementing the plan, not creating or designing it, it is important to have a clear understanding of the plan's directives. The RBT should routinely review behavior plans with their supervisor so there are regular opportunities to ask questions and clarify interventions. Because the plan often evolves over time, regular check-ins to ensure clarification can reduce the potential for mistakes and increase the opportunity to deepen understanding.

The RBT needs to report if the client demonstrates a change in behavior or a differing response to an intervention. Behavioral changes are very common and can offer a good opportunity to process how the RBT could modify their approach to interacting with the client. Bringing clear and thorough documentation of the session can help guide supervision, as it offers context for the supervisor to understand the RBT's experience.

An RBT may need to consult their supervisor immediately to seek guidance on how to defuse a crisis or advice on a higher level of intervention for their client. If the client has demonstrated a new behavior in session, the RBT should use clinical judgment to determine whether this requires immediate consultation with a supervisor or is something that can wait for the next regularly scheduled meeting. An example of a time when this might call for immediate consultation could be if the behavior plan needs immediate modification or there is abuse/neglect of a vulnerable person that needs to be reported to authorities.

RBTs should consult with their supervisor when they need access to materials required for their job, like data sheets, materials for skills acquisition, and reinforcers for behavior. RBTs should be forthcoming about their need for new materials to ensure they are not going into a session ill-prepared.

Per the RBT Ethics Code, there are specific situations in which the RBT is required to report to their supervisor and the BACB within 30 days. These situations impact an RBT's ability to do their job and include the following:

- The RBT receiving legal charges

- The RBT being investigated by previous or current employers, government agencies, educational institutions, or other third-party entities

- The RBT receiving disciplinary actions from a current or former employer, including suspension or termination

- The RBT having a physical condition, mental condition, or substance abuse concern that may impair their ability to provide services to the client

Reporting Variables Affecting the Client

Maintaining thorough documentation is essential, especially when a client has high and ever-evolving needs. Comprehensive documentation allows the client's treatment team to have a firm understanding of the treatment progress, particularly when navigating a multitude of variables. Part of routinely documenting interactions with the client is capturing the external and internal variables—including physical and mental health, medication, and environmental factors—that could impact the client's engagement or overall progress. This can offer a more robust understanding of how to support the client and engage them most effectively. It is part of an RBT's ethical responsibility to ensure they offer a comprehensive picture of the client's experience so treatment can be responsive to the client's needs.

Mental Health
Individuals diagnosed as being on the autism spectrum have a high probability of comorbidity; they often meet criteria for other mental health disorders, most commonly depression, anxiety, and

obsessive-compulsive disorder. Symptoms of these accompanying disorders can manifest in ways that might make it challenging for the client to engage in treatment. It's important to factor other potential disorders into treatment planning and detail the emergence or regression of symptoms as observed in interactions. There are many ways that this can manifest:

- **Anxiety:** Excessive worry, avoidance, or fear related to completing certain tasks or engaging with the RBT
- **Depression:** Decreased motivation, notable lack of energy, and increased levels of hopelessness that lead to lack of willingness to engage with the RBT or follow through with behavioral interventions
- **Obsessive-compulsive disorder:** Repetitive behaviors, intrusive thoughts, or rigid routines, leading the client to require a specific and thoughtful approach to behavioral intervention

Medication

The client's medication regimen should be considered throughout the treatment process. Often, clients receive treatment in conjunction with psychiatric care; it's common to work with clients experiencing regimen shifts. Skill acquisition and behavior reduction could be impacted by a change in dosage or the addition or removal of medications.

Medication changes can lead to shifts in the client's attention span, frustration tolerance, ability to regulate emotions, and energy levels. These shifts can often impact the client's ability to complete skill acquisition tasks or respond favorably to behavior reduction strategies. Documentation of medication changes and how they correlate to behavior and mood shifts can support collaboration with the client's parents or psychiatric team in advocating for a medication regimen that works more effectively for the client.

Physical Health

It is helpful to understand a client's acute and chronic health conditions, which could impact their level of engagement during sessions. For example, a client may be diagnosed with asthma and require in-session modifications to not exacerbate difficulty breathing. Other health issues may require modifications, such as flexibility in scheduling, modifying the length of sessions, changing activity structure, and rescheduling sessions to accommodate necessary medical appointments. Any modification to sessions—e.g., canceled or rescheduled sessions—must be thoroughly documented in order to understand their impact on the client's overall progress.

Session Attendees

There can sometimes be a change in attendees in a client's regular session, shifting the dynamics of the session by influencing a change in behavior for the client. A parent or guardian may bring the client's siblings to the session. Siblings often want to join in and engage/play during the session. If this is to be a regular occurrence, it's helpful to have it built into the behavior plan. If the object of a behavior plan is to strengthen social skills or familial relationships, including regular sibling participation could be a useful strategy. If this isn't the goal, it may be helpful to build strategies to minimize distractions while the siblings are in attendance. Regardless of the plan, it is important to thoroughly document via accurate, objective notes when there are other attendees so as to understand the impact that it has on the client.

Sleep

Individuals with autism often have atypical sleeping patterns, which can impact the client's behavior, mood, and engagement with others. Common struggles caused by difficulty sleeping are shortened attention span, low frustration tolerance, and difficulty remembering previously learned skills or retaining new information. Any reported or observed sleep disturbances or irregularities should be recorded in the session notes to offer insight into the client's level of functioning that day. Reports could come from the client themselves or from the parent, guardian, or adult bringing them to the session.

Environmental Changes

Any environmental changes for the client should be documented in session notes. This can include relocation (new house or school), familial changes (divorce, sibling addition, death of a family member, extended family moving in, etc.), a new pet, and more. Relocation can impact a client greatly, as their daily routine and relationships with those around them (new neighbors or peers) shift with the location. RBTs should be conscious of reporting these changes, as they can manifest differently for each client. Familial changes can cause emotional stress (confusion, anger, and grief) that can lead to behavioral changes in sessions.

Abuse or Neglect

RBTs are mandated reporters of the abuse or neglect of a child or vulnerable adult; they have a legal and ethical obligation to report. Mandated reporting laws ensure that providers are especially attentive to serving vulnerable populations—those who may not be able to protect and advocate for themselves.

If an RBT observes or suspects abuse or neglect, they should report this to their supervisor immediately, as well as to the appropriate authorities. Depending on the location, states have varying options for reporting, including online databases, phone numbers, fax, or email options. The RBT should be aware of their own state's reporting requirements prior to serving their clients. Complete and timely documentation of these concerns ensures that the most informed decision is made regarding the client.

Generating Objective Session Notes

Counselors must document their practice with the client. Counselors document sessions with clients as well as client legal mandates, such as visitation with minors in state custody. Documentation may be a combination of narrative and quantitative descriptions, depending on agency requirements. Records should be kept confidential either electronically or in a physical location. New laws require that all records be electronic, and they are called electronic health records. These records must be confidential as stated in the **Health Insurance Portability and Accountability Act of 1996 (HIPAA)**. It is crucial for the counselor to maintain accurate documentation.

Note-Taking Styles

Although each organization has a different set of rules and regulations governing the precise format of the note, the basic content of a treatment session note is standard across the industry. Notes should be written as soon as possible following the session, with the best practice being writing them at the end of session. This is because memories naturally fade over time, thus offering a less precise or inaccurate recollection of the session the longer the RBT waits to write. Treatment notes serve a variety of purposes. They not only fulfill legal, regulatory, organizational, and insurance purposes but are also useful for the treatment team to analyze on an ongoing basis to track the client's treatment. Several elements comprise a well-written, objective session note, including basic information, client affect and presentation, observations and interventions, data, and barriers to treatment.

Documenting and Reporting

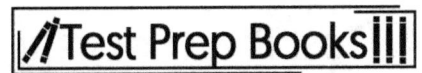

Information from both the subjective and objective data is combined to formulate a concise, yet comprehensive, assessment for the client. In some note-taking practices, the identification of the subjective and objective data along with assessment formation is required. This style of documentation is known as the **SOAP method**, an acronym that stands for Subjective, Objective, Assessment, and Plan. Another note-taking style that focuses on the subjective and objective data is the BIRP documentation method. **BIRP** stands for Behavior, Intervention, Response, and Plan. It is not as commonly used as SOAP.

Basic Information

The start of the session note should describe who was in attendance, where the session occurred, and the precise date and time. Putting this information first provides context for the reader to orient themselves properly. This information is also essential for billing purposes, given that insurance companies require precise times of services rendered. It can help to have a consistent format to begin each note with, such as:

Date: 3/2/2024
Time: 11:45 AM–12:30 PM
Attendees: [Client Name], [RBT]
Location: Treatment Center

Client Affect and Presentation

The RBT should describe how the client appeared during the session, specifically regarding the client's affect and presentation. This provides the reader with a deeper understanding of the client's emotional and physical state at the time of the session, which can offer some insight into the client's level of engagement with the treatment that day. Beyond simply indicating how the RBT thinks the client was feeling, which is subjective interpretation, an objective description of the client's affect and presentation relies on tangible facts, offering a measurable, observable description of behaviors.

Rather than offering vague, subjective interpretation like "The client was sad today," the RBT could write, "The client had downcast eyes, withdrawn body language, and a frown throughout the session. The client verbalized less often than is their typical baseline." This description offers concrete visual and behavioral descriptors, which can be helpful in further treatment planning.

The RBT is encouraged to avoid using vague terms, like sad, mad, or happy, opting instead for descriptors that paint a more accurate picture of the presentation. The RBT should aim to include factual information rather than their own personal assertion. In addition to observations regarding the client's emotional state, physical behavior and presence are also worth noting: "The client appeared more at ease today, as evidenced by lack of fidgeting and demonstrated ability to remain in their seat without requiring prompts to do so."

Observations and Interventions

At the core of the session note are the RBT's observations of the client's behaviors during the session. This includes the specific behaviors that the treatment is seeking to target and should also include any new or unanticipated behaviors that arise. Each behavior should have a description that is clear, objective, and factual. It can be easy to fall into the trap of offering subjective interpretations, which can infer what the client *might* be feeling, rather than offering tangible evidence. For example, the RBT might write, "The client got mad and started having a tantrum." This not only infers emotion but also uses subjective language that is open for multiple interpretations. A better description is, "The client

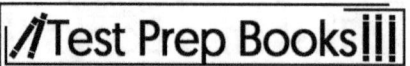

was playing with their preferred toy when the RBT asked them to put the toy away to prepare to go to lunch. The client began to cry, yell, and throw themselves to the ground. This lasted 90 seconds before the client was able to cease the behavior and engage in the RBT's request." This offers factual descriptions of not only the behavior but also the antecedent and aftermath.

The RBT should also include descriptions of interventions offered during the session, including responses to targeted behaviors. To continue the above example, the RBT might offer how they reacted or adjusted the environment in response to the client's struggle with being asked to put away their toy. "When the client began to cry, yell, and throw themselves on the ground, the RBT removed the siblings and other technician from the room, dimmed the lights, and sat next to the client without speaking."

Data

A full set of data from the session should always be included in the session note, as it offers further objective information to strengthen the note. The data—indicating the behavior's frequency, duration, and/or intensity—quantifies how effective the interventions have been and offers insight into behavioral changes. The type of data collected depends on the behavior plan. Examples of what this data could look like include the following:

- **Frequency and duration:** The client experienced 3 episodes of disruptive behavior during this session, each lasting 70–90 seconds.

- **Task completion:** The client filled their own cup of water successfully 3 out of 4 times during session.

- **Response accuracy:** The client responded to their name being called 7 out of 10 times during session. Of those 7 instances, all responses occurred within 15 seconds.

While data can be expressed narratively, it is important to know that utilizing graphs, charts, and other visual elements can enhance the reader's interpretation of the data. Offering visual elements in session notes can help the treatment team notice trends, which offer insight into whether the interventions being used are effective (behavior is decreasing, increasing, or remaining the same) or adjustments need to be made.

Certain elements, such as behavior intensity, are most effectively shared in a chart. For example, explaining intensity in a narrative form might look like: "The client experienced 4 instances of the targeted behavior during this session. The instances lasted approximately 3 minutes, 5 minutes, 7 minutes, and 9 minutes. This shows that the behavior increased by 2 minutes each time it occurred." This description is not as effective as a graph.

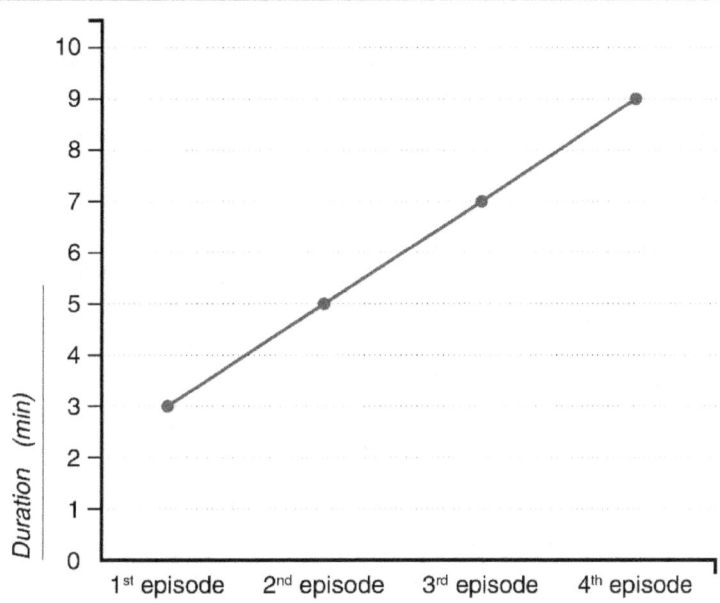

Each time a session occurs, it can be added to the chart to compare how the behavioral intensity looks over time.

Barriers

Barriers to implementing the behavior plan should be outlined in the note. Barriers are anything that could get in the way of the client participating in sessions or hinder the RBT's ability to engage the client effectively. External barriers could include environmental concerns (too much background noise, room is too hot or cold) and time constraints (tardiness). Barriers can also be internal, such as the client struggling with a lack of motivation, or cognitive or developmental considerations.

Data and Documentation Requirements

RBTs must be familiar with the Health Insurance Portability and Accountability Act of 1996 (HIPAA), which guides the safeguarding of clients' Protected Health Information (PHI). HIPAA is a federal law that stipulates how PHI is handled, collected, stored, and transported. All employees who work with clients in a healthcare setting are mandated to comply with HIPAA guidelines. HIPAA can be understood in the context of three primary rules that must be adhered to. The first is the Privacy Rule, which dictates that all clients have a right for their PHI to be kept private, with limits on who provided with access to it. Access is defined as seeing or hearing about client PHI. This rule can be broken accidentally or intentionally. For example, an employee who accesses a client's file without having a legitimate reason to do so and an employee who accidentally sends an email about a client's treatment plan to the incorrect person have both breached this rule.

The second rule is the Security Rule, which sets the standard for the safeguarding of PHI. All healthcare entities managing PHI must adhere to technical, physical, and administrative safeguards surrounding

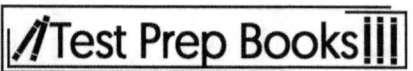

Documenting and Reporting

PHI. An example of this rule being breached is an employee sharing their password to company software with a colleague, who then accesses a client's file that they are not approved to view.

The last rule is the Breach Notification Rule, which dictates the need to notify individuals within 60 days if there is a data breach involving their PHI. In addition to needing to notify the individual themselves, the organization is often required to report a breach to the Department of Health and Human Services (HHS) and, in some cases, the media. For example, a treatment center finds out that an RBT emailed a treatment plan to the incorrect recipient. Instead of notifying the client in question within the required 60 days, the center notifies the client after a year has passed. This is a breach of this policy because the center waited a year to inform the client of its information breach.

Collection and Storage of Client Information

Organization and storage of client information varies greatly depending on the counselor, the institution, and the requirements of any external funding sources. Information may be stored electronically in online systems or on paper. Important components of information in counseling include: intake forms; personal, medical, and demographic information; assessments and reviews; any diagnoses, intervention, and treatment outlines with measurable goals; and discharge plans or paperwork. Since this is all highly sensitive and confidential information, counselors should be mindful to keep all information updated, accurate, and stored securely.

The most recommended data collection method is to input data and information directly into HIPAA-compliant software/systems, which are now employed by most companies. HIPAA-compliant software/systems are also referred to as electronic health records (EHR). When using email to communicate with or about clients, the email must be encrypted. This offers an extra element of protection.

Any physical notes must be kept secured in a locked cabinet or drawer inside a locked room when not actively being used during the session. After the notes are transferred to the electronic platform, they should immediately be shredded, so as to not risk having unnecessary duplicates of PHI.

All documentation and information pertaining to the client should be stored in compliance with applicable state and federal laws and policies and regulations by the organization servicing the client. All records and data are required by the BACB to be maintained for 7 years in case of an internal or external audit, for future reference for the treatment team, or in case the client reaches back out to inquire about accessing this information. Other state and federal laws, as well as company policies and regulations, may extend this storage beyond 7 years.

Transportation

RBTs sometimes conduct home-based work for a variety of reasons. Clients might be more comfortable in their home, have barriers to traveling to the center, or have targeted behaviors that benefit from intervention directly in the home. In those instances, the RBT is responsible for transporting PHI via written notes and/or an electronic device. If client documentation must be transported, the safest method is to have it locked in the trunk, ideally inside a safe or locked box. If the RBT is using a laptop or tablet that has access to PHI, the device should be protected by a passcode only known to the RBT. After the trip is complete, the written and/or electronic PHI should then be returned to a secured office.

Documentation

The documentation an RBT completes for each session becomes part of the client's medical history. Excluding subjectivity and only documenting vital, relevant information should be standard practice. The

RBT should only record information that is essential to the client's treatment process, including their progress and any applicable behavioral analysis. Depending on the organization, there will be a specific documentation format they need to adhere to. Documentation should be clear and objective to maintain the integrity of the session data for future analysis.

Disclosures

The RBT cannot disclose confidential information without the consent of the client. In many cases, the client is a minor, so the RBT should familiarize themselves with the client's parent, guardian, or other family members who are involved in the daily life and care of the client. Sometimes, RBTs work alongside other professionals—like doctors or teachers—to provide holistic care to the child. A release of information form should be on file for each person with whom the RBT needs to discuss the client. Maintaining thorough documentation, including all required forms, is essential to ensure that the client's privacy is upheld.

Practice Quiz

1. Janine is documenting her session with a client, Serena. Serena is working on reducing self-injurious behaviors in response to sharing her toys. During today's session, Serena's siblings were present and coloring with Serena's crayons. Serena had multiple episodes of hitting herself on the leg. What is the best description of this behavior?
    a. Serena was upset that her siblings attended the session, as evidenced by increased self-harm.
    b. Serena's self-harm leads us to conclude that she does not like to share her belongings.
    c. Serena exhibited self-injurious behavior 6 times when her siblings were using her crayons.
    d. Serena's siblings took her crayons, causing Serena to exhibit 6 instances of self-injurious behavior.

2. The BACB requires that client data be stored for ___ years.
    a. 2
    b. 10
    c. 3
    d. 7

3. Ursula, an RBT, has been emailing her client's father from her personal email to discuss the client's next session. Her personal email is not encrypted. Which HIPAA regulation does this breach?
    a. The Health Information Rule
    b. The Security Rule
    c. The Breach Notification Rule
    d. The Privacy Rule

4. Samara's client, who is a minor, shares that their stepfather was physically abusive to them 2 weeks ago. The child shows Samara a bruise on their leg that has almost faded. This stepfather has since left the state and no longer has access to the child. The child lives with their mother. What should Samara's next steps be in this instance?
    a. Samara should report this to her supervisor and the appropriate local/state authority.
    b. Samara should call the child's mother and ask for more information before reporting.
    c. Samara should call 911 to intervene, given the presence of child abuse.
    d. Samara does not need to report this, given the abuser's lack of access to the child.

5. Justin is an RBT and is establishing a supervisory relationship with Harold, a supervisor in his center. Justin has been an RBT for approximately 3 months. According to the BACB, how often must Harold provide Justin with supervision?
    a. At least weekly for the first 6 months, then on a monthly basis.
    b. The time must be equal to least 5 percent of Justin's direct client contact hours.
    c. Biweekly for full-time employees, monthly for part-time employees.
    d. This isn't mandated by the BACB but rather the organization itself.

See answers on the next page.

Answer Explanations

1. C: Choice C offers an objective, factual description of the information. Documentation should be objective and describe the actual behavior, without interjecting personal opinions or assumptions. Choice A is incorrect because it gives a subjective interpretation of Serena's mood. Choice B is incorrect because it offers a subjective interpretation of her opinion or preference. Choice D is incorrect, as this description infers that there is a causal relationship between Serena's siblings and her self-injurious behavior, which deviates from objective, factual descriptions.

2. D: The BACB requires that client data be stored for a period of 7 years. Choices A and C are incorrect, as 2 and 3 years are less than the mandated number of years. Choice B is incorrect, as this exceeds the BACB-mandated number of years, though state law or organizational policies may require longer than 7 years.

3. B: Using an unencrypted email to discuss client PHI breaches the HIPAA Security Rule. Choice A is incorrect, as this is not a HIPAA rule. Choice C is incorrect, as this rule dictates the need to notify individuals if there is a data breach involving their PHI. Choice D is incorrect, as this rule asserts that clients have a right for their PHI to be kept private and limited in who is provided with access to it.

4. A: Samara should both report this to the correct authorities and share it with her supervisor. Choice B is incorrect, as it is not Samara's responsibility to investigate this matter. While she might share with the mother what the child disclosed to her, it is not Samara's responsibility to seek more information on this incident. Choice C is incorrect, as the abuse does not appear to present imminent risk to the child, thus not requiring 911 intervention. Choice D is incorrect, as Samara is a mandated reporter of child abuse and neglect, meaning if she learns of child abuse, she must report it to the proper entity, regardless of imminence.

5. B: The amount of supervision must be equal to at least 5 percent of Justin's direct client contact hours. Choices A and C are incorrect, as supervision is not mandated to necessarily be on a weekly or monthly schedule. Choice D is incorrect, as although each organization may have differing regulations and guidelines, the BACB does have a mandate for supervision requirements.

Professional Conduct and Scope of Practice

The RBT's Role and Supervision Requirements

BACB Supervision Requirements for RBTs

Because of the Registered Behavior Technician's (RBT's) direct, one-on-one patient-care role, the Behavior Analysis Certification Board (BACB) has set specific rules and regulations that govern the RBT's practice as they work with clients to implement treatment plans and Applied Behavior Analysis (ABA) therapy. Treatment plans are typically written by a Board Certified Behavior Analyst (BCBA), and it is the RBT's responsibility to carry out these plans. Therefore, it is of upmost importance that the RBT and their supervisor maintain regular communication when it comes to client interaction to ensure ongoing, high-quality care and positive patient outcomes.

The BACB requires that the RBT be supervised by a BCBA, a Board Certified Assistant Behavior Analyst (BCaBA), or another licensed behavior health professional who is qualified to administer ABA therapy. The BACB sets supervision requirements that the RBT must adhere to in order to maintain their certification. It is vital to maintain accurate records and to ensure they are always stored safely.

To begin with, an RBT must be supervised by the BCBA or other designated supervisor for at least 5 percent of their work hours each month. On top of that, RBTs are required to have face-to-face communication with their supervisors at least two times per month. These face-to-face meeting help promote productive communication between the RBT and their supervisor regarding the implementation of the client's care plan and the quality of their outcomes.

In the event that an RBT is working as part of a group that is providing care for the same client, each RBT must have at least one monthly one-on-one meeting with their BCBA or other designated supervisor. Because in a group setting it is more likely for an individual to miss the opportunity to ask questions or receive personal feedback, the individual communication between each RBT and their supervisor helps to ensure the care plan is being followed and that all key information is being addressed appropriately.

RBTs are required to submit a report to the Behavior Analysis Certification Board if they ever do not meet the minimum requirements for supervision. However, if an RBT is on vacation or not working for a period of time, they are not required to meet supervision requirements during that time. In addition to this, if an RBT plans to take an extended leave of absence, they can put in an application for voluntary inactive status. **Voluntary inactive status** means that the RBT agrees not to practice as an RBT for a designated period, during which they are exempt from submitting their annual RBT Renewal Application. This includes exemptions from updated annual RBT competency assessments and any associated fees. Voluntary inactive status can provide these exemptions for up to two years at a time for the RBT.

Both the RBT and the BCBA or other supervisor are required to sign off on the monthly supervision log at the end of every month and are required to keep these supervision records for at least seven years. Failure to do so could result in the loss of the RBT's certification, so good record keeping is of utmost importance.

The Role of the RBT in the Service Delivery System

The RBT's main responsibility is to follow the treatment plan written by the BCBA to provide direct care to the client. It is important to remember that the RBT is not a behavior modification consultant. Rather, they are there to implement the care plan that has already been written. Furthermore, the RBT should never accept any additional jobs or duties that go beyond the specific scope of the written care plan they are meant to be following for their specific client, and they should provide service directly to the client only during designated times.

In addition to this, the RBT should always leave the care environment in the same condition as it was when they first entered it. It would be unprofessional and poor care to leave the treatment environment a mess and could even result in unforeseen hazards or effects on client outcomes. Finally, the RBT is responsible for continued, thorough documentation on the progress note as well as informing stakeholders of any additional needs or concerns, including any new reinforcers. A stakeholder is any person other than the client who is involved in the client's treatment plan, such as family members, caregivers, or collaborators. Good communication is vital to ensure that everyone stays on the same page and to provide the best possible outcomes for the client.

The number one priority for any RBT is to maintain the safety and well-being of their client. All duties performed should fall within their competence and scope of practice. All rules and regulations put in place by the BACB are to help ensure the safety of clients and reduce any risk of potential harm.

Responding to Feedback

Feedback in a Professional, Care Centered Environment

Constructive criticism in a professional environment should be handled respectfully and with the aim of fostering a positive environment of open communication. Professional feedback is an essential component of any work environment, but for the RBT it can mean the difference between a client receiving quality care or not. Feedback is necessary to help ensure good outcomes for the client when implementing care plans and should always be encouraged. Both positive feedback and constructive criticism should be expected, and the RBT should always aim to receive feedback in a respectful and professional manner.

A common problem that the RBT may run into is not understanding some of the feedback they receive. Sometimes, with all the specific details and technicalities that go into providing care—especially in ABA therapy—it is not uncommon for things to get lost in translation. Sometimes how one person phrases something may not make sense to someone else at first. When this happens, it's important to ask for clarification and ensure all parties involved are in full understanding with one another.

Clarifying questions should always be phrased professionally and respectfully. They should come from a place of genuine curiosity in order to better understand what the person is trying to say rather than from a place of animosity. It can be easy to get defensive when receiving constructive criticism, so the RBT should be aware of their tone, body language, and choice of words in such situations.

In order to provide the best possible care, some form of feedback should be communicated after each session. Even something as simple as the BCBA or other designated supervisor letting the RBT know that they are doing a good job and to keep up the good work lets them know they are on the right track with implementing the client's care plan as well as possible. A lack of feedback leads to confusion and a decline in the overall quality of care, so it is important to maintain open, ongoing communication throughout the process of implementing a client's care plan.

Many companies have rules regarding formal processes for receiving feedback, so it is important to keep up with one's company policy in this regard. At the very least, the BCBA or other supervisor should

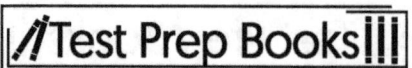

Professional Conduct and Scope of Practice

provide the RBT with some sort of detailed feedback on work performance during the one-on-one meetings that are required to take place face-to-face at least once per month, as per BACB regulatory standards. However, more feedback than that is always a positive thing and tends to enhance the quality of care provided to the client by the RBT.

Strategies for the RBT to Accept Feedback and Receive Constructive Criticism

When receiving constructive criticism, keep in mind that it is a learning opportunity and is not meant to be taken personally in any sort of negative way. It is merely professional critique given with the aim of helping the RBT improve the quality of their care. This is done for the good of the client and will ultimately help the RBT grow and improve in their professional career. For these reasons, constructive feedback should be embraced and looked at as an opportunity for improvement, and the RBT should always strive to go into the conversation with an open mind and not get discouraged.

Additionally, the RBT should engage in the conversation in a positive and constructive way when receiving feedback from their supervisor, even if they may perceive some of that feedback as negative. If applicable, inquire about any recommended strategies for improvement regarding the critique. Asking questions in a professional manner helps clarify any confusion and adds to the conversation. It shows that the RBT is genuinely open to receiving and using the feedback for their own improvement, which show their commitment to doing the best job possible and ensuring positive client outcomes.

One of the most important elements to successfully receiving constructive criticism in a work environment is for the RBT to take the time to thoughtfully process and act on the feedback that they have received. They should consider how their supervisor's input can be directly applied to their work and should develop a specific plan of action for improvement. The RBT should find ways to incorporate planned strategies and goals into their work. Additionally, the RBT should strive to be proactive in seeking future feedback on the subject and whether or not their strategies for improvement are working. This not only helps to ensure better client outcomes and professional improvement, but also shows the supervisor that the RBT took the criticism seriously and made a real effort to make positive changes to address any relevant issues and to improve.

Communicating with Stakeholders

Resident Rights

The resident has the right to have health information kept private, and only shared with those who are given permission to view it. The **Health Insurance Portability and Accountability Act (HIPAA)** was passed by Congress in 1996 to protect health information. The term HIPAA is often used to reference resident privacy. There are many different ways a resident's personal health information can be shared: verbally, digitally, over the phone or fax, or through written messages.

The nursing assistant plays an important role in keeping a resident's health information private. Sharing personal details—such as a resident's name, condition, and medical history—in an inappropriate way violates the person's right to privacy. For example, telling a friend who does not work in the facility that the nursing assistant took care of the friend's aunt, without the aunt's consent or knowledge, is considered a violation of privacy. Another way a nursing assistant could violate a resident's privacy is to access the medical record when they are not actually caring for that particular resident. For example, if a celebrity has been admitted to a different unit, and the nursing assistant—curious to find out the details—accesses the celebrity's electronic health record, then they are in violation of HIPAA. Those who violate HIPAA and are caught could lose their jobs, among other punitive actions.

Professional Conduct and Scope of Practice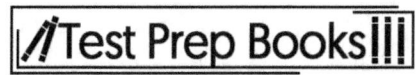

Limits of Confidentiality

Counselors have a duty to protect confidential information of clients. Ethically, client information should not be discussed with anyone other than the client. Legally, a client has a right to keep their medical and therapeutic information confidential. The **Health Insurance Portability and Accountability Act of 1996 (HIPAA)** requires that medical information (including therapeutic and mental health information) be protected and kept confidential. However, there are certain limitations to confidentiality. These generally involve risk of harm to the individual being served as well as to others. Counselors are not as protected as some other professionals when it comes to confidentiality and often find themselves being called to testify in court cases related to their clients. There are also certain situations in which counselors may have to release confidential information to protect the client or satisfy the duty to warn.

Minors

Providing services to minors can be challenging when it comes to confidentiality issues, especially since the legal rules and regulations vary from state to state. At times, there can be a conflict between the counselor's feeling of ethical responsibility to maintain the privacy of the minor and the legal right of parents to be informed of issues discussed. Adolescents in particular may discuss concerns with a counselor that they do not want their parents to be aware of, and it can be a violation of trust if these issues are subsequently revealed to parents. It is imperative that at the start of treatment, the expectations of the counselor's relationship with each person are discussed with the parents and minors, as well as the benefits and limits of confidentiality. Minors should never be promised confidentiality when the counselor cannot keep that promise, but the privacy and individuality of the minor should be maintained as much as possible. In cases where private information about the minor is going to be revealed, counselors should always inform the minor. This holds true whether it is with the client's consent, mandated reporting, or due to the parent utilizing their right to information.

Groups

Confidentiality also becomes more complicated when a counselor is working with two or more people, either in a family or group session. All participants must agree that any information shared within the context of treatment will be kept confidential and not shared with others. However, the counselor should stress with clients that they cannot force other members to abide by the confidentiality agreement and that breach of confidentiality is a risk.

Mandated Reporting

It's important to note that counselors are considered mandated reporters in all states. This means there is a legal and ethical obligation to break confidentiality to report any signs and symptoms of child and elder abuse or neglect. In some cases, it will be impossible to know for sure if abuse or neglect is happening. Often the counselor will have only a small amount of information that may raise concerns but must make a report so that an investigation can occur. Any professional who has a suspicion of abuse or neglect of a child or a vulnerable adult must legally make a report to either Child Protective Services or Adult Protective Services, and they cannot be held liable for reports made in good faith.

Self-Harm

Some clients may disclose intent to harm themselves. It is necessary in these situations to fully assess suicidal intent and determine if the client is serious about carrying out a plan for self-harm. It might be sufficient, in cases where a client has considered self-harm but has no clear plan, to complete a safety plan with the client. The safety plan will outline what the client agrees to do should they begin to experience the desire to engage in self-harm. However, if the client has a clear plan of action and access to items necessary to carry out the plan, then confidentiality should be broken to protect the client. This would involve notifying police and having the client committed for observation for their own protection.

Duty to Warn

In addition to protecting clients from themselves, counselors also have a duty to warn third-party individuals if there is threat of harm. **Duty to warn** was established by the 1976 case Tarasoff vs. Regents of the University of California. In this case, a graduate student at the University of California-Berkeley had become obsessed with Tatiana Tarasoff. After significant distress, he sought psychological treatment and disclosed to his therapist that he had a plan to kill Tarasoff. Although the psychologist did have the student temporarily committed, he was ultimately released. He eventually stopped seeking treatment and attacked and killed Tarasoff. Tarasoff's family sued the psychologist and various other individuals involved with the university. This case evolved into the duty to warn third parties of potential risk of harm. Satisfying the duty to warn can be done by notifying police or the individual who is the intended victim.

Because ethical dilemmas can involve legal situations, they may also have legal consequences for a counselor or necessitate involving the legal system. For example, a client may disclose that he frequently drinks large amounts of alcohol and then drives his children to school. Ethically, there is an obligation to keep what the client has said in confidence. However, the client's children are being placed in a situation in which they are in great danger of being injured or harmed. Due to laws protecting the welfare of children, the counselor would need to make a report to Child Protective Services. In some states, if someone has a good faith reason to believe that a child is being neglected or abused and does not report the situation, that person may face a civil lawsuit and even criminal charges.

Determining Clearly Established Threats

One of the difficulties associated with breaking confidentiality to protect a third party is that the threat isn't always clearly established. If a client discloses during treatment that he is going to go home and stab his neighbor, this is clearly a plan of intended harm. However, what about an HIV-positive client who fails to warn sexual partners of her HIV status? What if the client fully understands the risk to her partners and has no intention of disclosing her status? This is a situation which would require thorough documentation, thoughtful debate, and possibly conferencing with colleagues to decide upon the best course of action.

Technology

With technology being utilized extensively by counselors, confidentiality of electronic information is another important issue. Counseling sessions are now being provided by telephone, video chat, and online simulation, and these media open new possibilities for information abuse. If a counselor provides a video therapy session, they should be aware that it is possible for the client to have someone else in the room, off-camera, without informing the counselor or other participants. The same could be true with electronic communication such as texting or email. There is no way to know if a client is forwarding electronic information to third parties without the counselor's knowledge.

Storage of Records

Other issues relating to confidentiality include the storage and maintenance of records and charts. All confidential material should be kept in a secure location and locked at all times. For example, if a counselor takes a clipboard into client rooms to make notes for later documentation, that clipboard should be locked in a drawer when not in use so that no one can turn it over and see confidential information when the counselor is away from their desk. With the use of electronics and computers,

Professional Conduct and Scope of Practice

there should be policies in place to lock computers when away to avoid anyone seeing notes or other confidential information. Collaboration between colleagues in which clients may be discussed should be done behind closed doors to avoid anyone else hearing the conversation.

Sharing Client Information in Malpractice Lawsuits
There may be instances in which a counselor is sued for malpractice. In these cases, the Code of Ethics states that it is permissible for the counselor to share confidential client information to aid in self-defense, but only so far as is necessary to adequately defend oneself.

Legal and Ethical Issues Regarding Confidentiality
Disclosing Breaks in Confidentiality with Clients
Often when abuse or neglect is suspected, the concern about breaking confidentiality is at the forefront of the mind of the counselor. When disclosing information due to legal requirements, it is always important to discuss the situation with the client. It should be noted that the counselor should evaluate their own safety when discussing disclosure of confidential information with the client. If the counselor believes the situation to be unsafe if/when the client learns of the disclosure, then it is not necessary to alert the client prior to disclosing the confidential information. During informed consent, this requirement to report any signs of abuse or neglect should have been disclosed to the client. This is something that should be discussed in detail with clients during the informed consent process and throughout the relationship.

When such breaks in confidentiality occur, they can damage the relationship. In some cases, it may be necessary or appropriate to disclose to the client that a report is being made. For example, if a new mother has tested positive for cocaine and the infant has tested positive for cocaine while in the hospital, the infant will remain in the Neonatal Intensive Care Unit due to withdrawal. Disclosing to the mother that a report is being made, and why it's being made, could prepare her and create an opportunity to speak further with her about treatment options and other important considerations. It's important to note that counselors who fail to report suspected abuse or neglect can be subject to civil penalties and/or prosecution.

Maintaining Professional Boundaries

There are specific guidelines regarding professional boundaries in the RBT Ethics Code. It is important to maintain these boundaries to ensure a professional therapeutic relationship between the RBT and their clients and to maintain objectivity. Emotional attachments and personal bonds can disrupt the RBT's ability to provide the best care possible.

Dual Relationships
Dual relationships occur when separate relationship ties exist between an RBT and their client, a stakeholder, or a supervisor outside of providing care. These relationships can lead to a conflict of interest in the workplace and should be avoided at all costs. A **conflict of interest** is a situation in which the RBT may have multiple interests, one of which may work against the other. There are many examples of how a dual relationship can occur, and it can be easy to overlook something that could potentially lead to issues such as preferential treatment, which is why the importance of maintaining professional boundaries and following RBT Ethics Code guidelines should not be overlooked.

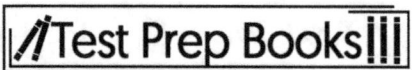

Professional Conduct and Scope of Practice

An RBT who spends time with a client or caregiver outside of therapy sessions by going to family events or other get-togethers has a dual relationship. Additionally, if an RBT is friends with or related to a client or coworker, this is also a conflict of interest in the workplace.

Another form of dual relationship is if the RBT works a second job that is connected to their client. For example, it would go against the RBT Ethics Code for the RBT to work with a client's father at a second desk job on the weekends. The RBT must be aware of their connections with the client and stakeholders so that they can properly maintain professional boundaries.

Social Media Connections
Being friends with a client or stakeholder on any online social media platform is a dual relationship and should be avoided. Living in the technology-centered culture of today's world, it can be easy to overlook social media connections and to do something as simple as accept a friend request or follow someone without thinking twice about it. However, this can lead to serious conflicts of interest in the workplace. The RBT should never connect with clients or their caregivers outside of the therapeutic work environment in any way, and this absolutely and irrefutably includes the internet.

After the Therapeutic Relationship is Over
According to the RBT Ethics Code, the RBT is free to establish whatever platonic relationships with whoever they wish if a therapeutic relationship no longer exists. Because they no longer provide care to a specific client, they are free to establish relationships with the client or a stakeholder.

The exception to this is relationships that are romantic or sexual in nature. The RBT Ethics Code states that the RBT must wait at least two years after the end of a therapeutic work relationship before any sort of romantic relationship can be established. This includes clients, their parents, and other caregivers or stakeholders. After at least two years have passed from the time the therapeutic relationship ends, the RBT is no longer limited by RBT Ethics Code regulations regarding their personal relationships to people connected with that client.

Additional Considerations
The RBT Ethics Code also has guidelines regarding the exchange of gifts in the workplace, which help prevent biases and conflicts of interest. The RBT may accept presents from clients or stakeholders only as long as any gift given does not exceed a total maximum monetary value of ten dollars. Additionally, any gifts given are prohibited from becoming a regular, expected source of value or income.

Expensive gifts, much like dual relationships, can lead to a conflict of interest and can cause a decline in the quality of care provided by the RBT, whether they realize it or not. It can affect their behavior in the workplace and can affect the implementation of proper ABA therapy. For example, if the RBT were to develop some form of personal bias or preference based on gifts they were given, they may show favoritism and ignore bad behaviors or give rewards or reinforcements at the wrong times.

What to Do When Boundaries are Crossed
If an RBT suspects that a professional boundary has been crossed, they should immediately contact their supervisor to discuss the issue and remedy the situation as quickly as possible. Similarly, if the RBT believes there is a reasonable likelihood that a boundary will be broken for any reason, they should reach out to their supervisor so that preventative measures can be taken.

It is important to keep in mind that the professional role of the RBT is to provide the best client-centered care possible. Positive client outcomes are reliant on the RBT performing their duties properly in a professional, objective manner. The client's needs and providing quality care should always be top priorities, and it is the responsibility of the RBT to hold themselves accountable for their conduct in the workplace.

Maintaining Client Dignity

Every human being deserves to be valued and treated with respect. It is vital for the RBT to keep this in mind when providing care to clients. Every client and stakeholder should always be treated with dignity. The RBT should strive to carry themselves in a dignified manner and be polite in any interactions that take place while on the job.

Guidelines for Ensuring Client Dignity is Maintained

There are several recommendations for RBTs to maintain the dignity of their clients over the course of their therapy. Two key guidelines to maintaining client dignity are respecting the client's privacy and ensuring that the proper informed consent is obtained before engaging in any form of treatment.

The RBT should always respect the client's right to personal autonomy. The **right to autonomy** refers to a client's right to make their own choices and decisions without being controlled by any other person. The RBT can help maintain the client's sense of autonomy by providing the client with choices whenever possible during therapy sessions and by allowing them to help come up with solutions to problems by thinking through issues themselves in order to help keep them engaged in the therapeutic process.

Moreover, the RBT should always be on the lookout for signs of assent and assent withdrawal. **Assent** is the client's agreement to participate in treatment, whether it be through verbal or nonverbal cues or methods of communication. **Assent withdrawal**, on the other hand, is the client's disapproval or unwillingness to continue their participation. Signs of assent withdrawal can be anything from verbally saying no to displaying a general negative attitude toward the RBT about receiving care. The RBT should be continually assessing whether the client is communicating assent, and assent withdrawal should always be respected. It is because of this concept that assent-based learning is now a standard for modern day ABA therapy. **Assent-based learning** is a method of providing care that heavily emphasizes the importance of the RBT gaining the client's permission and having them agree to continue treatment. This method helps maintain the client's dignity by encouraging a sense of independence throughout the care process.

The RBT should encourage the client to communicate and self-advocate as much as possible. The client should be able to express their personal feelings and emotions regarding their treatment. **Self-advocation** is the client's ability to express to the RBT what their own needs, rights, and interests are. The process of encouraging this may include teaching the client how to articulate their personal needs, making sure they know their rights, and allowing them to make informed decisions.

Another way to help ensure client dignity is maintained is to prioritize positive reinforcement throughout the therapeutic process. **Positive reinforcement** is a form of operant conditioning that utilizes rewards when a desired behavior is displayed in order to increase the likelihood of the desired behavior. It's proven to be one of the most effective methods of reinforcement, and it prioritizes dignity and client well-being in the process.

Additionally, it is extremely important that the RBT treat every client and stakeholder with the same level of respect and professionalism regardless of any personal, religious, or cultural differences that may exist. The RBT will encounter clients from a wide range of backgrounds. Any personal biases should be left at the door when one enters the workplace, and the RBT should always keep in mind the importance of treating everyone equally and respecting people's differences.

The simplest and most important concept for the RBT to constantly keep in mind is that every client should always be treated as a human being. When working in fields centered around client care, it can sometimes be easy to get wrapped up in completing one's tasks, especially when one is under stress. Prioritizing tasks over personal interactions, however, can negatively impact relationships, leading to a degradation of the client's trust in the RBT, which can lower the quality of the RBT-client therapeutic relationship and decrease the quality of care provided to the client. Every person deserves to always be treated with respect and dignity, and the RBT should go into their work environment ready to show their clients the compassion and empathy they deserve in the process of receiving their therapy.

Practice Quiz

1. An RBT is looking over their supervision logs for the past few months and wants to be sure they are complying with supervisory guidelines. Which of the following are BACB supervision requirements for RBTs?
    a. The RBT and their supervisor must meet face-to-face at least four times per month.
    b. The RBT must be supervised for at least 5 percent of their work hours.
    c. Monthly supervision records must be retained for at least three years.
    d. The monthly supervision records must be signed by the RBT and their supervisor twice per month.

2. An RBT is getting ready to start their first job and is nervous about what to expect when it comes to feedback and communication. Which of the following are possible sources of feedback or constructive criticism for the RBT that they can commonly expect to experience in the workplace?
    a. A supervisor
    b. A client
    c. A colleague
    d. All of the above

3. An RBT and their supervisor are discussing conflicts of interest in the workplace, and the RBT wants to ensure they avoid any situations that would be considered dual relationships. All of the following would be examples of dual relationships, EXCEPT:
    a. The RBT works for their client's parents as a tutor on the weekends as their side job.
    b. The RBT attends dinner parties on weekends with their client's caregiver.
    c. The RBT engages in a romantic relationship with someone who was their client four years ago.
    d. The RBT is the cousin of their client's caregiver.

4. Which of the following would be a breach of the RBT Ethics Code regulations for maintaining professional boundaries?
    a. The RBT becomes friends with the caregiver of a person that stopped being their client two months ago.
    b. The RBT accepts a gift card from their client's caregiver worth twenty dollars.
    c. The RBT becomes friends on Facebook with someone who stopped being their client three weeks ago.
    d. The RBT accepts a gift from their client worth five dollars in value

5. A colleague has asked the RBT for advice to get better at maintaining their client's dignity during their therapy sessions. Which of the following would NOT be a good recommendation?
    a. Decrease the use of positive reinforcement
    b. Respect personal, cultural, and religious differences
    c. Treat every client as a human being with empathy and compassion
    d. Encourage self-advocacy and communication

See answers on the next page.

Answer Explanations

1. B: BACB supervision guidelines require that the RBT be supervised for at least 5 percent of their work hours each month. Choice A is incorrect because the RBT and their supervisor only need to meet face-to-face twice per month. Choice C is incorrect because monthly supervision records must be retained by both the RBT and their supervisor for at least seven years according to the BACB. Choice D is not correct because the RBT and their supervisor only need to sign the records once at the end of each month.

2. D: Constructive feedback in the workplace can come from many sources. Supervisors, clients, and other colleagues can all be the source of constructive criticism, and the RBT should always strive to engage in each conversation with an open mind. Therefore, Choices A, B, and C are incorrect since Choice D is the most complete correct response.

3. C: Once the therapeutic relationship has been over for at least two years, an RBT's romantic or sexual relationships with people involved in that therapeutic relationship (clients, their parents, their other caregivers, and other family members of the client) are no longer restricted by the BACB's RBT Ethics Code. If the RBT is not providing therapy to the individual anymore, it would not create a dual relationship if they were to start dating four years later. Choices A, B, and D all give examples of situations in which the RBT is engaging in a relationship with a client, their caregiver, or their family member outside of their work environment, which is a dual relationship.

4. B: The RBT Ethics Code prohibits the RBT from accepting gifts from their clients or their clients' family members or caregivers worth more than ten dollars, so accepting a gift card worth twenty dollars would be against the rules. Choice A is not against the rules because the RBT is free to form platonic relationships with anyone they want as soon as the therapeutic relationship has ended. Choice C is incorrect because the RBT can be friends on social media with whomever they want after the therapeutic work relationship has ended. Choice D is incorrect because the RBT is free to accept gifts from their clients that are worth less than ten dollars in value.

5. A: Positive reinforcement is a useful tactic that encourages client dignity by maintaining a positive, reward-based form of behavior modification and does not necessitate the use of negative or discouraging tactics. Decreasing the use of positive reinforcement therefore would not help maintain client dignity. Choices B, C, and D are all recommended ways for the RBT to help maintain client dignity throughout the process of providing therapy.

RBT Practice Test #1

1. Which of the following statements is an example of quantitative data that may be included when documenting a client's behaviors?
    a. The client arrived with their parent 10 minutes before the session's scheduled start time.
    b. When I began putting away the puzzle, the client shouted "No!"
    c. The client reported completing their homework before playing video games after school three times in the past week.
    d. At the beginning of the session, the client's parent said that they felt that the client struck themselves more frequently than usual.

2. When collecting client data, the *rate* is defined as which of the following?
    a. How often a client exhibits a behavior
    b. The conditions in which a client's behavior changes
    c. A behavior's intensity, rated on a scale of 1 to 10
    d. The frequency of a behavior during a specific period

3. Which of the following data collection methods is a type of discontinuous measurement?
    a. Time sampling
    b. Inter-response time
    c. Event recording
    d. Permanent product recording

4. Which of the following is a key component of a behavior reduction plan?
    a. Competency evaluation
    b. Functional behavioral assessment
    c. Identification of target behavior
    d. Thought log

5. An RBT is reflecting on the supervision that they have been receiving recently. Which of the following is NOT a form of supervision?
    a. Meeting individually with a supervisor for a scheduled weekly session
    b. Meeting with a supervisor and group of peers that work for the same organization to consult on cases
    c. Engaging in the required observation sessions a few times a month
    d. Documenting sessions in the clinical record as part of the communication with other providers

6. During a preference assessment, an RBT observes a client's choice of toys and activities during recess. Which of the following methods is being used during this assessment?
    a. Open observation
    b. Free operant observation
    c. Incidental observation
    d. Paired stimulus

7. Which of the following is typically included in a client's skill acquisition plan?
   a. List of all goals completed in the past
   b. Specific object preferences for reinforcement
   c. Goals for maintaining achieved skills
   d. Date of next functional assessment

8. An RBT is working with a student in an elementary school. The RBT creates a document outlining the behavior that needs to be changed, its function, replacement behaviors, and interventions and teaching strategies. What type of document is this?
   a. Behavior reduction plan
   b. Functional behavioral assessment
   c. Behavior activation
   d. Neuropsychological exam

9. An RBT is leaving their position to go to another agency. They have a final meeting with their supervisor, and are reviewing that they have all the paperwork they need. What should they make sure they obtain from their supervisor?
   a. A reference letter
   b. Informed consent paperwork signed by the supervisor
   c. A supervision log documenting the hours of supervision provided
   d. Their RBT certification paperwork

10. A behavior technician engages in 100 hours of behavior analysis work with clients monthly. They receive regular supervision as part of their role. How many hours per month should their supervisor observe their sessions?
    a. 1
    b. 0
    c. 3
    d. 5

11. How does data collection help in assessing changes in behavior over the course of therapy?
    a. Data collected during the initial assessments defines how frequently particular behaviors occur.
    b. Initial data about the client helps with comparing their behavior to developmental norms.
    c. Collecting data in different locations is helpful in associating the client's behavior with their environment.
    d. Continuing to collect data during treatment is useful in tracking the frequency of desired and undesired behaviors.

12. A behavior technician's supervisor is working on a behavior reduction plan for a pediatric client to reduce aggressive behaviors and must decide what replacement behaviors to include in the plan. Which action would be most important in making this decision?
    a. Conducting a parental interview to obtain family history
    b. Collecting developmental history and documentation
    c. Identifying the function of the undesirable behavior
    d. Determining the child's stage of development

13. A behavior technician has a full caseload and sees 50 clients a month. They look at their calendar and realize that they have not met their monthly requirement of 2.5 hours of observation. What is the best response?
    a. Clearly document the reasons that they were unable to be observed this month.
    b. Ask an experienced peer to sit in for an observation as soon as possible.
    c. Contact their supervisor to schedule an observation session.
    d. Cancel client visits to reduce the number of observation hours needed to stay in compliance.

14. Which of the following best describes the milestone skills being tested during an individualized assessment?
    a. The client's effective age based on their abilities rather than their biological age
    b. The client's ability to participate in their school's academic curriculum
    c. The client's ability to understand language and social behavior, based on their age
    d. The client's competence in the skills currently being practiced on their skill acquisition plan

15. Permanent product recording is best suited for documenting which of the following behaviors?
    a. A client holds their breath when frustrated.
    b. A client recognizes a *walk* sign and crosses the street.
    c. A client cleans their bedroom on a Saturday.
    d. A client raises their hand to ask to use the bathroom.

16. What would be an important consideration when working on a behavior reduction plan for a child who is 6 years old?
    a. Including the intervention of a high-probability request sequence
    b. Referring the child to a pediatrician as part of the plan
    c. Stopping the intervention immediately if the negative behavior increases at all
    d. Obtaining parental or guardian consent

17. An RBT is taking family leave for 3 months and will not be seeing any clients during that time. How often should they obtain supervision to maintain their certification?
    a. They do not need supervision because they are not seeing clients.
    b. It is up to their supervisor to determine frequency and document the decision.
    c. They are required to have monthly supervision to maintain their certification.
    d. They should follow the requirements for supervision based on their years of certification as an RBT.

18. Which of the following statements best documents a client's behavior?
    a. "Tripping on his untied shoelace made Dylan angry and aggressive."
    b. "After Dylan tripped, his face turned red, he shouted, and he punched the floor twice."
    c. "When Dylan was verbally prompted, he refused to tie his shoe."
    d. "Dylan was obstinate about his untied shoelaces, so I did not argue, and we left the classroom."

19. A behavior technician engages in behavioral interventions and analysis with clients for 20 hours per week and receives 1 hour of observation each week. Weekly observation is the only contact that the RBT has with their supervisor. Why have they NOT met the requirements for supervision?
    a. RBTs require a minimum of 2 hours of observation weekly.
    b. Supervision involves regular communication in addition to observation.
    c. The supervisor should be observing at least 10% of the RBT's sessions.
    d. The supervisor should also be writing a note for each of the RBT's sessions.

20. A behavior technician is working with a young client on reducing undesirable behavior. They have been using food as a positive reinforcement for replacing undesirable behaviors with desired ones. The technician chooses to try this intervention in the late morning, prior to the child's lunch break at school. What concept best explains the choice in time of day?
   a. Motivating operations
   b. Positive reinforcement
   c. Informed consent
   d. Motivational interviewing

21. An RBT is managing their files that are saved on their work computer. They are reviewing supervision records and deciding what to save. For how long should they maintain their supervision records?
   a. It is recommended to keep records for as long as they are with a particular agency.
   b. They are required to keep a supervision record for 7 years.
   c. They are required to keep a supervision record for 6 months.
   d. They do not need to maintain a supervision record beyond the case file.

22. Which of the following should always be documented during permanent product recording?
   a. The date on which the behavior occurred
   b. The consequence of the behavior
   c. The client's goal in performing the behavior
   d. The time between a prompt and the behavior

23. During partial interval time sampling, how often should the RBT document a targeted behavior?
   a. Every time the behavior occurs during that interval
   b. The first time the behavior occurs during that interval, with the latency period
   c. Only whether the behavior occurred at all during that interval
   d. Only whether the behavior was ongoing at the end of the interval

24. Which of the following situations is the MOST likely to result in the termination of the RBT's certification?
   a. The RBT files a complaint about their supervisor for inappropriate actions.
   b. A client's family reports that they are frustrated with the RBT's work.
   c. The RBT takes a leave from work and does not maintain their supervision hours.
   d. The RBT is out of compliance during a supervision audit.

25. Which of the following best defines a behavior's duration in a continuous measurement procedure?
   a. The length of time between an antecedent and the client's behavior
   b. The length of time between directing a client to perform a task and assisting the client with a prompt
   c. The length of time between the client's accurate use of a skill and the reinforcement of that behavior
   d. The length of time between the beginning and end of a particular behavior

26. During the last three sessions, Benny consistently became dysregulated after the RBT removed the superhero toy that had been provided for reinforcement. When preparing for the next session, the RBT should do which of the following?
    a. Choose a second toy for reinforcement and offer Benny a choice between the two toys when reinforcing his behavior.
    b. Set the superhero toy aside and plan to invite Benny to pick a different toy from the shelf at the start of the session.
    c. Leave the superhero toy on the shelf and select another toy to give to Benny during the session.
    d. Continue using the superhero toy and try to shape Benny's behavior when it is removed.

27. Which of the following would be the most appropriate backup reinforcer in a token economy?
    a. Physical coins, stars, or other objects
    b. An edible treat, like a piece of candy
    c. Verbal praise to encourage the behavior
    d. Going on a special outing with the RBT

28. Which of the following types of data would be most useful when documenting the eating habits of a client who is experiencing health problems that may be related to an eating disorder?
    a. Latency
    b. Inter-response time
    c. Duration
    d. Interval recording

29. What is an important difference between one-on-one and group supervision?
    a. Group supervision is not permitted for RBTs who have been practicing less than one year.
    b. Group supervision cannot be the only format in which supervision is provided.
    c. Group supervision does not need to be included in the supervision log.
    d. Group supervision is preferred by insurance payors because it is more efficient.

30. Which of the following is NOT a function of behavior?
    a. Escape
    b. Attention
    c. Tangible
    d. Abstract

31. An RBT is planning to conduct a new intervention this week with a 5-year-old client. The RBT has conducted this intervention in the past with clients who were young adults, but never a child of this age. The RBT is unsure of how to adapt the intervention based on the client's age. What is the best next step for the RBT to take?
    a. Review the research to determine the best practice to implement the intervention with the client.
    b. Ask that a peer familiar with this age group work with the client instead.
    c. Seek supervision prior to implementing the intervention with the client.
    d. Take detailed notes during the intervention to be able to seek supervision afterward.

32. Which of the following best explains why consistency is important when using discrete trial training?
   a. Discrete trial training works best when the RBT controls for just one variable.
   b. Most clients will become confused if the RBT presents tasks with unfamiliar variables.
   c. Highly consistent discrete trials help clients to associate their behavior with the reinforcement.
   d. Performing the same task consistently assists clients in memorizing how to perform new skills.

33. An RBT is working on a behavior plan with a client that they are struggling to build rapport with. They meet with the client two times per week, and often feel like things change so frequently with the client between their weekly supervision sessions that it is difficult to seek feedback. What would be an appropriate next step?
   a. Discuss the situation with the supervisor and request more frequent feedback to support their work with this client.
   b. Request an additional supervisor to be able to have more regular meetings.
   c. Reduce the client's sessions to weekly to be able to have supervision occur between each session to obtain feedback.
   d. Alter the behavior intervention plan to better meet the needs of the client.

34. Which of the following is the best example of an indirect functional assessment?
   a. Discussing a client's disruptive behaviors with a teacher or principal
   b. Asking a client's parents to complete a checklist about when the client uses particular behaviors
   c. Observing the client in their day-to-day routine without providing direct support
   d. Prompting a client to use a particular skill and then observing their use of the skill

35. An RBT is documenting when a client raises their voice while in the classroom. Which of the following statements provides the best documentation of the frequency of this behavior?
   a. "The client raised their voice four times during the school day."
   b. "Throughout the day, the client raised their voice twice per hour."
   c. "The client did not raise their voice during math class."
   d. "On average, the client raised their voice for 25 seconds."

36. Naturalistic teaching is best demonstrated by conducting which of the following activities?
   a. Driving a client to the grocery store so they can buy their own groceries
   b. Encouraging a client to speak with the cashier while visiting a bookstore
   c. Playing a board game with a client while discussing their treatment plan
   d. Pulling the client aside during a kickball game to help them calm down when their team is losing

37. An RBT is teaching a client to brush their teeth. Based on task analysis, which of the following steps in this task will the RBT most likely teach during a therapy session?
   a. Walk to the bathroom
   b. Pick up the toothbrush
   c. Floss and then rinse
   d. Brush teeth for 2 minutes

38. An RBT meets with their supervisor regularly and has received only positive feedback on their client work. However, at the annual review required by the organization, the RBT receives feedback that they need to improve their documentation skills. What should the RBT do next?
   a. File a complaint with the organization because they have not received adequate support.
   b. Inform the supervisor that their documentation skills are up to the organization standard.
   c. Review the notes of a peer to ensure that their documentation is correct before raising an issue.
   d. Ask clarifying questions about how they can improve and request more frequent feedback moving forward.

39. An RBT is using discrimination training to help a client practice identifying colors. Which of the following sets of objects would be most useful for this purpose?
   a. Banana, lemon, red apple
   b. Red dinosaur, blue car, green truck
   c. Stop sign, walk sign, street sign
   d. Wooden pencil, white pen, mechanical pencil

40. A behavior technician is working with a teenage client who disrupts their classroom by overturning furniture. The teacher states that they have no idea why the student does this; it seems to happen at different times of day without a clear pattern. What would be the best next step for the technician to take?
   a. Explain to the teacher than this type of behavior has an escape function, and plan the intervention accordingly.
   b. Work with the student to develop a behavior reduction plan that identifies the behavior's function, and work to reduce it.
   c. Conduct a functional behavioral assessment to gather more information on the behavior's function.
   d. Collaborate with the teacher and school administration to develop an appropriate disciplinary plan because the student is breaking school rules.

41. Which of the following client skills is a prerequisite for the effective use of all multiple stimulus preference assessments?
   a. The ability to recognize and discriminate between objects
   b. The ability to physically navigate the environment
   c. The ability to remember different persons that the client meets
   d. The ability to self-regulate when a stimulus is removed

42. Which of the following is NOT an appropriate use of supervision?
   a. Obtaining feedback on interventions to improve skills
   b. Discussing changes the client is experiencing, such as an illness or school change
   c. Informing a supervisor that more support is needed to learn a particular skill
   d. Building a friendship with the supervisor and spending time together outside of work

43. Which of the following is a benefit of using graphs to interpret data collected during assessments?
   a. Graphs are a way to take raw data and present it to other people.
   b. Graphs assist with data analysis by providing a visual representation of the data.
   c. Graphs can lead to discovering new data about the client's behavior.
   d. Graphing data instructs the behavior analyst about required changes to the client's treatment.

44. A client independently drinks from their water bottle. Which of the following is the most likely antecedent to this behavior?
    a. The RBT prompted the client to maintain hydration.
    b. The client realized that they were feeling thirsty.
    c. The RBT drank from their own water bottle.
    d. The client remembered their goal of drinking more water.

45. A gesture prompt is best exemplified by which of the following?
    a. Physically helping the client wave goodbye
    b. Tapping the client on the shoulder as a reminder
    c. Waving at a person to encourage the client to do the same
    d. Pointing at a person the client recognizes

46. When conducting an individualized assessment, how often should the RBT prompt the client to perform a tested skill?
    a. The RBT should never prompt the client during an assessment.
    b. The RBT should prompt the client only when specified by the test.
    c. The RBT should only give the client a single prompt to use the skill.
    d. The RBT should use prompts as needed to help the client perform the skill.

47. What is the difference between positive and negative automatic functions of behavior?
    a. Positive automatic behaviors are a choice, while negative automatic behaviors are unconscious.
    b. Positive automatic behaviors creative a positive stimulus, while negative automatic behaviors remove or stop a negative one.
    c. Positive automatic behaviors are reinforcement, while negative automatic behaviors are punishment.
    d. Positive automatic behaviors can be observed by others, while negative automatic behaviors are internal and cannot be observed.

48. An RBT discusses a challenging case in both individual and peer supervision. They share about a client that has struggled to engage, and seek input. They receive conflicting feedback from their individual supervisor and the peers in their group. What is the best response?
    a. Document the conflicting supervision received and the justification for how they choose to proceed.
    b. Review the issue in their next individual supervision session to obtain further feedback on how to move forward.
    c. Follow the advice of the peer supervision session because the perspective of multiple people is more likely to be correct.
    d. Bring the feedback to the next client session and work with the client to alter the behavior reduction plan to something they are comfortable with.

49. An RBT is teaching a client to use appropriate social greetings with people they do not recognize, and the client has demonstrated competence in this skill in the RBT's classroom. Which of the following activities is best for teaching the client to generalize this skill?
    a. Greeting an unfamiliar teacher while running an errand to their classroom
    b. Prompting the client to greet a friend at the beginning of recess
    c. Asking the client's parents to prompt greetings while interacting with a cashier at a grocery store
    d. Encouraging the client to greet a school employee they do not recognize

50. An RBT is working with a client who enjoys watching sports and is motivated to learn to play basketball. The RBT plans to use shaping to teach the client how to dribble a basketball down the court. Which of the following skills is most important for shaping into the new skill?
   a. Walking at a consistent gait
   b. Bouncing and catching a ball
   c. Throwing a basketball accurately
   d. Understanding the lines on the court

51. What is the BEST explanation for why data collection is an important part of the supervisory relationship for an RBT?
   a. It is part of a complete session note, which is a component of the insurance reimbursement process.
   b. It provides information about the work with the client that should be reviewed and discussed during supervision to improve the RBT's practice.
   c. The supervisor is the only other person allowed to read the data section of session notes due to confidentiality laws.
   d. Supervisors need to write the session notes for each RBT they supervise, and data collection is important information to include.

52. Which of the following is an everyday example of the tokens used in a token economy?
   a. Pieces of candy
   b. A trip to the zoo
   c. Toy building bricks
   d. Paper money

53. Which of the following best exemplifies a visual prompt?
   a. Holding up a picture of a stop sign
   b. Waving at a stranger so the client will do the same
   c. Motioning with one hand for the client to continue talking
   d. Raising an eyebrow after asking a question

54. A technician is meeting with a young adult client for a routine session. They have been working with the client for a few months. The client updates the technician that they are meeting with their psychiatrist next month and may begin a new medication for anxiety. What should the technician do next?
   a. Call their supervisor after the session ends to update them on this change.
   b. Contact the client's parent to discuss the potential impact of this change on their work with the client.
   c. Document the change and discuss with their supervisor during the weekly supervision meeting.
   d. Abstain from including this information in the client record or during supervision because medication changes fall under confidentiality law.

55. A technician is observing a child for a functional behavioral assessment. In the classroom, the technician observes the child raising their hand several times with increasing frustration because the teacher is busy with other students and does not call on them. The child then pokes the student next to them with their pencil, which results in the teacher rushing over to intervene. The original concern was that the child is often aggressive towards peers in this way. What is the antecedent of the behavior?
   a. The child poking the other student with the pencil
   b. The child's developmental, psychiatric, and family history
   c. The child's inability to wait patiently in the classroom
   d. The child not being called on when they wanted to speak to the teacher

56. An RBT is conducting discrimination training with a 5-year-old. Which of the following environments is most appropriate for these exercises?
   a. A playground the client enjoys visiting
   b. The living room of the client's home
   c. An empty classroom at the client's school
   d. The school cafeteria during lunch hour

57. An RBT is playing a board game with a client as a method of naturalistic teaching. What social skill is the RBT most likely trying to teach via this activity?
   a. Sharing toys
   b. Taking turns
   c. Reading instructions
   d. Accepting loss

58. Which of the following is NOT typically included in a client's skill acquisition plan?
   a. Communication methods among stakeholders
   b. Prompts to be used with the client during behavioral therapy
   c. Diagnoses made as the result of individualized assessments
   d. Graphs of the client's progress during a previous treatment plan

59. Which of the following describes *chaining* as used during behavioral therapy?
   a. Attaching one task to another in sequence to teach a skill
   b. Incentivizing correct behavior with a desirable reward
   c. Linking specific environments to the use of certain skills
   d. Connecting the use of a skill to a particular antecedent

60. A parent is working with their child on the behavior interventions assigned by their RBT. The parent is working to get the child to practice proper hand washing hygiene. They leave soap next to every sink the child uses, and praise the child when they wash their hands on their own. What intervention are the parents using to support the behavior change?
   a. Functional communication training
   b. Discriminative stimulus
   c. High probability request sequence
   d. Punishment

61. A technician is engaging in an intervention with an adolescent client. During the intervention, the client's aggressive behavior escalates in a way that is not usual for them. The technician is concerned they will harm themselves, engages in a de-escalation protocol to bring them back to safety, and ends the session early. What should the technician do next?
   a. Talk to their supervisor during their next scheduled meeting about ways to handle this situation moving forward.
   b. Document the situation and contact their supervisor promptly to discuss how to support the client.
   c. Meet with the client's caregiver to discontinue services because safety is at risk.
   d. File a mandated report because the client is being harmed and child protective services needs to be aware.

62. Which of the following conditions is most helpful for using shaping to teach a client a new physical skill?
   a. The client can walk and navigate their environment independently.
   b. The client possesses sufficient language skills to understand the intended outcome.
   c. The client has chosen which physical skill to learn and is motivated to succeed.
   d. The client can currently perform one basic step of the new skill.

63. Which of the following is necessary for a stimulus control transfer procedure to be effective?
   a. The RBT can control for the antecedent to remain the same while the behavior changes.
   b. The client consistently performs the same behavior in response to a particular antecedent.
   c. The RBT can control for the behavior to remain the same while the antecedent changes.
   d. The client consistently receives a desired consequence when they perform the behavior.

64. A young client is dropped off for a session by their parent. In the waiting room, the RBT observes the parent engaging in behavior that is a known trigger for the client. The RBT intervenes and the parent becomes upset, but allows the session to proceed normally. Afterward, the RBT discusses this incident with their supervisor. What should the RBT do next?
   a. Implement the feedback provided by the supervisor to repair the relationship with the family during the next session.
   b. Discuss the situation with a trusted peer to process their feelings about the difficult interaction.
   c. Educate the parent on how their triggering behavior is limiting the effectiveness of the behavior reduction plan and sessions with the child.
   d. Contact the child's teachers to find out if this behavior is a pattern before discussing during supervision.

65. What is the *consequence* in documentation of a client's behaviors during a descriptive functional assessment?
   a. The stimulus that reinforces a client's use of the target behavior
   b. The client's intended goal in using the target behavior
   c. A description of how the client behaved in response to the antecedent
   d. Whatever happened directly after the client engaged in the target behavior

66. A behavior technician is working with a client to brush their teeth, a challenging task for the client. They give the client the following prompts: high five, stand up, smile, brush your teeth. What intervention best describes this interaction?
    a. High probability request sequence
    b. Positive praise
    c. Stages of change
    d. Extinction burst

67. How frequently should an RBT review a client's documentation as part of preparing for a therapy session?
    a. Whenever they receive a new skill acquisition plan
    b. Before every session of behavioral therapy
    c. Only if another provider recently wrote the documentation
    d. Only when planning to teach a new skill

68. Which of the following would be a reason to contact a supervisor urgently outside of regularly scheduled supervision meetings?
    a. The client is tired and does not want to complete a full session.
    b. The client's mother shares that they will be changing schools next month.
    c. The client appears to be having an increase in acute mental health symptoms.
    d. The client's parent has been joining the sessions, and this causes the client to be distracted.

69. Which of the following is a conditioned positive reinforcer of behavior?
    a. Drinking water out of a favorite water bottle
    b. Leaving a noisy construction site
    c. Visiting a friend's house after school
    d. Eating a piece of a preferred type of candy

70. A technician is working with an adolescent client on reducing some challenging behaviors. For the past few sessions, the client's parent has been meeting with the technician for the first few minutes to share about difficult behavior at home. The client becomes distressed during this time, making the session less productive. How should the technician proceed?
    a. Tell the parent that this behavior is causing the client distress, and it needs to stop.
    b. Meet with the parent in another room so the client does not hear what the parent is saying.
    c. Seek supervision to discuss the parent's behavior, how it is impacting the client, and how to respond.
    d. Document the parent's behavior in notes but do not otherwise interfere because it is important to work together with the family.

71. A teacher has a student who often shouts out and interrupts. The teacher is practicing differential reinforcement to work on the behavior. What is the best example of this?
    a. The teacher avoids the behavior by separating the student from the environment that leads to the aggression.
    b. The teacher observes the student to identify the antecedent and function of the behavior.
    c. The teacher ignores the student when he shouts, and rewards him when he raises his hand.
    d. The teacher creates a behavior plan for the student's parents to reinforce the good behavior at home.

72. An RBT wants their client to use a particular behavior more frequently. Which of the following categories is best to use as a consequence for performing the behavior?
   a. Negative reinforcement
   b. Positive punishment
   c. Unconditioned reinforcement
   d. Conditioned punishment

73. An RBT drives a client on a trip to visit their grandmother. During the visit, the RBT nods their head several times to encourage the client to continue telling a story. This is an example of which type of prompt?
   a. Modeling prompt
   b. Facial prompt
   c. Verbal prompt
   d. Gesture prompt

74. A new RBT is working with a client in a high school setting. The RBT is tasked with engaging in different interventions to work toward extinction of a negative behavior. The interventions are new to the RBT. What is the best explanation for why seeking supervision is important in this situation?
   a. Ongoing observation is a supervision requirement when working with clients who are high-school-aged and younger.
   b. Supervision can help ease the anxiety that RBTs may feel when they are new to their role.
   c. Part of the supervisory relationship includes the supervisor teaching and providing feedback to the RBT before they implement a new skill with a client.
   d. The supervisor needs to verify the RBT's licensure as soon as possible.

75. Which of the following factors is most important when deciding which type of object to use as a generalized reinforcer, or token, in a token economy?
   a. Ease of recordkeeping
   b. Client preference
   c. Availability of the tokens
   d. The targeted behavior

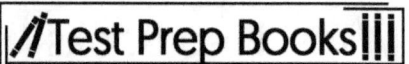

Answer Explanations #1

1. C: Quantitative data provides a description of a client's behavior in terms of a numerical measurement such as frequency, duration, or another quantity-based metric. Choice C is correct because this documentation provides a specific *frequency* with which the client performed a behavior (in this case, completing homework before playing videogames). Choice A is incorrect because the client and their parent's arrival time does not necessarily constitute documentation of the *client's* behavior. Choice B is incorrect because this statement documents a particular instance of behavior (shouting "No!"), but it does not use a measurable, quantity-based metric. Without a numerical measurement, such as how frequently the client shouts "No!" when toys are removed, there is no quantitative data. Choice D is incorrect because the parent's report does not include the specificity needed for this to constitute data. Rather, the parent's report conveys a subjective feeling about the frequency of the behavior.

2. D: The rate of a behavior is its frequency during a specific length of time. Choice A is incorrect because how often a client performs a behavior is that behavior's frequency. Choice B is incorrect because the client's environment may be part of a behavior's antecedents but is not what the rate measures. Choice C is incorrect because, while behavioral intensity is a type of *qualitative data*, rating the behavior is not synonymous with that behavior's rate. For example, if observing a client who engages in yelling, rating the behavior's *intensity* would include how loud they yelled, while the behavior's *rate* would be how many times they yelled in a particular time period.

3. A: Time sampling is a type of discontinuous measurement because the RBT only records data for a set period of time (for example, counting the number of times a client snaps their fingers during a 10-second interval). Choice B is incorrect because a client's inter-response time is the time between two instances of behavior; it is a type of data, not a data collection method. Choice C is incorrect because event recording is a type of continuous measurement in which the RBT documents each instance of the studied behavior. Choice D is incorrect because permanent product recording collects data over a long period by studying the objective products (outcomes) that a client produces (such as completed homework assignments).

4. C: The identification of a target behavior is one of the first components of a behavior reduction plan; it highlights the behavior that will be reduced or eliminated by following the plan. Choice A is incorrect because a competency evaluation determines the client's ability to make decisions and is not a part of this plan. Choice B is incorrect because a functional behavioral assessment (FBA) is often conducted prior to a behavior reduction plan, not as a part of one. Choice D is incorrect because a thought log is a therapeutic tool to track cognitions, not a behavior reduction intervention or a standard part of a behavior reduction plan.

5. D: While documentation is a key task for an RBT and may be reviewed as a part of supervision, the task itself is not a part of the supervision and has a purpose outside of the feedback that might be provided. Choices A, B, and C are incorrect because they are all forms of supervision. One-on-one meetings are regular individualized support provided by the supervisor on a scheduled basis. Group supervision is a format in which multiple technicians receive supervision together; this is allowable but should not be the only format of supervision being received. Observation is also a form of supervision; RBTs are required to have their supervisor observe a portion of their sessions.

Answer Explanations #1

6. B: Choice *B* is correct because the client, or the *operant*, is allowed to freely choose toys and activities based on their personal preferences during this assessment. *Open observation*, choice *A*, is incorrect because the term does not describe a typical method of preference assessment. Choice *C* is incorrect because *incidental observation* is not a method of assessment; in an assessment, RBTs intentionally observe the client's preferences. Choice *D* is incorrect because this situation does not present specific stimuli in order to determine the client's preferences.

7. C: A skill acquisition plan (SAP) will often include a goal to encourage maintenance of skills the client has already accomplished in order to avoid backsliding. This is most common in long-term behavioral treatment. Choice *A* is incorrect because, while the SAP may occasionally reference a past goal (such as in a maintenance goal), it does not list *all* of a client's past goals. Choice *B* is incorrect because, while the SAP often lists reinforcement methods, it is uncommon for it to *specify* what objects should be used for reinforcement. Choice *D* is incorrect because functional assessments are conducted based on the client's needs, not at a routine interval.

8. A: A behavior reduction plan (BRP) is a standard intervention focused on replacing, reducing, or eliminating a challenging or undesirable behavior. A BRP includes identification of the target behavior, the behavior's function, replacement behaviors, and interventions. Choices *B*, *C*, and *D* are incorrect because they all describe different types of behavioral assessments or interventions. A functional behavioral assessment occurs prior to a BRP and involves identifying the antecedent and functions of behavior through observation. Behavior activation is a therapeutic strategy to encourage engagement and activity. A neuropsychological exam includes a variety of diagnostic tests used to diagnose brain or neurological disorders.

9. C: RBTs need to maintain a record proving that they received appropriate supervision for any behavior analysis work they have done because this is a licensure requirement. When transitioning to a new organization, an RBT should obtain all needed documentation of supervision prior to leaving. Choice *A* is incorrect because, while a reference letter may be useful for the future, it is not required. Choice *B* is incorrect because informed consent paperwork is something a client signs at the start of treatment, and it is not signed by the RBT's supervisor. Choice *D* is incorrect because a certified RBT is responsible for maintaining their own records of certification; their supervisor would not be the one holding this document.

10. D: A supervisor must observe at least 5% of an RBT's direct client work, which would be 5 hours in a month with 100 working hours. This is a requirement of the profession. Choice *B* is incorrect because it indicates that behavior technicians do not require observation as part of the supervision requirements, which is false. Choices *A* and *C* are incorrect because neither 1 nor 3 hours meets the minimum requirements for observation by a supervisor. It is allowable to have more sessions observed, but it must be at least 5%.

11. D: Tracking the frequency of desired and undesired behaviors over the course of behavioral therapy helps in assessing whether the behaviors targeted during therapy are becoming more or less frequent. This information allows stakeholders to further individualize the client's treatment. Choice *A* is incorrect because data from the initial assessments must be paired with new data to assess changes. Choice *B* is incorrect because comparison *to developmental norms* does not necessarily help the stakeholders understand how the client's behaviors have changed during treatment. Choice *C* is incorrect because it only involves tracking behavioral changes based on location and does not mention tracking changes over the time spent in therapy.

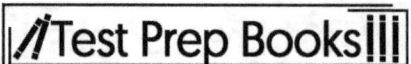

Answer Explanations #1

12. C: Identifying the function of the undesirable behavior is very important when working to reduce, change, or eliminate it. When the behavior's function is known, it is possible to identify how that need can be met in another way and thus determine appropriate replacement behaviors. Choices A and B are incorrect because, while this background information may be useful and could be part of a plan, it does not guarantee that the behavioral function would be identified. Choice D is incorrect because, while understanding the developmental stage may be important for selecting appropriate interventions and replacement behaviors, it does not provide the reason behind the undesirable behavior.

13. C: RBTs must have at least 5% of their client hours observed directly by their supervisor. In this situation, the RBT should contact their supervisor as soon as possible to plan for the needed observation hours. Choice A is incorrect because observation is a requirement for licensure, and documenting barriers to observation is not adequate. Choice B is incorrect because observation must be done by the supervisor, not a peer. Choice D is incorrect because, while it is true that the number of observation hours is tied to the number of client hours, cancelling sessions is not in the best interest of the client.

14. C: A *milestone skill* is a developmental skill that individuals of a particular age are typically able to perform. For example, babies often begin to recognize their names between 6 and 9 months of age. Thus, choice C is correct because language skills are developmental milestones tested in individualized assessments. Choice A is incorrect because this is the definition of a client's *developmental age*, not a description of milestone skills. Choice B is incorrect because an individualized assessment examines the client's abilities without comparison to an academic curriculum. Choice D is incorrect because, while an individualized assessment might be conducted while the behavior analyst prepares a new skill acquisition plan, the assessment does not test only the skills that were being practiced on the prior plan.

15. C: A permanent product is data that can be objectively identified as indicating whether a behavior did or did not occur, typically due to the client producing a concrete object that can be documented. Choice C is correct because a clean bedroom is objective data exemplifying a permanent product. Whether the bedroom is clean is a concrete outcome of the client's behavior because the RBT can directly observe the bedroom's cleanliness. Choice A is incorrect because holding one's breath does not produce a concrete outcome—it can be observed in the moment, but its results cannot be observed after the behavior occurs. Choices B and D are incorrect for the same reason: these behaviors do not produce a permanent product.

16. D: When working with a child, parental or guardian consent is required and important for efficacy; it should be obtained as part of the initial stages of the intervention. Choice A is incorrect because, while a high-probability request sequence is a behavioral intervention, it is not specific to a child that age and it is not a required part of the plan. Choice B is incorrect because, while some situations warrant a referral to a pediatrician, a referral is not a routine piece of the behavior reduction plan. Choice C is incorrect because it is not uncommon for negative behavior to temporarily increase when working toward reduction. This temporary increase is also known as an extinction burst.

17. A: If an RBT is taking a leave or break from their work and does not have any client contact, they do not need to have regular supervision to maintain their certification. If they take an extended leave, they can also consider applying for voluntary inactive status. Choices B, C, and D are incorrect because the RBT does not require supervision when not seeing clients; this is not a decision of their supervisor or connected to their years of work experience. Once they resume client work, they must return to the required supervision hours.

18. B: The best documentation of a client's behavior includes data that is both observable and measurable. Choice *B* is correct because this statement uses objective descriptions to document Dylan's behavior (i.e., his face turned red) and provides the frequency with which he engaged in a behavior (punching the floor twice). Choice *A* is incorrect because emotional adjectives like *angry* convey a subjective interpretation of the client's behavior. Choice *C* is incorrect because, while this statement does provide appropriate documentation, the quality of documentation in Choice *B* is superior due to its precision about Dylan's behaviors. Choice *D* is incorrect because it makes a subjective claim that the client was obstinate and because it unnecessarily documents the author's behavior (not arguing).

19. B: While it is correct that supervisors should observe at least 5% of the time that the RBT spends performing direct interventions, this is not the only supervision requirement. Supervision must also include regular communication and feedback to improve practice and discuss ongoing care being provided. Choice *A* is incorrect because there is not an hourly observation requirement; the minimum is based on a percentage of overall work with clients. Choice *C* is incorrect because the requirement is for supervisors to observe a minimum of 5% of service hours, not 10% of sessions. Choice *D* is incorrect because, while documentation is critical, the technician should write a note after every session, not the supervisor.

20. A: *Motivating operations* is the concept that the environment has an impact on the value of a reinforcement, which can increase or decrease the chance of it working as a motivator. Food is a common example of this concept; it is a stronger motivator if someone is hungry, and less motivating if they are full. Choice *B* is incorrect because, while positive reinforcement is occurring, it is unrelated to the time of day, whereas *motivating operations* specifically refers to the role of the environment in changing motivation. Choices *C* and *D* are incorrect because neither informed consent nor motivational interviewing are concepts in behavioral interventions.

21. B: RBTs are required to keep a record of their supervision hours and content for at least 7 years, according to Behavior Analyst Certification Board (BACB) guidelines. These records must be kept in case the RBT is audited. Choice *A* is incorrect because the requirement is to maintain the records for 7 years, regardless of whether the RBT changes organizations or employers in that time frame. Choice *C* is incorrect because 6 months is not long enough; the requirement is 7 years. Choice *D* is incorrect because RBTs are required to keep a supervision log with details about supervision received. Their case notes do not qualify as a supervision log.

22. A: Permanent product recording is used to measure concrete objects or outcomes produced by a client as the result of a behavior, such as the completion of homework. The date on which the behavior led to a permanent product is relevant for establishing the frequency of the behavior during the recording period. Choice *B* is incorrect because recording permanent products does not necessarily mean that the RBT observed the consequence that immediately followed the client's behavior. Choice *C* is incorrect because permanent product recording documents only concrete outcomes, not the client's goal. Choice *D* is incorrect because permanent product recording is typically used for outcomes that do not occur while the client is being directly observed.

23. C: When using partial interval recording, a method of discontinuous measurement, the RBT records whether the behavior occurred during the specified period. Choice *A* is incorrect because none of the discontinuous measurement methods document the frequency of behavior within the designated interval. Choice *B* is incorrect because interval recording is not combined with monitoring the latency period between an antecedent and a client's subsequent behavior. Choice *D* is incorrect because recording the presence of a behavior at the end of each interval describes the use of momentary time sampling, not partial interval recording.

24. D: RBTs have strict requirements for maintaining their certification to provide services. One of these requirements is receiving and documenting the required supervision hours. If a supervision audit is conducted and the RBT was found to be noncompliant, they could have their certification terminated. Choice *A* is incorrect because the RBT has the right to report their supervisor for inappropriate behavior, and doing so should not result in negative consequences to the RBT. Choice *B* is incorrect because, while the family's complaint would need to be investigated depending on what has been said, routine conflict with a client or family is worked through during supervision, and would not typically result in loss of ability to practice. Choice *C* is incorrect because RBTs do not need to receive supervision when on a leave and not seeing clients.

25. D: The duration of a behavior is the length of time that the client engages in that behavior. For example, the RBT might record that the client flapped their arms for 12 seconds when excited about the next activity. Choice *A* is incorrect because the amount of time between the antecedent stimulus and the client's behavior is called *latency*. Choice *B* is incorrect because the time between giving directions and then prompting the client is not part of the behavior itself; it is therefore generally not recorded during continuous measurement procedures. Choice *C* is incorrect because the length of time between a client's behavior and reinforcement is also not part of the behavior; it is also generally not recorded (in particular, because the immediate consequence of behavior is more significant than a reinforcement, which occurs after a small period of time).

26. A: Offering a second toy allows the RBT to determine whether Benny's behavior is due to the removal of the *superhero* toy or due to the removal of *any* toy. Additional preparations, such as placing the new toy nearer and the superhero toy farther away, can further help in discerning Benny's preferred methods of reinforcement. Choice *B* is incorrect because inviting Benny to pick a different toy at the beginning of the session provides reinforcement without connection to a desired behavior. Additionally, the new toy's removal to begin the session may result in further dysregulation. Choice *C* is incorrect because leaving the superhero toy on the shelf does not experimentally remove it from the therapy session's environment—it is still visible to the client. Choice *D* is incorrect because *shaping* is not an effective teaching procedure when a client is dysregulated due to its emphasis on learning a skill through small steps, which a dysregulated individual is typically unable to perform.

27. D: A variety of backup reinforcers can be used as part of a token economy. A special outing exemplifies a backup reinforcer that is a privilege exchanged for a certain number of tokens. Such privileges are not commonly used as reinforcement in other treatment contexts. Thus, Choice *D* is correct. Choice *A* is incorrect because *coins* are an example of *tokens*, not a backup reinforcer. Choice *B* is incorrect because, while an edible treat is often an available reward in a token economy, it is not as significant a reward as a special outing is. Choice *C* is incorrect because verbal praise is used as primary reinforcement in almost all contexts and therefore would not be an appropriate backup reinforcer.

28. B: Inter-response time is the length of time between multiple instances of a behavior. In the behavior of a client with a possible eating disorder, this data helps determine whether the frequency of meals contributes to the client's health challenges. Choice *A* is incorrect because *latency* is the time between a stimulus (such as being hungry) and the behavior (eating). This is not likely to help when documenting eating habits because a client's hunger is not necessarily observable. Choice *C* is incorrect because *duration* measures how long a behavior (such as eating) occurs, but this is less useful in this context than determining how often the client performs the behavior (eating). Choice *D* is incorrect because interval recording is a method of data collection, not a type of data.

29. B: Group supervision cannot be the only format in which supervision is provided. While there are many benefits of group supervision, RBTs must also receive one-on-one in-person supervision to comply with their certification requirements. Choice *A* is incorrect because group supervision is allowable and is unconnected to years of practice experience. Choice *C* is incorrect because all forms of supervision should be documented in case there is an audit. Choice *D* is incorrect because the insurance payor does not play a role in the supervision of RBTs; supervision requirements are determined by certification requirements and agency protocol.

30. D: *Abstract* is not a behavior function. All behaviors are understood to have at least one function, and some behaviors serve multiple functions. A function is the purpose of a behavior; it is why a behavior occurs. There are four common behavior functions: escape, sensory, tangible, and attention. An example of escape function is a child who throws a tantrum while getting dressed to avoid wearing uncomfortable clothing. A sensory function example would be a client who engages in rocking behavior to self-soothe. A tangible behavior function example would be a child who screams because the noise leads to their parents becoming frustrated and letting them watch television. An example of an attention behavior function would be a student who has outbursts to become their teacher's focus.

31. C: An RBT should be in frequent communication with their supervisor, especially if they are conducting an intervention that they are unfamiliar with or have questions about. It is important to discuss this with a supervisor prior to working with the client in order to minimize the risk of causing harm or distress to the client. Choice *A* is incorrect because, while reviewing research and evidence-based practices may be a helpful learning tool, the RBT also needs to also seek supervision promptly. Choice *B* is incorrect because the RBT should seek supervision before determining that the client should work with a different provider; this change is not necessarily warranted based on the information provided. They need to speak with a supervisor to determine if it would be in the client's best interest. Choice *D* is incorrect because they should seek supervision prior to working with the client on the intervention, not afterward.

32. C: If the RBT is consistent when using discrete trial training, they will reduce the number of variables that the client must navigate. This helps clients associate their behavior with both the stimulus and the reinforcement because the rest of the stimuli have remained the same. Thus, choice *C* is correct. Choice *A* is incorrect because it does not explain why consistency benefits discrete trial training. Choice *B* is incorrect because it incorrectly generalizes clients' struggle with unfamiliar variables. Adaptability is individualized from one client to another and cannot be generalized to explain why consistency is important in discrete trial training. Choice *D* is incorrect because discrete trial training teaches a client how to perform a new skill by specifically associating a behavior with a reinforcement. While a client may memorize how to complete the task, it is more important that they learn to associate the behavior with a reinforcement and are able to understand their new skills in order to help with generalization. Therefore, choice *C* is a better answer than choice *D*.

33. A: Regular feedback is an important part of supervision that RBTs should use to improve their skills and work with clients. In this case, more frequent communication is needed to get the feedback needed to provide the best possible services to the client. Choice *B* is incorrect because there should be more frequent communication with the supervisor in place rather than an additional supervisor. Choice *C* is incorrect because the RBT should not alter session frequency without consulting the supervisor, and it is

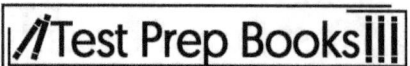

Answer Explanations #1

typically not best practice to alter session frequency unless it would be in the client's best interest. Choice D is incorrect because the RBT should not alter the plan without consulting their supervisor.

34. B: An *indirect functional assessment* gathers the observations of parents, teachers, and other stakeholders using questionnaires and interviews. Choice B is correct because an indirect method (the checklist) is being used, and the purpose is to determine the function of the client's particular behaviors. Choice A is incorrect because this discussion lacks sufficient rigor to count as an interview for the purposes of an indirect functional assessment. Choices C and D are incorrect because these actions are direct assessment of the client through observation (choice C) or prompting the client to perform a task (choice D).

35. A: During continuous recording, a behavior's *frequency* is simply how many times that behavior occurs during the entire recording period. Choice B is incorrect because how often a client performs a behavior during a particular, shorter period of time (such as "twice per hour") is the *rate* of the behavior. Choice C is incorrect because this statement documents the behavior during math class as a *partial interval*, assessing whether it occurred during that discrete period of time. Choice D is incorrect because it records the *duration* of the behavior, not how many times it occurred.

36. B: Encouraging a client to speak with a cashier demonstrates naturalistic teaching by providing a verbal prompt in a situation the client might encounter in their everyday life. Choice A is incorrect because, while buying groceries is a day-to-day activity, the RBT is not described as providing teaching or support. Choice C is incorrect because, although the board game is a day-to-day activity, the RBT is not using it as a teaching method. Instead, they are discussing treatment while playing the board game. Choice D is incorrect because, while a kickball game is a natural activity, asking the client to fully step away from the activity is a weaker example of naturalistic teaching than Choice B—the client is being removed from the activity rather than being provided support while continuing the activity.

37. B: When using task analysis, the RBT tries to break down a skill into the simplest steps possible so that it is easier for the client to learn. Picking up the toothbrush is a single, simple action that can be taught during a therapy session. Choice A is incorrect because walking to the bathroom is not only used for brushing one's teeth; other bathroom tasks include using the toilet or taking a shower. Task analysis should include the specific steps that go into the task. In the case of brushing teeth, this includes picking up the toothbrush, opening the toothpaste, and putting toothpaste on the toothbrush. Walking to the bathroom is a separate skill that the client should already know before moving to brushing teeth and therefore would not be taught in this chain of behaviors. Choice C is incorrect because it describes larger tasks (flossing and rinsing) that would be broken down into much smaller steps for teaching; in addition, these are not necessarily steps in brushing one's teeth. Choice D is incorrect because it describes a complex task (brushing teeth), rather than a single, simple step (brushing a particular side of the mouth).

38. D: RBTs should be able to take feedback from their supervisor and apply it to improving their skills. In this case, it would be appropriate to ask questions to understand what needs to improve and advocate for more consistent feedback on a regular basis rather than just in an annual review. Choice A is incorrect because there is not enough information to justify a complaint; feedback on documentation is an appropriate comment from a supervisor even if best practice would have been more ongoing feedback. Choice B is incorrect because the RBT should take and apply feedback from a supervisor, not argue back about it. Choice C is incorrect because reviewing a peer's notes without cause could impact client privacy, and it does not reflect accepting and applying supervisor feedback.

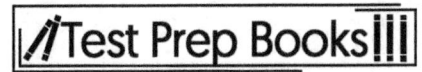

39. A: The set of three fruits features two objects with similar colors (banana, lemon) and one with a different color (red apple). This is useful in discrimination training because the distinction between the selected objects is clear, helping the client identify differences between colors. Choice *B* is incorrect because all three objects have different colors. Choice *C* is incorrect because it is not clear what color two of the objects are—walk signs and street signs are not always uniform in color. Choice *D* is incorrect for the same reason. It is reasonable to infer that the wooden pencil is the common yellow color, but there is no information to make a reasonable inference about the color of the mechanical pencil.

40. C: The next step is to conduct a functional behavioral assessment to gather more information on the behavior's function. The function of the behavior needs to be identified before a behavior reduction plan can be created and before working to change or replace the undesirable behavior. Choices *A* and *B* are incorrect because they make assumptions about the function of the behavior without gathering appropriate data. The behavior described here could be serving many different possible functions. Choice *D* is incorrect because enforcing discipline is not the goal of a behavior technician's work.

41. A: *Multiple stimulus preference assessments* are used to study a client's preferences by providing them with several desirable objects—such as toys or food—and then recording which options the client chooses first. Choice *A* is correct because all multiple stimulus assessments require the client to be able to use basic recognition and discrimination skills to discern preferential objects. Choices *B* and *C* are incorrect because neither physical navigation nor recognition of persons is required to perform a multiple stimulus assessment with desirable objects. Choice *D* is incorrect because, while self-regulation is a necessary skill for some assessments, such as multiple stimulus without replacement, this skill is not a prerequisite to all multiple stimulus methods; some assessments involve replacing the desired object, thereby allowing the client to select it again if they wish.

42. D: A supervision relationship is a professional one, and both the technician and the supervisor are prohibited from participating in a dual relationship by becoming friends outside of the working relationship. Choices *A*, *B*, and *C* are incorrect because obtaining feedback, discussing the client, and requesting more support are all common and appropriate uses of supervision.

43. B: A graph's visual representation of data makes analysis more intuitive. For example, a line graph of a behavior's rate over time indicates whether the behavior is increasing or decreasing over the course of treatment. Choice *A* is incorrect because being able to present data is not a benefit of *interpreting* that data. Choice *C* is incorrect because a graph uses data that is already available. Even if analysis of the graphed data provides new insights, it has not provided new data. Choice *D* is incorrect because a graph does not tell the behavior analyst what changes are required. Rather, treatment changes are determined by the behavior analyst after interpreting the graphed data.

44. B: The antecedent to a behavior is the immediate stimulus that triggers a person to perform the behavior. It is most likely that the client drank from their water bottle in response to the antecedent of feeling thirsty. Choice *A* is incorrect because the client drank independently; therefore, the RBT did not prompt the client to drink. Choice *C* is incorrect because the answer describes a modeling prompt, but as noted previously the client drank independently, without a prompt. Choice *D* is incorrect because it is less likely that the client drank due to their conditioned need to accomplish a goal than to the unconditioned need (i.e., biological need) for hydration.

45. D: A gesture prompt uses physical cues without a verbal component to remind or encourage the client to perform a desired behavior. Pointing at someone is a gesture prompt. Choice *A* is incorrect because physically helping the client to perform a skill is a physical prompt, not a gesture prompt.

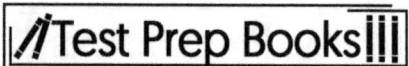

Choice *B* is incorrect because tapping the client's shoulder is also a type of physical prompt. Choice *C* is incorrect because performing a behavior so the client will copy it is a modeling prompt, not a gesture prompt.

46. B: In general, the RBT should not prompt a client during an individualized assessment because the test assesses the client's independent use of particular skills. However, it is appropriate to use a prompt if the assessment specifies the prompt as part of the procedure. Thus, choice *B* is correct, and choices *A*, *C*, and *D* are incorrect.

47. B: Positive automatic behaviors create a positive stimulus, while negative automatic behaviors remove or stop a negative one. Automatic behaviors produce a sensory reaction. If the behavior is positive, it adds a reaction, such as rocking that provides comfort. If the behavior is negative, it removes an undesired stimulus, such as taking off bothersome clothing. Choice *A* is incorrect because both positive and negative automatic behaviors can be either conscious or unconscious actions. Choice *C* is incorrect because both types of behavior are forms of reinforcement. Choice *D* is incorrect because there is no difference in these behaviors' visibility.

48. B: The RBT should review the issue in their next individual supervision session to obtain further feedback on how to move forward. An important part of the supervisory relationship is that the RBT should take and apply their supervisor's feedback. While peer supervision and input can be valuable, if the feedback or advice is conflicting, the RBT should follow up with the primary supervisor to clarify and be sure that they understand the recommended guidance. Choice *A* is incorrect because this would be unnecessary documentation, and because further supervision is needed. Choice *C* is incorrect because the feedback from the primary supervisor should override that of a peer. Choice *D* is incorrect because further supervision is needed, and it is not appropriate for the RBT to change the behavior reduction plan on their own.

49. C: Because the client has been demonstrating competence in the RBT's classroom, the next step in generalizing this skill is for the client to practice using it in other environments. Choice *C* is correct because using the skill while interacting with a cashier will help the client learn to generalize it outside of the school environment. Choices *A* and *D* are incorrect because the activity still takes place within the school, so practicing the behavior there would not be as helpful for generalizing the skill as practicing it in the grocery store. Choice *B* is incorrect because the client's friend is someone they recognize.

50. B: The client's ability to bounce and catch a ball can be shaped into dribbling a ball via learning to bounce the ball repeatedly. Choice *A* is incorrect because, while this skill is relevant, it is not the most important skill when learning to dribble (i.e., walk and bounce a ball at the same time). Choice *C* is incorrect because throwing a basketball does not utilize the coordination skills that can be shaped into dribbling. Choice *D* is incorrect because knowing the rules—such as understanding the lines—is not a physical skill that can be shaped into a new skill.

51. B: Data provides information about the work with the client that should be reviewed and discussed during supervision to improve practice. Since the supervisor does not observe every session, data collection is one of the tools that can be shared to discuss how things are going with each client, provide feedback for the technician on their practice, and work to improve their interventions in the client's best interest. Regular and active communication, such as sharing this information, is a key part of good supervision. Choice *A* is incorrect because, while session notes may be used as part of insurance claims, reimbursement is not directly related to the supervisory relationship. Choice *C* is incorrect because, while notes are subject to confidentiality laws, other people such as the client or caregiver, organizational staff, providers with a release of information, or insurance providers may be able to view them in certain circumstances. Choice D is incorrect because, while a supervisor may read or review notes, the technicians write their own session notes, not the supervisor.

52. D: Paper money used in day-to-day life is a symbolic object—a token—that serves as a generalized conditioned reinforcer. It is desirable and can serve as a learned reinforcer because it can be exchanged for unconditioned or terminal reinforcers such as food, shelter, and so on. This can be replicated in a behavioral therapy setting using either real or fake money, which can then be exchanged for backup, or terminal, reinforcers. Choice A is incorrect because candy, as an unconditioned reinforcer (something that serves as reinforcement without having to be learned), is more likely to be used as a backup, or terminal, reinforcer that can be gained in exchange for a certain number of tokens in the token economy. Choice B is incorrect because a trip to the zoo is an example of a backup reinforcer, not a token. Choice C is incorrect because, while toy building bricks could serve as tokens, they are more likely to be used as backup reinforcers, or terminal rewards.

53. A: A visual prompt uses an image or text to encourage a client to use one of their skills without speaking aloud; a picture of a stop sign exemplifies such an image. Choice B is incorrect because waving is an example of a modeling prompt. Choices C and D are incorrect because the hand motion and facial expression are both examples of gesture prompts.

54. C: The technician should document the change and discuss it with their supervisor during the weekly supervision meeting. Medication changes are important to consider when working on behavior analysis; it is appropriate to include this information in the notes, and it is something that should be communicated to the supervisor. Choice A is incorrect because the situation does not present a crisis, and the weekly supervision meeting will occur before the proposed medication change, so there is no urgent need to contact the supervisor. Choice B is incorrect because the client is an adult, so the technician would likely not contact the parent in this situation. There may be times when there is a release to speak to family members, but that information is not included here. Choice D is incorrect because, while medication information is considered protected health information, confidential patient information is still able and expected to be included in session notes or shared in supervision.

55. D: The child not being called on when they wanted to speak to the teacher is the antecedent. An antecedent is the trigger or cause of the behavior. Understanding the antecedent helps identify the function. In this case, the child poked the other student to get the teacher's attention. This behavior appeared to be triggered by the client not receiving the teacher's attention when they raised their hand. Choice A is incorrect because it describes the behavior itself, not its cause. Choice B is incorrect because, while this is important background information to consider, it does not explain the cause of the behavior at this moment. Choice C is incorrect because the child's inability to wait patiently is not the cause of the behavior, although it contributed to the situation.

56. C: During discrimination training, it is important for the exercises to be conducted in a calm and structured environment. This reduces the background "noise" that may increase the difficulty in discriminating between objects presented by the RBT. An empty classroom provides the least extraneous stimuli and thus is most suitable for conducting discrimination training. Choice A is incorrect because a playground has a large number of variables that the RBT cannot control (such as how many other children are present). Choice B is incorrect because the living room of the client's home likely has familiar stimuli that may distract the client (such as toys, pets, family members, etc.). Choice D is incorrect because the school cafeteria is likely a noisy, chaotic environment, which is not at all suitable for discrimination training.

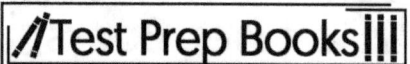

Answer Explanations #1

57. B: Taking turns is a common rule in board games, and practicing taking turns in this context will improve a client's ability to take turns outside of the structured rules of the board game. Of all of the answer choices, taking turns is the skill most frequently used when playing a board game. Not every board game requires sharing, and the client will not lose every game they play; thus, Choices *A* and *D* are incorrect. Choice *C* is incorrect because not every game requires reading instructions; for example, if the client is already familiar with the game, or if another player is explaining the rules.

58. D: The skill acquisition plan (SAP) is typically a short document that does not include graphs or other detailed data about the client. Choice *A* is incorrect because communication methods are often specified in the SAP to improve the transmission of information among members of the client's support group. Choice *B* is incorrect because preferred prompts will often be included on the SAP both for the client's general preferences and for prompts to be used with specific skill goals. Choice *C* is incorrect because any psychological diagnoses will always be included on the SAP as relevant information for the RBT and other providers working with the client.

59. A: In behavior therapy, *chaining* is a concept used in conjunction with task analysis. Task analysis breaks a skill down into its simplest steps, which are then chained together in sequence as the client's abilities improve. Thus, Choice *A* is correct. Choice *B* is incorrect because such an incentive is a method of reinforcement. Choice *C* is incorrect because there is no standard terminology in applied behavior analysis for connecting environment and behavior. Choice *D* is incorrect because altering the connection between a skill and its antecedent describes the goal of stimulus control transfer.

60. B: Discriminative stimulus is an intervention that uses environmental, object, or verbal cues to prompt a behavior; the presence of these cues signals the reinforcement of the behavior. In this example, the behavior is cued by the soap being out, and reinforced by the child engaging in the desired behavior and being praised. Choice *A* is incorrect because functional communication training is a behavior change intervention that involves teaching the client a verbal cue that they can use to meet their need. This cue replaces the challenging behavior. Choice *C* is incorrect because high probability request sequence is an intervention that involves prompting the desired behavior after multiple other known and accessible behaviors; an example would be "smile, high five, shake hands, wash your hands." Choice *D* is incorrect because the behavior is reinforced without punishment or negative consequence.

61. B: The technician should document the situation and contact their supervisor promptly to discuss how to support the client. This is a situation where there was unexpected behavior and safety was at risk, which warrants urgent supervisor communication rather than waiting until the next scheduled meeting. Immediate documentation is also important. Choice *A* is incorrect because, due to the behavioral and safety concerns, the technician should contact their supervisor quickly after the session rather than waiting until a routine meeting. Choice *C* is incorrect because the technician should speak to their supervisor before determining if services can continue. Behavior escalation is an anticipated part of behavioral interventions so it is not a guarantee that this would warrant stopping services altogether, and this is a decision that would not be made without supervision. Choice *D* is incorrect because there is no indication that the client is experiencing abuse or neglect, nor are they at imminent risk of seriously harming themself or someone else, so a mandated report to protective services is not needed at this time.

62. D: When using shaping, an RBT works with a skill the client already possesses and uses reinforcement to shape the client toward being able to use a new, similar skill. For example, if a client can walk independently, the RBT can use shaping to teach the client how to skip by teaching them to alter their gait. Thus, Choice *D* is correct. Choice *A* is incorrect because not all physical skills require a client to be able to walk independently (for example, raising one's hand). Choice B is incorrect because language skills are not necessarily required to learn to perform physical skills. Choice C is incorrect because, while client preference and motivation improve the outcome of behavioral therapy, they are not strict prerequisites to using shaping. For example, a client may not be motivated to learn a physical hygiene skill, but shaping could still be used to teach them to perform the necessary tasks.

63. B: For stimulus control transfer to be effective, a consistent cause-and-effect relationship between the antecedent and the client's behavior must already exist. The RBT can then attempt to alter either the antecedent or the behavior in order to transfer the behavior to a new antecedent or a new behavior to the current antecedent. Choice B is correct because the consistent relationship between a specific behavior and an antecedent is necessary. Choices A and C are incorrect because the RBT can control for either situation described in these answers. Choice D is incorrect because, while understanding consequences is important for effective stimulus control transfer, the relationship between the behavior and its consequence does not need to be consistent in the same fashion as the relationship between antecedent and behavior.

64. A: The RBT's next step is to implement their supervisor's feedback to repair the relationship with the family during the next session. When faced with a challenging interaction such as the one described in this example, RBTs should consult with their supervisor and then implement the feedback provided to guide their work moving forward. Choice B is incorrect because, while the RBT may need to process their feelings, they should seek feedback from their supervisor, not a peer. This is important because of client confidentiality and also because supervisor feedback is essential to providing good services. Choice C is incorrect; this type of parental interaction would likely be had by the supervisor, not the RBT, and the RBT would at the very least require supervision before engaging in this type of interaction. Choice D is incorrect because an RBT should seek supervision and receive feedback prior to engaging in this level of stakeholder contact.

65. D: In applied behavior analysis, the term *consequence* always refers to whatever happens immediately after the client performs a target behavior. This consequence might be another client behavior, a response from the RBT, or a change in the environment. Consequences are often structured reinforcement or punishment to help shape behavior. Thus, Choice D is correct. Choice A is incorrect because the consequence that follows a target behavior is not necessarily a reinforcement of that behavior. Choice B is incorrect because a functional assessment does not attempt to determine a client's *goals* in using behaviors. Instead, it simply describes their behaviors with cause and effect. Choice C is incorrect because the term *consequence*, when used in applied behavior analysis, refers to the consequence of the client's target behavior rather than to how the client behaved as a consequence of an antecedent.

66. A: A high probability request sequence is an intervention that involves prompting simple behaviors that are known to the client in quick succession before prompting the desired behavior that there is resistance toward. Choice B is incorrect because there is no praise being given. Choice C is incorrect because the term *stages of change* refers to the framework for identifying readiness to change behavior. Choice D is incorrect because an extinction burst is an expected temporary increase in an undesired behavior when engaging in interventions to reduce it.

67. B: RBTs ought to review the client's documentation—their skill acquisition plan (SAP), observation notes, and so on—prior to every session. Consistent reviewing habits support treatment by keeping providers up-to-date with the most recent information about a client. Choice A is incorrect because an RBT should review not only the SAP but also the most recent documentation of therapy sessions with

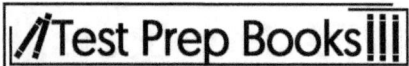

the client. Choice C is incorrect because the RBT should not assume that they only need to review the documentation of other providers, even with a long-term client. Refreshing their memory regarding the most recent information improves the consistency of care. Choice D is incorrect because a client's documentation is not only relevant when teaching a new skill—it is relevant in all sessions.

68. C: Part of the role of the technician is to make appropriate use of supervision, which involves knowing when the supervisor should be contacted outside of normal communication or meetings. An increase in acute mental health symptoms is the most urgent of the answer choices, and would warrant contacting the supervisor promptly. Choices A and B are incorrect because, while this information should be documented in the note, situations like occasional tiredness or a school change can wait until routine supervision. Choice D is incorrect because, while this should be documented in the note, it appears to be an ongoing challenge rather than an acute one, and does not require urgent communication prior to the next routine supervision contact.

69. C: A *conditioned positive reinforcer* is a consequence for behavior that is desirable because the individual has learned that it is desirable (conditioned) and because it provides something to the individual (positive). Visiting a friend is a social interaction that an individual has learned—through experience or conditioning—is pleasant and, therefore, can be used as a positive reinforcer for a client performing a desired behavior. Choices A and D are incorrect because biological reinforcers like drinking water or eating candy are examples of unconditioned reinforcers. Choice B is incorrect because leaving the presence of unpleasant stimuli exemplifies negative reinforcement: the individual is rewarded for their behavior by the lack of the undesirable circumstance rather than the addition of a desirable circumstance.

70. C: The technician should seek supervision to discuss the parent's behavior, how it is impacting the client, and how to respond. Interference or barriers in treatment are an important topic for an RBT to bring to their supervisor. Choice A is incorrect because the technician did not seek supervision before intervening with the parent, and while a change is needed, telling the parent what to do is not the most appropriate intervention. Choice B is incorrect because the technician did not obtain supervision, and there is no guarantee that meeting with the parent in another room would lessen the client's distress. Choice D is incorrect because, while this should be documented, it is a barrier to care and needs to be addressed. Working through challenges with a family is an expected part of care, and collaboration does not mean ignoring behaviors that negatively impact the treatment progress.

71. C: The best example is when the teacher ignores the student when he shouts, and rewards him when he raises his hand. Differential reinforcement is an intervention that rewards or reinforces the desired behavior rather than the challenging behavior. In this case, the teacher is reinforcing the student raising his hand rather than the outburst. Choice A is incorrect because separating the student from the trigger does not reinforce positive behavior. Choice B is incorrect because it describes a functional behavioral assessment, not differential reinforcement. Choice D is incorrect because, while the parents could engage in this intervention, creating a behavior plan for someone else to implement is not part of the intervention.

72. A: Choice A is correct because a reinforcement is a consequence that is likely to make a behavior occur more frequently. In this case, negative reinforcement encourages the behavior by providing a consequence in which something is removed to encourage the behavior. Choice B is incorrect because a positive punishment adds a consequence that is intended to discourage the use of a behavior. Choice C is incorrect because the term *unconditioned reinforcement* describes a reinforcement that happens naturally (i.e., eating when you feel hungry). This is a behavior that occurs naturally without being taught; therefore, the RBT cannot teach the client how to behave using this method. Choice D is incorrect for the same reason that Choice B is incorrect: a punishment is intended to reduce a behavior's frequency, not to increase it.

73. D: Nodding one's head is a nonverbal gesture using the RBT's body to prompt the client to continue speaking. Choice A is incorrect because the RBT is not modeling a behavior to prompt the client to mimic their actions. Choice B is incorrect because *facial prompt* is not a prompting category; any nonverbal prompt using one's head or face is considered a type of gesture prompt. Choice C is incorrect because the RBT has not spoken and therefore the prompt cannot be considered verbal.

74. C: Part of the supervisory relationship includes the supervisor teaching and providing feedback to the RBT before they implement a new skill with a client. This is an important part of supervision, and it is why supervision should be sought prior to attempting an unfamiliar or new intervention with a client. Choice A is incorrect because observation is a requirement of supervision for any behavior analysis work, not just when working with children and adolescents. Choice B is incorrect because, while reduced anxiety may be a positive outcome of supervision, it is not the primary reason that supervision is needed in this situation. Choice D is incorrect because licensure verification should happen as a part of the hiring process; it is not an ongoing need.

75. B: When determining what type of object to use as a generalized reinforcer, or token, in a token economy, the client's preference is the most important factor because the object needs to be something that they find appealing in itself so that earning the token serves as a small reinforcer; this way, the client will have a desire to earn and retain their tokens before exchanging them for backup reinforcers. Thus, Choice B is correct. Choice A is incorrect because a token that is easy to record may not be the most effective object if the client is not able to engage with it. For example, an abstract token like checkmarks on a sheet of paper may be easy to record but more difficult for a client to engage with than a physical token. Choice C is incorrect because the client's preferred type of token is more important than the token's availability. Choice D is incorrect because, in general, the behavior being targeted in a token economy is not significant when deciding which type of token to use.

RBT Practice Test #2

1. Which of the following statements is the best description of a client's behavior for use in documentation notes?
    a. "Cassie used appropriate social skills during class (for example, raising her hand twice) and I praised the behavior."
    b. "Each time Cassie received verbal reinforcement during class, she clapped her hands for several seconds, then stopped independently."
    c. "Cassie's ability to raise her hand in class continues to improve, as was demonstrated by two uses of the skill today and no instances of blurting out a question."
    d. "Cassie raised her hand to ask questions twice during class, then clapped her hands for 3 seconds and 4 seconds after I provided verbal reinforcement."

2. An RBT is teaching various skills to a client diagnosed with autism spectrum disorder. Which of the following skills is NOT taught effectively by using discrimination training?
    a. Identifying parts of the human body
    b. Recognizing the faces of family members
    c. Throwing different types of sports balls
    d. Recognizing the shapes of different letters

3. An RBT is meeting with a 10-year-old client for their weekly session. They have no signed release of information forms for this client. The client's guardian picks the client up and asks how the session went. How should the RBT respond?
    a. Request that a release of information be signed so client information can be discussed.
    b. Discuss with a supervisor whether the guardian can be given client information.
    c. Provide the guardian with a brief update on the session and confirm the next appointment.
    d. Explain that they don't have time between sessions to provide these kinds of updates.

4. Momentary time sampling is most useful for determining which of the following characteristics of a behavior?
    a. Latency
    b. Frequency
    c. Duration
    d. Rate

5. What makes the use of motivating operations an effective tool in behavior interventions?
    a. It relies on environmental factors to change the value of the reinforcement.
    b. It is specifically targeted to be effective in children under the age of 3.
    c. It uses punishment to rapidly decrease the negative behavior.
    d. It teaches the client to voice their need rather than relying on negative behavior.

6. Services are being provided in an elementary school setting, and referrals often come from school staff. Which stakeholder would NOT require a release of information in order for the RBT to speak to them regarding a 5-year-old client?
    a. Referring party
    b. School counselor
    c. Guardian
    d. Primary care physician

7. A technician is meeting with a teenage client to work on reducing the negative behavior of aggression. The client typically engages in aggressive behavior with peers when they want to speak to the teacher, and the replacement behavior is to raise their hand instead. The technician learns that the client has stopped the aggressive behavior, but has developed a new behavior of frequent and intense verbal outbursts. What should the technician do?
    a. Seek immediate guidance to determine if this type of behavior is allowed to be documented in the session notes.
    b. Document that the client is making progress and that the intervention is effective because the aggression has stopped.
    c. Document the session and seek supervision to discuss the new behavior of verbal outbursts.
    d. Contact the client's mental health provider because the behavior change indicates a psychiatric concern.

8. An RBT is reading a behavior analyst's directions prior to performing an individualized assessment. Which of the following best defines an *operational definition* in the instructions?
    a. A description of generalized behavior using specific, objective examples
    b. The aspects of a behavior described using the metrics of applied behavior analysis
    c. Shorthand words or phrases used colloquially by stakeholders, but not in documentation
    d. The definition of a term used by behavior analysts to describe a client's behavior

9. Which of the following preference assessment methods would be most appropriate when working with a client who exhibits emotional dysregulation when toys are removed?
    a. Paired stimulus
    b. Rank order
    c. Single stimulus
    d. Open-ended questions

10. Which of the following situations would require a release of information?
    a. An RBT needs to contact the school counselor on behalf of a client to discuss a scheduling issue.
    b. An RBT needs to better organize client information to share with their supervisor.
    c. An RBT is engaging in documentation required to maintain their certification.
    d. An RBT is working with a new client and needs to ensure that they understand the services.

11. A child often grabs onto their parent's legs when out in public to signal that they want to be picked up. The parent starts ignoring the grabbing behavior and does not pick the child up. They do pick up the child and hold them at other times when the child is not engaging in the grabbing behavior. What is the likely result of the parent's response?
    a. Escape behavior
    b. Extinction
    c. Insecure attachment
    d. Crisis intervention

12. Which of the following statements best documents the duration of a client's behavior?
    a. "Shantelle took 45 seconds, on average, between bites while eating lunch."
    b. "Shantelle spent 1 hour eating lunch today and remained in the cafeteria for 10 minutes after her peers."
    c. "Shantelle ate most of her food during the first 30 minutes of lunch today."
    d. "Shantelle spoke with her peers two times while she had food in her mouth during the first 15 minutes of lunch."

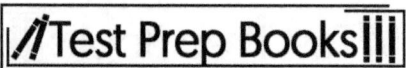

13. An RBT is working with an 11-year-old client. The RBT has been struggling to complete the behavior reduction plan because every time they attempt to begin the planned behavior change intervention activities, the client engages in something distracting, such as playing with their phone or asking to go to the bathroom. What is the best strategy to work through this challenge?
    a. Ask a peer to demonstrate a different approach.
    b. Request an observation session from their supervisor for feedback.
    c. Tell the client that they are getting in the way of their own progress.
    d. Consistently document the barrier and circumstances in the session notes.

14. Permanent product recording would be best suited for documenting which of the following behaviors?
    a. Punching a hole in the drywall
    b. Punctual arrival to the classroom
    c. Attending basketball practice regularly
    d. Independently completing a daily exercise routine

15. An RBT is working with an eight-year-old client who has an Individualized Education Program (IEP) at their school. The parent asks the RBT to attend the upcoming IEP meeting to provide insights into the client's progress and share about the behavior reduction plan that is in place. What is the best response?
    a. Explain that they are unable to attend because that would involve sharing private client information, which goes against protocol.
    b. Discuss the matter in supervision and communicate that this may be more appropriate for the supervisor or BCBA to attend.
    c. Ask the child if they are comfortable with the RBT attending the meeting to ensure that client wishes are respected.
    d. Decline because an IEP is not relevant to the work being conducted by the RBT.

16. Which of the following is an example of a behavior with an escape function?
    a. Engaging in aggression toward a sibling when the parent is busy working because it results in the parent coming into the room to intervene
    b. Washing one's hands repeatedly to remove any dirt or grime after going outside
    c. Entering a room that they are not allowed to access because a favorite toy is inside
    d. Having an outburst during a disliked class at school to get sent to the principal's office

17. An RBT has used task analysis to determine simple steps for teaching their client to take a shower. The client wants to change the order of the steps: they want to rinse their body before washing their hair instead of washing their hair first. Which of the following is the best way to account for the client's preference?
    a. Change the order of steps in the chain to accommodate the client's desired alteration.
    b. Change the order of steps so that the client washes their hair and body at the same time.
    c. Ask the client why they prefer this change, to acquire more information.
    d. Continue teaching the client to wash their hair before rinsing their body.

18. A parent reaches out between sessions and requests a letter to give to the client's school to verify the services that are being provided. A release of information has been signed for the school. The client is 12 years old. How should the RBT respond?
   a. Inquire as to why the school is requesting this information.
   b. Offer to call the school directly to give them an update and then notify their supervisor.
   c. Refuse to contact the school because they cannot share private information.
   d. Inform the parent that they will contact their supervisor to follow up, and promptly request their supervisor's assistance.

19. An RBT is documenting client data during a functional assessment. Which of the following is NOT typically included in the documentation?
   a. Graphs
   b. Tables
   c. Operational definitions
   d. Target skills

20. What is the most likely reason a supervisor would conduct an observation session?
   a. RBTs must have a portion of their sessions observed for feedback.
   b. The client is a child, which means that two staff members are always required to be in the session.
   c. The supervisor needs to observe the RBT's practice to recommend them for a promotion.
   d. The RBT is on a performance improvement plan due to concerns with their practice.

21. Which of the following describes an effective reinforcement?
   a. The reinforcement takes the recipient by surprise
   b. The reinforcement is implemented consistently
   c. The reinforcement is complex, with multiple steps
   d. The reinforcement prompts a response of confusion

22. What is the intended age range for the Verbal Behavior Milestones Assessment and Placement Program (VB-MAPP) language assessment?
   a. Up to 48 months old
   b. From 24 to 48 months old
   c. Up to 6 years old
   d. Up to 12 years old

23. Which of the following statements best documents the environment around a client?
   a. "The client sat on the floor behind the office's table with their back toward the wall."
   b. "I met the client in their clean and tidy living room. The client sat on the couch while I sat on a chair."
   c. "The client's bed was made, but two piles of dirty clothing covered 50% of the floor."
   d. "Prior to the session, I set out a puzzle and a toy tractor to engage the client."

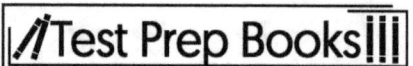

24. An RBT is sitting with several peers in a group supervision session led by their supervisor. Their organization sees clients in different locations based on the need, with RBTs often traveling to the client's school or home for sessions. The clinic sees pediatric clients of all ages. During group supervision, the RBT shares that their primary stakeholder communication is with their client's teachers. A peer states that they don't have any advice because they typically work only with the parents as stakeholders. What is the best explanation for this difference in the care provided?
    a. One of the technicians is not as experienced and therefore is not engaging in appropriate stakeholder communication.
    b. The parents of the clients may have signed different releases of information.
    c. The practice setting and client circumstances inform the need for and nature and frequency of stakeholder contact.
    d. One of the technicians is overstepping their role in communicating with the client's teachers.

25. A client is showing improvement in their social skills. According to the data, 30% of the time they require no prompting to use a social greeting, 60% of the time they require one prompt, and 10% of the time they require two or more prompts. How can the RBT best use prompt fading to continue encouraging this client's improvement?
    a. Never provide two or more prompts.
    b. Only use modeling prompts for this skill.
    c. Increase the time between the antecedent and the prompt.
    d. Always provide a modeling prompt before a verbal prompt.

26. An RBT is documenting a client's ability to meet their hydration needs. Which of the following statements describes the client's inter-response time in this situation?
    a. The time between when the client expresses feeling thirsty and when they directly ask for their water bottle
    b. The total time that the client spends drinking from their water bottle between asking for it and returning it to the RBT
    c. The number of times the client drinks from their water bottle throughout the day
    d. The time between each drink that the client takes while using their water bottle

27. Which of the following is NOT an appropriate topic for an RBT to discuss with their supervisor?
    a. Advice on a difficult relationship with a client's parent
    b. A request for feedback on session notes
    c. Help with processing a personal relationship issue
    d. A request for materials needed for interventions

28. Which of the following assessments experimentally alters variables to evaluate a client's behaviors?
    a. Functional analysis
    b. Free operant observations
    c. Developmental assessment
    d. Descriptive assessment

29. An RBT is working with a child in a small town in a rural area. They discover that the child's guardian works as a nurse at the pediatrician's office that they bring their own child to for care. What is the best next step?
   a. Consult with a supervisor to discuss whether this is a dual relationship and how to move forward.
   b. Discontinue services to avoid a dual relationship that puts the child at risk.
   c. Move their child to a pediatrician's office in another town to avoid a dual relationship while not impacting the behavior analysis services being provided.
   d. Meet with the guardian, determine if this relationship makes them uncomfortable, and ask what they would like to do.

30. A behavior technician is using differential reinforcement of alternative behavior. The client knocks over classroom furniture, which leads to being escorted out of class to a quiet space or to the main office. Which alternative behavior is the most likely to help replace this behavior?
   a. Allowing the child to eat lunch in the classroom because they are likely hungry
   b. Creating options for the child to work independently in the quiet space
   c. Removing all furniture that could be dangerous if knocked over
   d. Requiring the child to stay after class to complete any work they missed while having the outburst

31. An RBT is documenting changes made to their office to prepare for a therapy session. Which of the following best describes the session's environment?
   a. "I set two toys out on the desk for Karl to pick from during the therapy session."
   b. "The office was clean and tidy when Karl and his father arrived."
   c. "Karl made a nonverbal high-pitched noise and reached for the red dinosaur toy."
   d. "I placed a green truck close to Karl's seat and a red dinosaur farther away."

32. Which of the following is a benefit of teaching a client's parents to perform maintenance exercises with their child?
   a. Maintenance exercises will no longer be required in sessions with the RBT.
   b. Receiving verbal praise from a parent during maintenance serves as an unconditioned reinforcer.
   c. The client will be more motivated to participate in the maintenance exercises.
   d. Parental involvement will improve the client's skill retention after treatment ends.

33. An RBT's supervisor gives constructive feedback on how the RBT handled a tough situation during a recent observation session, and suggests alternative ways for them to build rapport with their client. The RBT does not agree with the supervisor's feedback. What is the best response?
   a. Report the supervisor because providing subjective feedback is not appropriate.
   b. Ask clarifying questions to understand and reflect on the feedback before responding.
   c. Get a second opinion on the interaction from an experienced peer.
   d. Document the disagreement in the client's session notes.

34. Which of the following data collection methods is most efficient when providing services in a group setting?
   a. Event recording
   b. Momentary time sampling
   c. Whole interval sampling
   d. Open-ended questioning

35. A behavior technician works with a 5-year-old client in an elementary school setting. Their services are completed and the client no longer needs behavior analysis support. A few years later, the RBT runs into the client's guardian and they hit it off. The guardian asks the RBT out on a date. Which of the following details would determine whether the date would pose an ethical conflict?
    a. The nature of behavior services provided to the child
    b. If the supervisor consents to this relationship
    c. The length of time that has passed between ending services and the new relationship
    d. If both parties are interested in a serious relationship

36. A young adult client is working on behavior reduction for their loud outbursts and interrupting others. Their behavior technician creates a plan with them: each time they attend a class without engaging in this behavior, they can earn 20 minutes of playing their favorite game. What intervention is being used to reduce the negative behavior?
    a. Differential reinforcement of alternative behavior
    b. Noncontingent reinforcement
    c. Differential reinforcement of other behavior
    d. Functional communication training

37. In applied behavior analysis, individualized assessments are primarily conducted to evaluate which of the following?
    a. Logical reasoning
    b. Reading comprehension
    c. Language comprehension
    d. Spatial reasoning

38. Which of the following best defines a discriminative stimulus?
    a. The stimulus that a client is intended to select during a therapy session for a desired consequence
    b. The stimulus that a client is intended to avoid during a therapy session
    c. The stimulus that occurs after a client performs a particular behavior
    d. The stimulus that occurs before a client performs a particular behavior

39. An RBT works in an outpatient setting with adult clients. At the holidays, one of their clients gives them a gift of a $100 gift card to a favorite restaurant. How should the RBT respond?
    a. Accept the gift, then notify their supervisor and document the gift.
    b. Thank the client and explain that they are unable to accept the gift.
    c. Ask their supervisor if they would be allowed to accept this gift.
    d. Accept the gift because refusing may hurt the client's feelings and impact services.

40. Which of the following variables could impact a client and their session, and would thus warrant updating a supervisor?
    a. The client's age
    b. The client has a history of insomnia.
    c. The client is starting an anxiety medication.
    d. The client is homeschooled.

41. What type of graph is best used to visually represent changes in a single metric over a period of time?
    a. Bar graph
    b. Line graph
    c. Pie chart
    d. Area chart

42. A behavior technician performs a task analysis to prepare to teach a client to play checkers. Which of the following steps must happen first?
    a. Sit down at the table.
    b. Pick up the checkerboard.
    c. Set up the pieces on the board.
    d. Move one of the pieces diagonally.

43. A behavior technician is working with a client using an intervention of differential reinforcement of alternative behavior. They are working to select an appropriate alternative behavior. What is NOT a criterion of an appropriate replacement behavior?
    a. A behavior that the client knows how to do
    b. A behavior that is simple
    c. A behavior that requires significant focus
    d. A behavior that can be done in many settings

44. Which of the following statements best exemplifies documentation of the antecedent to a behavior in a descriptive functional assessment?
    a. "The client was playing with building blocks when the doorbell rang."
    b. "The client hid inside the apartment's bathroom."
    c. "The client's mother gave them a high five and verbal praise."
    d. "The client's behavior did not change in response to their father's prompt."

45. A behavior technician is beginning a new job with an organization that works in a school setting. On their first day of work, they discover that their supervisor is their former girlfriend. They broke up 4 months ago but have remained on amicable terms. They only dated for about 2 months. How should the RBT proceed?
    a. Discuss with the supervisor if they are both able to set aside their personal relationship to be able to work together.
    b. Document the past relationship and report it to management before proceeding.
    c. Proceed with the supervisory relationship because it was not a serious romantic relationship.
    d. Notify the organization that alternative supervisory arrangements are needed.

46. A technician is meeting with an adolescent client that they have been working with for several months. During their weekly session, the client is not engaged and refuses to participate, which is unusual for them. At the end of the session, the client's mother tells the technician that the client has been sick all week and it is impacting their mood and sleep. What is the best response?
    a. Tell the parent they should not have had the client come in for a session.
    b. Advise that the client be given medication to get the needed sleep.
    c. Document the session, including the discussion with the parent, and update the supervisor.
    d. Follow protocol to not bill insurance for the session because the client was not engaged.

47. An RBT is using discrete trial training to teach a child to identify different shapes drawn on a sheet of paper. Which of the following tasks is best to use first when teaching this skill?
    a. "Touch any of the page's circles."
    b. "Point at each square on the page."
    c. "Count how many triangles were drawn."
    d. "Find two circles that are adjacent."

48. Which of the following examples of data collection is best suited for use in a clinical setting?
    a. Using continuous measurement to document the frequency with which a client appears distracted
    b. Using momentary time sampling to measure the latency between an antecedent and a client's behavior
    c. Using partial interval sampling to study the duration of a client's dysregulated behaviors
    d. Using permanent product recording to document the intensity of a client's dysregulation

49. A client has demonstrated the ability to share toys when playing with the RBT or with other students in a classroom. However, they do not successfully share toys in other settings, like while outside for recess. The client is struggling to achieve which of the following?
    a. Maintenance of the skill
    b. Stimulus control
    c. Generalization of the skill
    d. Independent use of the skill

50. What is the most likely way to achieve extinction of an automatic behavior?
    a. Conduct a functional behavioral assessment to understand the function of the behavior.
    b. Identify and reinforce a replacement behavior that creates a similar physical response.
    c. Limit the client's access to the behavior by taking away their favorite toys when they engage in it.
    d. It is not possible to achieve extinction of an automatic behavior.

51. When connecting the steps of a new skill together, which of the following methods should the RBT NOT use to sequence the steps?
    a. Forward chaining
    b. Non-sequential chaining
    c. Backward chaining
    d. Mid-sequence chaining

52. An RBT is meeting with an elementary-school-aged client who is in child protective custody. The client's behavior is more escalated than usual, and many of the behavioral interventions that had been progressing in past sessions are ineffective. At the end of the session, the RBT finds out that the client moved to a new foster home this week. What is the best response?
    a. Document the session, including the changes in the client's living situation, and speak to a supervisor promptly.
    b. Revise the client's behavioral intervention plan to reflect the ineffective interventions, indicate new ones to try next session, and get feedback from a supervisor.
    c. Contact the client's teachers to find out if the change in their living situation is also impacting them in other settings, and update a supervisor on the situation.
    d. Revisit rapport-building with the client because their behavior escalation is an indication that they don't feel comfortable, and ask a supervisor to observe the next session.

53. An RBT works with adolescent clients in a high school setting. One of their clients, an 18-year-old high school senior, adds them as a contact on a social media site. The client says that this is their preferred way to be contacted. What is the best response?
    a. Explain that this is not an appropriate contact method for their relationship and decline the social media request.
    b. Accept the request because adult clients can make the decision to engage in social media contact.
    c. Discuss with the client the pros and cons of becoming friends on social media and how that could impact services before letting them proceed.
    d. Discontinue services with the client because they are unable to hold appropriate boundaries.

54. Which of the following skill goals is best suited for a client's skill acquisition plan?
    a. "When feeling frustrated, the client will take a deep breath before speaking 5 out of 10 times."
    b. "During each therapy session, the client will practice raising their hand when they want to ask a question."
    c. "The client will accept sharing toys with other students during recess 9 times out of 10."
    d. "During each therapy session, the client will identify ways that they implemented new skills during the past week."

55. Which of the following actions is crucial to the crisis planning component of a behavior reduction plan?
    a. Only implementing a behavior reduction plan for clients over the age of 18
    b. Mandatory staff training on de-escalation methods during onboarding
    c. Requiring that all staff understand and comply with their role as mandated reporters
    d. Developing a relationship with local counseling agencies to refer clients who need more support

56. Incidental teaching is best demonstrated by which of the following?
    a. Going to the playground with a client and practicing physical skills on the jungle gym
    b. Verbally prompting a client to wave back at a teacher when passing them in the hallway
    c. Organizing a kickball game with a group of clients as a way of practicing good sportsmanship
    d. Praising a client's improved grades when encountering them at a grocery store with their family

57. Shaping procedures are most effective for teaching which type of skill?
    a. Physical
    b. Academic
    c. Emotional
    d. Social

58. What does AFLS stand for in the term *AFLS individualized assessment*?
    a. Analytic Full Language Survey
    b. Assessment of Functional Living Skills
    c. Assessment of Fundamental Language Skills
    d. Alternate for Foreign Language Students

59. The use of a positional prompt is most effective during which of the following teaching activities?
    a. Discrete trial training
    b. Discrimination training
    c. Generalizing a skill
    d. Socializing with a stranger

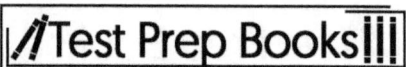

60. A behavior technician is working with a client on a behavior reduction plan that includes a food-based reward for abstaining from aggressive behavior. During the intervention, the client becomes extremely upset when they do not get a reward. Their behavior increases to the point where the technician is worried about the safety of themselves and the client. The technician is unable to re-engage the client in their intervention. What should the technician do next?
    a. Wait for the behavior to pass; an extinction burst is expected during the behavior reduction process.
    b. Discontinue services with the client and make a referral to another provider because they do not seem to be the right fit.
    c. Implement the de-escalation or crisis protocol outlined in the behavior reduction plan.
    d. Give the client the food-based reward because safety is the most important factor in this situation.

61. An RBT is working with a 10-year-old client who refuses to engage in the session and appears agitated. The RBT notices a bruise on the client's arm. The client discloses that they are experiencing physical abuse at home from their parent. What should the RBT do next?
    a. Update a supervisor and file a child protective services report in accordance with state and organizational protocol.
    b. Obtain consent from the client to contact child protective services and document their consent in the medical record.
    c. Contact a supervisor immediately to determine if the supervisor thinks that a child protective services report should be filed.
    d. File an anonymous child protective services report and document it in the medical record.

62. Which of the following activities best demonstrates the use of naturalistic teaching?
    a. Visiting another group home to play a board game with the clients who reside there
    b. Taking a client on a special outing because they received ten gold star stickers
    c. Attending the school play so a client can practice social skills while also watching their friends perform
    d. Teaching a client to use a calculator to prepare them to purchase their own groceries

63. *Play teaching* is an example of which of the following teaching methods?
    a. Naturalistic teaching
    b. Incidental teaching
    c. Discrete trial training
    d. Maintenance exercises

64. A client has learned how to accurately kick a soccer ball at the goal. Which of the following activities would best demonstrate the client's generalization of this skill?
    a. Throwing a football back and forth with the RBT
    b. Shooting a basketball into the net in gym class
    c. Talking about a soccer match on TV with their parents
    d. Playing a game of kickball with friends during recess

65. A client consistently claps their hands when they have a question to ask the RBT. If the RBT wanted to modify this skill into a new skill using shaping, which of the following new skills would be easiest to teach using this method?
   a. Applauding a friend's success when playing a game
   b. Raising their hand when they want their water bottle
   c. Catching a ball in gym class with both hands
   d. Waiting for eye contact prior to asking the RBT a question

66. A behavior technician is meeting with the parents of a teenage client. The parents say that they do not know why their child is constantly having outbursts and similar challenging behavior whenever they need to leave the house. They state that they have told him to stop and don't understand why his behavior continues. What is the best response?
   a. Tell the parents that this is developmentally appropriate for an adolescent.
   b. Provide psychoeducation on the functions of behavior.
   c. Tell the parents that they should stop reprimanding their child for behavior out of their control.
   d. Refer the parents to a support group for other parents having a similar experience.

67. An RBT is teaching a client the steps required to independently put away their lunch tray. Which of the following uses forward chaining to order the listed steps?
   a. Scrape off the tray; put the fork in the bin; set the tray on the stack
   b. Put the fork in the bin; set the tray on the stack; walk to the cleanup station
   c. Set the tray on the stack; put the fork in the bin; scrape off the tray
   d. Walk to the cleanup station; pick up the tray; put the fork in the bin

68. A client and their family are preparing for summer break, during which they will meet with the RBT monthly instead of weekly. Teaching the parents to conduct maintenance exercises with the client will be most effective for retaining which of the following skills?
   a. Raising their hand and waiting to be called on while in class
   b. Staying close to the teacher during school outings and field trips
   c. Spending at least 15 minutes on homework before playing video games after school
   d. Following the rules to play a dodgeball game during gym class

69. Which member of a client's treatment team is responsible for writing the goals in the client's skill acquisition plan?
   a. The Registered Behavior Technician
   b. The client's parents
   c. The Board Certified Behavior Analyst
   d. The client themself

70. An RBT has been working with an adult client for several months and is making progress in behavior change. The client informs the RBT that they will be beginning a new intensive outpatient therapy program where they will be receiving services several hours a day to treat an ongoing mental health condition. What should the RBT do next?
    a. Seek supervision to discuss how this might impact services and if a release of information should be obtained to coordinate care.
    b. Seek supervision to plan to discontinue services because this presents a conflict of interest.
    c. Work with the client to schedule sessions on days when they do not have other treatments, so they will not be too tired to participate.
    d. Ask the client to provide more information about the mental health diagnosis prompting this intensive treatment.

71. A behavior reduction plan has been implemented for a 10-year-old client who is engaging in aggressive behavior in the classroom that often results in the teacher taking the child to the principal's office. The technician believes the child's actions represent an escape behavior and works on an intervention to meet that need in a more appropriate way, which is unsuccessful. The next intervention requires the child to check in with the teacher at the start of class. This is successful in ending the aggressive behavior. Why did the first intervention not work?
    a. It typically takes at least two attempts to reduce challenging behavior.
    b. The first intervention was too advanced for a young child.
    c. There was no consistency in the first intervention.
    d. The assumed function of behavior was incorrect.

72. Which of the following is NOT true of the tokens used in a token economy?
    a. The tokens should be objects that, themselves, provide significant positive reinforcement to the client.
    b. The system's tokens can be exchanged for a variety of rewards or privileges based on the client's interests.
    c. The best objects to use as tokens are easy for both the client and the RBT to track and record.
    d. Tokens are effective when used to exchange for either conditioned or unconditioned reinforcers.

73. Which of the following statements best exemplifies one of a client's overall goals in their skill acquisition plan?
    a. The client will turn assignments in to the teacher on time 8 out of 10 times.
    b. The client will improve their social skills in order to maintain positive, healthy friendships with their peers.
    c. The client will advocate for their own needs (such as taking a break) during the school day.
    d. During each therapy session, the client will identify two instances of having used their coping skills during the previous week.

74. A client expresses low motivation to participate in behavior therapy and reports feeling frustrated that they are asked to perform tasks that they struggle to accomplish. Which of the following teaching methods should the RBT implement to try to improve the client's motivation?
    a. Discrete trial training
    b. Discrimination training
    c. Incidental teaching
    d. Shaping procedures

75. Which of the following cases shows the most generalization of a skill?
    a. The client can brush their teeth while in the bathroom at home as well as while in a hotel bathroom.
    b. The client takes a deep breath when feeling frustrated during games at home or at school and uses the same behavior after hearing bad news.
    c. The client always raises their hand before asking a question in the classroom and also does so while visiting the grocery store with their parents.
    d. The client recognizes uppercase letters when written on the whiteboard and also recognizes them on billboards.

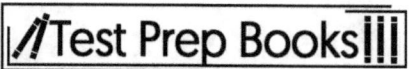

Answer Explanations #2

1. D: Choice *D* provides the best documentation of observable and measurable data because it describes the frequency and duration of Cassie's behaviors. Choice *A* is incorrect because the statement uses a generalization ("appropriate social skills") with the specific behavior as an example rather than strictly documenting the client's behavior. Choice *B* is incorrect because the statement could be strengthened with quantitative measurements of the behavior. Choice *C* is incorrect because choice *D* provides stronger documentation—choice *D* not only quantifies the behavior, it quantifies the duration of Cassie's response to verbal reinforcement as well.

2. C: Discrimination training is used to help a client distinguish differences among multiple objects and to improve their sensory skills. While some discrimination ability is necessary for the task of recognizing different sports balls, discrimination training is not effective for learning to throw. Choice *A* is incorrect because discrimination training is effective and frequently used to help children learn different parts of the body. Choice *B* is incorrect because discrimination training is effective for learning to distinguish different facial features, such as the size of someone's nose or the color of their eyes, as a means of recognizing family members. Choice *D* is incorrect because discrimination training is effective and regularly used while teaching a student to read by teaching them to distinguish the shapes of different letters.

3. C: The RBT should provide the guardian with a brief update on the session and confirm the next appointment. RBTs are responsible for managing stakeholder communication, and the guardian of a client is a critical stakeholder. In this situation, it is appropriate to answer the guardian's question, as well as confirm the follow-up plan. If the information were to go more in-depth, the Board Certified Behavior Analyst (BCBA) or supervisor may need to be looped in, but this is a simple inquiry. Choice *A* is incorrect because a guardian does not require a release of information if the communication is about a minor child in their custody. Choice *B* is incorrect because it can be assumed that the guardian has access to the client's information, and this does not need to be confirmed in supervision. Choice *D* is incorrect because RBTs should be polite and engaging with stakeholders, and this response dismisses a valid request from a guardian. While there may not be time for a detailed discussion, it is appropriate to answer questions and provide support.

4. C: When using momentary time sampling as a method of discontinuous recording, the RBT checks at regular intervals to see if a behavior is ongoing *at the end of that interval*. This is often utilized with very short intervals as a means of documenting how long a behavior is used. For example, a client might clap for several seconds, ask a question, and then continue clapping. Momentary time sampling is useful for documenting the overall duration of the clapping episode rather than the duration of each instance of clapping during the episode. Choice *A* is incorrect because recording ongoing behavior at the end of an interval does not help document the latency between an antecedent and the client's behavior. Choice *B* is incorrect because momentary time sampling is not effective for recording the frequency at which a behavior occurs during an interval. Choice *D* is incorrect for a similar reason: the behavior's rate is not recorded with momentary time sampling because only the end of the interval is recorded.

5. A: The use of motivating operations relies on environmental factors to change the value of the reinforcement. *Motivating operations* is a concept that incorporates environmental context to make a reinforcement either more or less desirable. For example, if food is a reinforcement, the client's hunger level will change how effective food is as a reinforcer of behavior. This makes it a useful factor to consider when designing an intervention for behavior change. Choice *B* is incorrect because there is no specific age range for using motivating operations. Choice C is incorrect because motivating operations are a factor in reinforcement, not punishment. Choice D is incorrect because using motivating operations does not rely on a verbal cue from the client.

6. C: A release of information is a form that allows private patient (client) information to be shared between parties with the consent of either the client or their guardian. RBTs need to understand their legal obligations and have the proper paperwork in place before sharing any client information. A guardian of a minor child can be contacted without that form. Choice A is incorrect because, while a release of information may be a part of the referral process in some cases, it cannot be assumed that communication with the referring agent is allowed without confirming that a release is in place. Choice B is incorrect because, even in a school setting, sharing information with the school counselor requires a signed release. Choice D is incorrect because sharing information with the pediatrician would also require a signed release.

7. C: The technician should seek supervision to discuss the new behavior of verbal outbursts. New or worsening negative behavior is a reason to seek supervision. The technician should also document this change in the session notes. Choice A is incorrect because behavior changes are a standard and expected component of session notes; there is no need to seek guidance on this topic. Choice B is incorrect because, while this should be documented, this is a more nuanced situation that requires supervision due to the presentation of a new and challenging behavior. Supervision is needed and the note should be objective rather than state that the intervention was effective without further context. Choice D is incorrect because, while there may be a need to coordinate care with other providers at various times, the first steps needed are documentation of the behavior and supervision. While behavior can be related to mental health, there is no information provided that suggests that mental health is known to be the cause in this example.

8. A: An *operational definition* is used to describe a general trend in the client's behavior by defining a term using specific instances of the behavior. For example, *patience* might have the operational definition of "waits to be called on, raises their hand, stands in line." Choice B is incorrect because an operational definition is used to define a word more precisely in an individualized context, not to describe the behavior's frequency, duration, etc. Choice C is incorrect because words used in casual conversation by the RBT and other stakeholders typically do not require a formal definition. Choice D is incorrect because the term *operational definition* denotes a word's meaning in the context of assessing and treating a particular client; it is not the definition of a technical term used throughout applied behavior analysis.

9. C: In a single stimulus assessment, a client is allowed to engage with a particular object (usually a toy) for as long as they wish. Their preferences are then ranked based on the duration of time that the client engages with the object. This method is well suited to working with a client who struggles with self-regulation because it avoids the conflict involved in removing a toy. Choice A is incorrect because a paired stimulus preference assessment requires removing one of the objects to pair it with another. Choices B and D are incorrect because rank order and open-ended questions are not considered preference assessment methods.

10. A: An RBT who needs to contact the school counselor on behalf of a client to discuss a scheduling issue first needs a release of information. A release of information is documentation that allows for contact with other stakeholders without violating patient (client) privacy laws. The client or their guardian must sign the document to provide that consent, which would allow the RBT to talk to a stakeholder such as school staff. Choice B is incorrect because a release of information is not needed in

supervision; the supervisor has access to the same client records. Choice C is incorrect because a release of information form is unrelated to certifications; it is focused on the stakeholder communication and information sharing. Choice D is incorrect because, while it is possible a that release of information would be signed when working with a new client, the focus of this document is not about understanding behavioral services.

11. B: *Extinction* refers to the concept that most behaviors will disappear eventually if they are not reinforced, especially if a positive alternative behavior is being reinforced instead. In this example, the child wants attention and to be picked up. If the child is not picked up when they grab the parent's legs, this lack of response will stop reinforcing the behavior. Choice A is incorrect because escape behavior is a function of behavior, not a type of response. Choice C is incorrect because not picking a child up during a planned intervention period is not the type of parental neglect that leads to attachment concerns between a child and caregiver. Choice D is incorrect because there is no indication that the child is in crisis.

12. B: Choice B is correct because it measures the duration of the time that Shantelle spent eating her lunch. The additional information about Shantelle remaining in the cafeteria after her peers may provide helpful contextual data but is not directly related to the measurement of the duration of the behavior specified in this choice (eating lunch). Choice A is incorrect because this statement records the inter-response time between each of Shantelle's bites while eating. Choice C is incorrect because this statement is most relevant to the rate at which Shantelle ate during the specified interval. Choice D is incorrect because this statement records the frequency with which Shantelle spoke with food in her mouth during the specified interval.

13. B: The best strategy is to request an observation session from their supervisor for feedback. Technicians are expected to have ongoing observation from their supervisor, and this would be a good opportunity to request feedback on a specific barrier that they are experiencing. This is the role of the supervisor. Choice A is incorrect because, while peer support can be useful, the best response here is to seek supervision. Choice C is incorrect because, even if the barrier is related to the client's behavior, blaming the client is not a professional or appropriate response. The technician is the professional, and it is their responsibility to work through and overcome barriers to implementation in a way that does not damage their relationship with the client. Choice D is incorrect because, while this information should be documented in the record, documentation alone will not address or overcome the barrier.

14. A: A hole in the wall is a permanent product that can be observed and documented independent of the client's presence or their active engagement in a specific behavior (hitting the wall). Choices B and C are incorrect because attendance, on its own, does not have a concrete object or outcome to document with permanent product recording. Choice D is incorrect because the results of exercise cannot be readily observed as a permanent product immediately after any one instance of completing an exercise routine.

15. B: While the RBT is responsible for implementing different interventions and some of the stakeholder communication, this activity may be more appropriate for the supervisor or BCBA in charge of the plan. The best choice is to seek supervision to confirm this. Choice A is incorrect because client information can be shared among stakeholders with signed consent from the client or guardian. Because the parent is asking for participation in the meeting, it can be assumed they have given or would give that permission. Choice C is incorrect because, while it would be best for the child to be comfortable, with a child this age, it is the parents' decision who to involve in such a meeting. Choice D is incorrect because, while the RBT should seek supervision to determine who should attend the meeting, there is a likely connection between an IEP and behavioral services.

16. D: Having an outburst during a disliked class at school to get sent to the principal's office is an example of a behavior with an escape function. The child is escaping participation in the disliked class by getting sent to the principal's office. Choice A is incorrect because the behavior is caused by wanting the attention of the working parent. Choice B is incorrect because the function of washing dirt off one's hands repeatedly is an automatic function. Choice C is incorrect because breaking a rule to get a favorite toy has a tangible function.

17. A: In the skill being taught, the order of the specified steps is not significant. Thus, it is best to allow for the client's alteration in accordance with their own preferences. Learning to chain these steps together is more important than chaining them in the order determined by the RBT. Choice B is incorrect because changing the order in this way does not accommodate the client's preference or otherwise resolve the situation. Choice C is incorrect because, in a minor change like this, acquiring more information is not necessary—it is simpler to accommodate the client's preference. Choice D is incorrect because continuing the same sequence despite the client's objection is likely to slow down the client's ability to learn this skill compared to allowing them to use the steps in their preferred order.

18. D: This is a reasonable request and should be followed up on. The release of information that is in place allows information to be shared and the client is a minor, which means that the parent can make this request. Stakeholder communication such as this is an important part of services. Choice A is incorrect because it is the parent's decision to request such a letter to verify services, and it does not warrant questioning. Choice B is incorrect because this type of communication would likely need to come from a supervisor and follow organizational protocol. Notifying the supervisor after speaking with the school would be incorrect. Additionally, offering to call ignores the parent's request for a letter. Choice C is incorrect because the question indicates that a release of information to communicate with the child's school has been signed.

19. D: The documentation from a functional assessment will typically include the data collected during that assessment, whereas a client's target skills are typically described in the skill acquisition plan (SAP) that is developed using the assessment's data. Choice A is incorrect because an RBT may use an ongoing graph of client behavior to track the behavior in relation to another variable (usually time). Choice B is incorrect because tables of numbers, symbols, or other methods of tracking behavior are almost always included in a functional assessment. Choice C is incorrect because the operational definitions of the behaviors that the RBT ought to document are often included for ease of reference.

20. A: RBT certification requires a portion of the RBT's sessions to be observed for feedback. Choice B is incorrect because working with children does not require a supervisor to be present, and sessions with clients of all ages are included in the observation requirements. Choices C and D are incorrect because, while it is possible a supervisor could use what they learned through observation to learn more about the RBT's practice and either recommend promotion or a need for improvement, neither a promotion nor a performance issue are the most common reason for the ongoing observation requirement.

21. B: For a reinforcement to effectively change behavior, it should be consistent and something the client can expect to occur. Consistency and predictability are important because that will allow the client to know that the reinforcement will be a reward for either engaging in a positive behavior or abstaining from a negative one, which increases the motivation to do so. Choices A and D are incorrect because if a reinforcement causes surprise or confusion, it will likely be ineffective; a reinforcement's efficacy relies

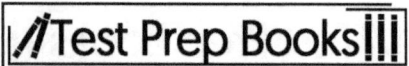

on it being a predictable outcome. Choice C is incorrect because if the reinforcement is too complex or does not occur quickly enough it will likely be ineffective, as the client will not make the connection between behavior and reward.

22. A: The Verbal Behavior Milestones Assessment and Placement Program (VB-MAPP) language assessment is used to determine the language skills of individuals from 0 to 18 months of age, 18 to 30 months of age, or 30 to 48 months of age. While it is often used in applied behavior analysis to assess older individuals who exhibit behaviors typical of someone 48 months of age or younger, the intended age range for the VB-MAPP is up to 48 months old. Therefore, choice A is correct, and choices B, C, and D are incorrect.

23. C: Choice C does the best job describing observable and measurable metrics of cleanliness in the client's bedroom. Choice A is incorrect because this statement documents the client's behavior, not the environment around the client. Choice B is incorrect because the phrase *clean and tidy* is subjective; it is not an objective description of the room. Choice D is incorrect because, while this statement does document the RBT's change in the environment prior to the session, it lacks a description of how the objects were set to engage the client and so is less precise than choice C.

24. C: Every client and situation is unique, and the RBT should work with their supervisor to determine stakeholder communication needs for each client. It is common for the setting to impact this communication. For example, an RBT who works in the school setting may have more communication with school staff, while in an outpatient clinic or in a home setting, the parents would likely be the primary contact. Choice A is incorrect because both forms of communication are appropriate depending on client need and context. While a release of information would also factor into what communication happens, choice B is incorrect because the better answer is that practice setting impacts communication with stakeholders. Choice D is incorrect because it is not overstepping to communicate with teachers, especially when services are provided in the school setting.

25. C: Prompt fading is most effective when the strength and frequency of the prompts used is decreased to encourage a client to use a particular skill. Increasing the time before using a prompt gives the client a longer time window to recognize that they need to use a social greeting. Over time, continuing to increase the time between the antecedent and the prompt will further fade the prompts and improve the client's generalization of the skill. Choice A is incorrect because never providing multiple prompts is unlikely to meaningfully improve the client's skill because they already rarely need two or more prompts. Choice B is incorrect because a modeling prompt may not be the best prompt to use in every circumstance. Choice D is incorrect because, while the use of a less intrusive prompt (modeling) before a more intrusive prompt (verbal) is an effective method of prompt fading, it would be less effective in this context than increasing the time between the antecedent and the prompt.

26. D: The inter-response time of a behavior is the time that elapses between discrete instances of that behavior. Choice D is correct because it describes the inter-response time between each drink that the client takes while using their water bottle. Choice A is incorrect because this answer describes the latency between the client's expression of thirst and their active request for the water bottle. Choice B is incorrect because this answer describes the duration during which the client uses their water bottle. Choice C is incorrect because this answer describes the frequency with which the client is meeting their hydration needs.

27. C: The focus of supervision should be professional issues that impact services provided, not personal issues. While there may be exceptions where a personal issue should be shared, such as a request for medical leave, this is not typically an appropriate use of supervision. Choice A is incorrect because, while it also involves a relationship, it is appropriate to discuss the dynamics between the technician and the client or their family, especially if it is presenting a barrier. Choice B is incorrect because it is appropriate and expected for a supervisor to provide guidance on clinical notes. Choice D is incorrect because obtaining needed materials, such as data sheets, is a routine supervision request.

28. A: A functional analysis is conducted by a behavior analyst (often with the assistance of an RBT) to determine the causation of a client's behaviors via experimental methods. Other methods of assessment establish *correlation,* but not causation. Thus, choice A is correct. Choice B is incorrect because *free operant observations* are a method of preference assessment. Choice C is incorrect because *developmental assessment* is a method of individualized assessment. Choice D is incorrect because, while a *descriptive assessment* is a type of functional assessment, it does not use an experimental method to test different variables.

29. A: A dual relationship is when a provider has a relationship with a client or key stakeholder outside of the professional relationship. This can be especially common in small towns or rural areas. There are ethical considerations for dual relationships, which risk harm to the client and must be avoided. The best choice here is to seek supervision and determine if this constitutes a dual relationship that could harm the client, and work with a supervisor on how to move forward in a way that is ethical and supportive of the client. Choices B and C are incorrect because supervision should be sought before immediately discontinuing services or making significant changes. Choice D is incorrect because supervision should be sought, and behaving ethically is the responsibility of the RBT, not a decision made with the guardian.

30. B: Creating options for the child to choose to work independently in the quiet space is most likely to help replace the undesirable behavior. Knocking over furniture serves an escape function, so the replacement behavior should offer a way to meet that function without engaging in the undesired behavior: choosing to leave the classroom in an appropriate manner. Choice A is incorrect because there is no indication that this behavior is due to hunger. Choice C is incorrect because it makes the environment safer but does not address behavior change. Choice D is incorrect because this involves punishment of the behavior, not reinforcing behavior change through supporting a replacement behavior.

31. D: Choice D is correct because this answer describes a measurable change in the session's environment by specifying which toy is placed nearer to the client's seat. This measurement is relevant documentation because it helps identify the client's preferences. For example, if Karl were to reach for the red dinosaur (which is farther away than the green truck), this would indicate that he prefers that toy and that it will be more useful as a reinforcer in the future. Choice A is incorrect because the statement lacks specificity about the toys and their positions in the environment. Choice B is incorrect because *clean and tidy* is a subjective description of the office—the evaluation of cleanliness varies from person to person. Choice C is incorrect because, while this statement is an appropriate description of the client's behavior, it does not describe the session's environment.

32. D: The goal of maintenance exercises is skill retention. If the client's parents learn how to perform these exercises, the client is more likely to retain the skills learned even after their treatment is over. Choice A is incorrect because it is still important for the RBT to occasionally perform maintenance exercises with the client to ensure that their at-home exercises are being performed correctly. Choice B is incorrect because verbal praise is not a form of unconditioned reinforcement. Choice C is incorrect because a client is not necessarily more motivated to perform exercises with a parent than with the RBT.

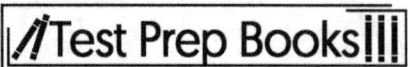

For example, adolescent clients are more likely to engage with non-parental adults than with their parents.

33. B: The best response is to ask clarifying questions to understand and reflect on the feedback before responding. Part of the supervision relationship is to take feedback, including negative or constructive feedback, as this is part of improving one's practice. In this instance, it is best to reflect on and ask questions to understand the feedback before pushing back. Choice A is incorrect because there is no indication that this interaction was inappropriate and does not warrant a report. Choice C is incorrect because guidance should be sought primarily from the supervisor, not a peer. Choice D is incorrect because this interaction is not something that would be documented in the client's medical record.

34. B: Momentary time sampling is the most appropriate option for a group setting (such as a classroom) because the RBT or other service provider is only required to document the client(s) behavior at the end of specific intervals. This enables the RBT to record detailed information while also providing other therapeutic services during the observation session. Choice A is incorrect because documenting every instance of a behavior with event recording consumes more time and requires the RBT's undivided attention. Choice C is incorrect because documenting whether a behavior occurs for the entire length of each time interval during the observation session presents inefficiencies similar to event recording. Choice D is incorrect because open-ended questioning is best suited to conducting an individualized assessment, not while recording data in a group setting.

35. C: RBTs should not engage in a sexual or romantic relationship with a client or stakeholder for at least 2 years after the professional relationship has concluded. Additionally, the relationship should not be the reason that the professional services are terminated. If more than 2 years have passed, going on a date with the guardian of a former client would not constitute an ethical violation. Choice A is incorrect because the 2-year rule is in place regardless of what services were provided. Choice B is incorrect because this is not a current client, so this would not be an issue overseen by the supervisor. Choice D is incorrect because the length or nature of the relationship is irrelevant to the ethical obligations.

36. C: Differential reinforcement of other behavior uses a reinforcement when the undesirable behavior is avoided for a set amount of time. In this case, playing the favorite game is the reinforcement to reduce the negative behavior. Choice A is incorrect because, while differential reinforcement of alternative behavior (DRA) involves reinforcement following a positive replacement behavior or lack of negative behavior, it does not focus on a specific time of avoidance to receive the reward. Choice B is incorrect because noncontingent reinforcement is a technique that involves giving the reinforcement or reward randomly and frequently, rather than connecting it to a behavior. Choice D is incorrect because functional communication training is a form of DRA that involves the client using a verbal cue rather than the negative behavior to meet the desired function.

37. C: The purpose of an individualized assessment is to evaluate a client's language skills, social skills, and other developmental milestones. These assessments do not evaluate a client's reasoning skills. Therefore, choices A and D are incorrect. Choice B is incorrect because, while reading comprehension might be considered part of language comprehension, the emphasis in an individualized assessment is on a client's ability to understand and use spoken language, not written language.

38. A: *Discriminative stimulus* is a term used in discrimination training to denote the stimulus that the client should select out of a group of stimuli for a desired consequence. Choice B is incorrect because the client is not intended to avoid a discriminative stimulus. Choice C is incorrect because this is the definition of a consequence of behavior. Choice D is incorrect because this is the definition of the antecedent that triggers a behavior.

39. B: An RBT may not accept money or gifts that are valued over $10 from clients. Accepting such gifts could create a dynamic that could impact the services provided and is therefore prohibited. There is often organizational policy on this topic in addition to the professional ethical guidelines. The best response is to thank the client for their gesture and explain that this gift cannot be accepted. Choice A is incorrect because gifts of this value cannot be accepted regardless of documentation or supervisor consultation. Choice C is incorrect because this does not require supervision; not accepting a gift such as this is clearly stated in the RBT ethical code. Choice D is incorrect because, while it is important to maintain a good working relationship, not offending the client is not an appropriate reason for an ethical violation such as accepting a $100 gift.

40. C: RBTs should be aware of variables that could impact a client's a session or progress and communicate these changes to their supervisor promptly. The client starting a new medication is a change that the supervisor would be unaware of and may impact services. Choices A, B, and D are incorrect because they are not new information or changes. Age, a history of a long-term condition, or an ongoing status would be information collected in an initial intake, not new variables that could change the services being provided or alter the effectiveness of a session.

41. B: A line graph is an effective means of showing the change in a client's behavior by graphing a metric indicating intensity, frequency, or duration of the behavior on the y-axis and showing how this metric changed during treatment by graphing time on the x-axis. Choice A is incorrect because a bar graph is best suited for comparing total quantities of different metrics rather than representing changes over time. Choice C is incorrect because a pie chart is best used to show the relative proportions of different metrics as a percentage (such as the percentage of days a client turns in their homework). Choice D is incorrect because an area chart is best used to compare multiple metrics over time.

42. C: The first step in learning to play a game is to set up the game board as required by the game's rules. Choice A is incorrect because, while logically this step must occur first, sitting down at the table is not a step that task analysis would define as part of playing a game of checkers. Choice B is incorrect because there isn't sufficient context about whether picking up the board is for the sake of setting up the pieces or cleaning up the game. Choice D is incorrect because setting up the board must happen prior to moving the pieces.

43. C: Replacement behavior should be accessible and easy for the client to do so that there is not an extra level of complication of engaging in a new behavior when they are already engaging in the challenging work of behavior reduction. A behavior that takes a lot of focus and is difficult would not be a good choice. Choices A, B, and D are incorrect because they all describe appropriate features of alternate behavior; they should be known, simple, and applicable in many environments.

44. A: Stating that the client "was playing … when the doorbell rang" indicates that this is the antecedent to a behavior exhibited by the client. Choice B is incorrect because it describes the client's behavior, not the antecedent. Choice C is incorrect because this reinforcement is an example of a consequence for behavior, not an antecedent. Choice D is incorrect because this statement also describes the client's behavior—in this case, the lack of change in their behavior.

45. D: The RBT should notify the organization that alternative supervisory arrangements are needed. Just as it is unethical to engage in a dual relationship with a client, RBTs and supervisors both have an

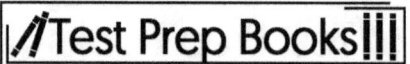

ethical obligation to not have a dual relationship with each other that could impair their professional work. It is not appropriate to receive supervision from a former partner, especially if the relationship ended recently. An alternative arrangement must be found. Choice A is incorrect because this is a dual relationship regardless of how well the RBT and supervisor work together. Choice B is incorrect because this is an ethical issue that needs to be addressed, and simply documenting the relationship is not an adequate intervention. Choice C is incorrect because the length or intensity of the relationship does not matter for this ethical issue to be a concern.

46. C: All sessions should be documented with an objective description of what occurred and what interventions were offered. The discussion with the parent about the client's sleep challenges is relevant and should be included in the note, and this is information that should be communicated to a supervisor. Choice A is incorrect because telling the parent what to do is not appropriate. Choice B is incorrect because an RBT is not qualified to advise on medications. Choice D is incorrect because it is typical to bill insurance as usual if a session is completed; the client's lack of engagement would be documented in the clinical notes but should not impact billing.

47. A: When conducting discrete trials, the RBT ought to begin by instructing the client to perform the simplest possible task. In this case, identifying a single shape is the simplest task. Choices B and D are incorrect because identifying shapes that are similar to one another—whether across the whole page or adjacent shapes—is a more complex task than identifying a single shape. Choice C is incorrect because the task is even more complex—it requires both identifying shapes and counting the number of shapes.

48. A: A clinical setting—such as a formal therapy session—is the best setting for the RBT to use data collection methods that require a lot of attention. Choice A is correct because continuous measurement of a client's attention span may not be feasible in other settings (like a classroom). Choice B is incorrect because momentary time sampling is not an effective method for measuring a client's latency; this method documents the occurrence of a behavior only at the ends of the specified intervals. Choice C is incorrect because partial interval sampling can be used effectively in a variety of settings (for example, to document whether dysregulated behavior occurred during each class throughout a school day). Choice D is incorrect because permanent product recording for this behavior is well suited for use in variety of settings. Intensity is measured by whether the dysregulation resulted in a permanent product (i.e., did the client break an object?). This data can be collected in the clinical setting but should also be collected in other settings.

49. C: The client in question is able to use the skill—sharing—in certain environments but struggles to use it in other environments. This demonstrates that they have not generalized the skill for use in a variety of settings and situations. Choice A is incorrect because maintenance is a concept used for retaining current skills, and no indication is given that the client is struggling to maintain their ability to share. Choice B is incorrect because stimulus control is not generally an educational goal. Rather, it is a concept used by the RBT while conducting behavior therapy exercises (such as in stimulus control transfer). Choice D is incorrect because the client is able to use the skill independently.

50. B: Reinforcement of a replacement behavior is a method to achieve extinction of the negative behavior, especially if the replacement behavior meets the same function. For example, if a child has an escape behavior of aggression in the classroom to get to leave the room, creating a way for the child to ask to take a break or go to a quiet room would be an effective replacement behavior. Choice A is incorrect because, while it is a helpful part of the process to gather information, a functional behavioral assessment alone won't lead to extinction. Choice C is incorrect because this is a form of punishment

Answer Explanations #2

and does not replace the behavior's function. Choice D is incorrect because it is possible to achieve extinction of a behavior regardless of its function.

51. B: When using chaining to connect the independent steps of a skill that has been broken down via task analysis, it is important that the steps are always connected in the sequence in which they are to be used. Non-sequential exercises do not help the client understand a chain of steps that occur in a particular sequence. Choice A is incorrect because forward chaining connects the steps in the order required to complete the target skill. Choice C is incorrect because in backward chaining, the client learns the steps in reverse, starting with the last step. Choice D is incorrect because beginning a task at a step in the middle of the sequence rather than at the beginning is still an effective way to improve a client's ability to chain steps together, especially if they are struggling in the middle of performing the skill.

52. A: RBTs need to be aware of and assess for any variables or changes in the client's life that may impact their response to behavioral interventions. A change in living situation is a significant change that would understandably impact the client, and the RBT needs to include this in the medical record and seek prompt supervision for guidance on how to proceed. Choice B is incorrect because it is reasonable to assume that the external changes factored into the client's behavior. This should be explored further before making significant changes to the behavior plan, especially if it had previously been working. Choice C is incorrect because there is no indication that the RBT has the needed release of information paperwork to contact the child's teachers. Choice D is incorrect because it is much more likely that the behavior escalation is due to the change in the client's living situation rather than their relationship with the RBT. While supervisor observation might be useful to get input on how to best support the client, it is unlikely that rapport is the primary issue in this situation.

53. A: RBTs should maintain professional and appropriate boundaries with clients. Engaging on social media is not an appropriate interaction for this relationship, and the best choice is to uphold and explain this boundary to the client. Choice B is incorrect because this is a boundary issue regardless of the client's age. Choice C is incorrect because it is the RBT's responsibility to uphold the boundaries, not to discuss the consequences with the client and allow them to choose. Choice D is incorrect because, while the RBT needs to hold the boundary here, this is a reasonable interaction with a high-school-aged client. The RBT should be prepared to respond, but this alone would not justify discontinuing services.

54. A: Taking a deep breath makes this skill goal both objective and measurable. While an RBT cannot directly observe a client's emotions, they can record symptoms of dysregulation (such as a red face) and can record how often the client takes a deep breath prior to speaking while experiencing those symptoms. This allows the treatment team to collect data about the client's progress in self-regulation. Choice B is incorrect because it lacks parameters to make it measurable. Choice C is incorrect because the goal is about the client's emotions ("will accept"), rather than an objective behavior that can be observed (such as sharing the first time another student asks for the toy). Choice D is incorrect because it is imprecise and lacks measurable parameters.

55. B: Mandatory staff training on de-escalation methods during onboarding is crucial to crisis planning. Crisis planning should be a part of every behavior reduction plan; the term *crisis planning* refers to having an individualized plan to recognize, support, and de-escalate a client if they reach a crisis state during an intervention. Following a standard de-escalation protocol that staff are trained for in advance is a best practice in crisis intervention. Many models exist, and staff should follow agency procedures and training. Choice A is incorrect because behavior reduction plans are appropriate for clients of all ages. Choice C is incorrect because, while staff members may be mandated reporters, this refers to their

Answer Explanations #2

legal requirement to report situations of harm, neglect, or abuse, and is not directly related to crisis planning. Choice *D* is incorrect because, while it is possible that a client who is frequently in crisis may need a referral for more intensive therapeutic services, developing this referral relationship would not be a part of the crisis plan section of the behavior reduction plan.

56. B: Incidental teaching is a naturalistic teaching method that seizes opportunities to encourage the use of a client's skills during day-to-day activities. The verbal prompt demonstrates incidental teaching by encouraging the client to use their social skills to return the teacher's wave. Choices *A* and *C* are incorrect because, while intentionally going to the playground or playing a kickball game demonstrates naturalistic teaching, it does not demonstrate incidental teaching. Choice *D* is incorrect because the RBT is not using the incidental encounter to encourage the use of a client's skills. Rather, they are providing verbal praise as reinforcement during the incidental encounter.

57. A: Shaping is used to take a basic skill and guide that capacity toward performing a new skill. Physical skills are easily shaped by directing a client to perform familiar motions in slightly different ways. Over time, the client learns to perform the new set of physical motions. For example, a client who can wave their hand might be directed to wave their hand while holding an object. The RBT slowly changes how the client holds the object and waves their hand until the client is able to perform the waving action required to brush their teeth. Thus, choice *A* is correct. Choice *B* is incorrect because a client's academic abilities are less easily shaped toward unfamiliar skills (for example, the ability to read cannot necessarily be shaped into improving arithmetic). Choice *C* is incorrect because shaping is typically less effective for teaching emotional skills—like self-regulation—than procedures like stimulus control transfer are. Choice *D* is incorrect because, while social skills can effectively be shaped from less effective behavior toward more effective behavior, doing so is typically slower and more complex than using shaping to teach a physical skill.

58. B: The Assessment of Functional Living Skills (AFLS) is an individualized assessment that evaluates a client's ability to perform day-to-day tasks such as personal hygiene tasks or vocational skills. Despite the use of *functional* in the name, it is not a functional behavior assessment. The AFLS assesses a client's overall ability to function rather than analyzing how a specific behavior functions for the client. Thus, choice *B* is correct, and choices *A*, *C,* and *D* are incorrect.

59. B: A positional prompt is useful in discrimination training to highlight the object that is the correct choice by moving it closer to the client or farther away from the other objects. Choice *A* is incorrect because the efficacy of a positional prompt during a discrete trial depends on the type of trial being conducted. Choice *C* is incorrect because no particular prompt type is most effective when generalizing an unspecified skill. The best type of prompt will depend on the skill to be generalized. Choice *D* is incorrect because changing the position of an object is not typically an effective prompt in social situations. A modeling prompt or a gesture prompt is usually the best option.

60. C: The next step is to implement the de-escalation protocol outlined in the crisis section of the behavior reduction plan. Behavior reduction plans should include a crisis planning section that describes potential triggers and what to do in the event of an escalation such as this. A standard de-escalation protocol is typically included; it may involve verbal or physical interventions to maintain safety and support the client. Choice *A* is incorrect because, while an extinction burst during behavior reduction is a known possibility, this situation involves a safety concern and a crisis response is needed. Choice *B* is incorrect because handling this sort of crisis is part of the intervention. A possible escalation of this type is possible during behavior reduction, and does not suggest any fault on the part of the technician.

Choice D is incorrect because, while safety is the focus, the technician should follow the de-escalation protocol.

61. A: RBTs are mandated reporters, which means that they are required to report instances of abuse and neglect. A child experiencing physical harm from a parent requires a child protective services report, so the correct response is to notify a supervisor and promptly file that report. Choice B is incorrect because the report must be filed whether the client consents or not; the risk of harm overrides the typical right to privacy. Choice C is incorrect because, while a supervisor should be notified, this is not the supervisor's decision. The client disclosed clear physical abuse to the RBT, so a report must be filed. Choice D is incorrect because mandated reporters include their contact information when they file a child protective services report; it would not be anonymous.

62. C: Naturalistic teaching utilizes day-to-day activities or mimics day-to-day activities to help clients practice using their skills in a context that provides them with additional motivation to succeed. Attending the school play is an activity that the RBT can organize to help the client practice their social skills and also provides the client with motivation to succeed (the desire to support one's friends). Choice A is incorrect because, while playing a board game demonstrates naturalistic teaching, the group home setting, based on the information given, is less likely to provide the same motivation to succeed as would attending a play in which the client's friends will perform. Choice B is incorrect because this activity is a reward for participation in a token economy, not an activity chosen for naturalistic teaching. Choice D is incorrect because this activity is not naturalistic—it is preparing for a day-to-day activity, not actually engaging in one.

63. A: Play teaching is a form of naturalistic teaching used to engage children in play activities as a method of teaching them new skills, often social skills. For example, the RBT might use building blocks with a child to create an opportunity for learning to share toys (the blocks). Practicing this skill with an adult improves the child's ability to share toys when playing with other children. Choice B is incorrect because, while incidental teaching can occur during play, *play teaching* refers to intentionally using play activities during behavior therapy. Choice C is incorrect because discrete trial training typically is not used in conjunction with play teaching—children tend to want to remain engaged in the play activity rather than continue to perform discrete trials. Choice D is incorrect because, while play teaching can be used as part of a maintenance exercise, it is generally used to teach new skills.

64. D: By playing a game of kickball, the client would be using their new skill (kicking a ball) in a different context (a kickball game instead of a soccer game). This demonstrates generalization. Choices A and B are incorrect because throwing a ball is a different skill than kicking a ball. Choice C is incorrect because discussing a soccer match is not a generalization of the client's ability to accurately kick a soccer ball.

65. B: The client is consistently using this physical behavior to communicate a need to the RBT (in this case, asking a question). Shaping can be used effectively in this case to modify the client's clapping behavior in such a way that they begin raising their hand instead (for example, beginning by lifting both hands higher up while clapping). Choice A is incorrect because shaping is best used to adapt a current behavior into a different behavior within the same context, and cheering on a friend is a different context than asking a question. Choice C is incorrect because the purpose of clapping their hands is to get attention. Catching a ball does not achieve the same goal as getting attention to ask a question. Choice D is incorrect because, while the social context is the same, making eye contact is not a new behavior that uses the client's current behavior (clapping their hands). Consequently, shaping would not be effective to teach the new skill.

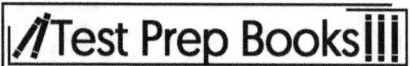

66. B: The best response is to provide psychoeducation on the functions of behavior. Helping the family or support system understand behavior and the behavior reduction process is important. Because the parents say that they don't understand why the behavior is continuing, the best response is to help them understand the concept of behavior functions. Choice A is incorrect because the behavior described is not developmentally typical. Choice C is incorrect because, while there may be useful guidance to help the parents support their child, the role of the technician is not to tell the parents what to do. Choice D is incorrect because, while it is possible that a support group would be helpful, it does not provide education on behavior or function.

67. A: In task analysis, forward chaining is used to connect steps together in the sequence used when performing the actual skill. Choice A is correct because the steps listed represent a logical, sequentially arranged set of actions that could constitute putting away a lunch tray. Choices B, C, and D are incorrect because the steps are in non-sequential order.

68. B: Among the options given, Choice B is the skill that would be easiest to practice while vacationing with family because maintenance exercises could be used by the parents during day-to-day activities, such as running errands, to continue practicing the skill of staying close to one's caretaker in public. Choices A, C, and D are incorrect because these skills are used in settings and situations that are more difficult to replicate while vacationing as a family.

69. C: The skill acquisition plan (SAP) is written by the treatment team's behavior analyst with the support and feedback of other members of the team, including the RBT, the parents, and the client themself. Choice C is correct because the behavior analyst ultimately determines the final language and metrics of the SAP's skill goals. Choices A, B, and D are incorrect because, while these team members contribute to the goal-setting process, they are not directly responsible for writing the skill goals.

70. A: The RBT should seek supervision to discuss how this might impact services and if a release of information should be obtained to coordinate care. The client starting new treatment or mental health care is the type of variable an RBT should be aware of, and the RBT should discuss with their supervisor how it could impact care and get guidance on how to proceed. It would also be appropriate to discuss a release of information to coordinate care as part of that conversation. Choice B is incorrect because, while supervision should be obtained, there is not enough information to assume that services must be discontinued. Choice C is incorrect because it does not involve seeking supervision. Choice D is also incorrect because it does not involve seeking supervision, and it is not appropriate to ask more about a client's diagnosis than what is clinically needed to know.

71. D: The first intervention likely failed because the function of the behavior was identified incorrectly. Identifying the function of a behavior is important in reducing or eliminating it. While behavior can have multiple functions, in this example it appears that the primary function was attention, not escape. A need for attention is addressed through the second intervention. Choice A is incorrect because it does not necessarily take multiple interventions to reduce behavior. Choice B is incorrect because there is no indication that the first intervention was beyond the child's abilities. Choice C is incorrect because, although consistency is important, nothing in the example indicates that the first intervention was inconsistent.

72. A: The tokens in a token economy should not themselves be terminal reinforcers of client behavior. Instead, they are symbolic objects that have acquired value to the client by repeatedly having been paired with unconditioned or terminal reinforcers These tokens can be exchanged for the client's desired, terminal reinforcer. Choices B, C, and D are all true of token economies. Tokens can be effective in systems that offer a variety of methods of reinforcement to the client, the most effective tokens are easy to use by both the client and the RBT or other providers, and the rewards in a token economy may include both types of reinforcers (for example, pieces of candy or access to a toy).

73. B: An overall goal is an objective identified as the desired outcome of participation in behavior therapy. It is what the client and their treatment team hope that therapy as a whole will achieve long-term. Skill goals are smaller, specific, measurable objectives that, when combined, help to achieve the overall goal. Therefore, Choice B is the best example of an overall goal on a client's skill acquisition plan, while Choices A and D both exemplify appropriate skill goals rather than overall goals and are therefore incorrect. Choice C is incorrect because it more closely resembles a skill goal than an overall goal, though it lacks the metrics required to be an effective skill goal.

74. D: Shaping builds new skills based on a client's current abilities. If the client feels frustrated that they cannot perform the tasks given during a therapy session, shaping procedures may be a more effective teaching method because they focus on using the client's current abilities in a new way. Choice A is incorrect because, although discrete trials are simple, they won't necessarily boost the client's self-esteem if the trial is beyond the client's current abilities. Choice B is incorrect because discrimination training is only effective for particular types of tasks, and the question does not provide enough information to know whether improving the client's ability to discriminate will improve their motivation. Choice C is incorrect because, while incidental teaching does often increase a client's motivation, it may be less effective in this situation because the client is struggling to perform their current goals.

75. B: In this case, the client has generalized their coping skill for use in different environments and in response to different stimuli (feeling frustrated and feeling sad). Choice A is incorrect because the client generalizes the skill for use only in different settings (different bathrooms). Choice C is incorrect because the client has not generalized the skill effectively—raising one's hand is not a normative way to ask parents questions in a grocery store. Choice D is incorrect because the client recognizes uppercase letters in different circumstances but is not described as generalizing the skill further (for example, recognizing uppercase letters in a decorative font).

RBT Practice Test #3

1. What intervention uses the method of withholding reinforcement for a negative behavior in order to eliminate it?
    a. Extinction
    b. Avoidance
    c. Compartmentalization
    d. Positive punishment

2. An RBT has a caseload of fifteen clients, all of whom they see weekly. When should the RBT write their session notes?
    a. Determining note frequency is up to the supervisor and billing agent.
    b. A note should be written following each session.
    c. They should submit a monthly report documenting all work done.
    d. They should complete a session note whenever there is a clinical change to report.

3. Which of the following can be used as a permanent product when recording client data?
    a. Progress
    b. Behaviors
    c. Outcomes
    d. Tokens

4. An RBT works with children, providing behavioral services in an outpatient setting. A contractor working on renovations in the RBT's home says that they need to find behavioral services for their own child, who is 5 years old. They state that the child has trouble trusting new people and inquire whether the RBT would be able to work with the child at the outpatient organization. What is the best response?
    a. Explain that this would not be appropriate and provide resources to help the contractor find services for their child.
    b. Agree as long as the relationship is documented, because this is in the best interest of the child.
    c. Offer to work with the child one-on-one before engaging with the organization to determine if it is a good fit.
    d. Agree as long as the child has insurance coverage, so there is no conflict of interest with payment.

5. When preparing for a therapy session, the RBT should always do which of the following?
    a. Ensure that the session's activities will provide an opportunity to practice at least one skill goal.
    b. Adjust the therapy session's environment to engage the client's interests.
    c. Identify informal ways to help the client practice their social skills during the session.
    d. Review the client's most recent individualized assessment.

6. Which of the following statements about the graph is true?

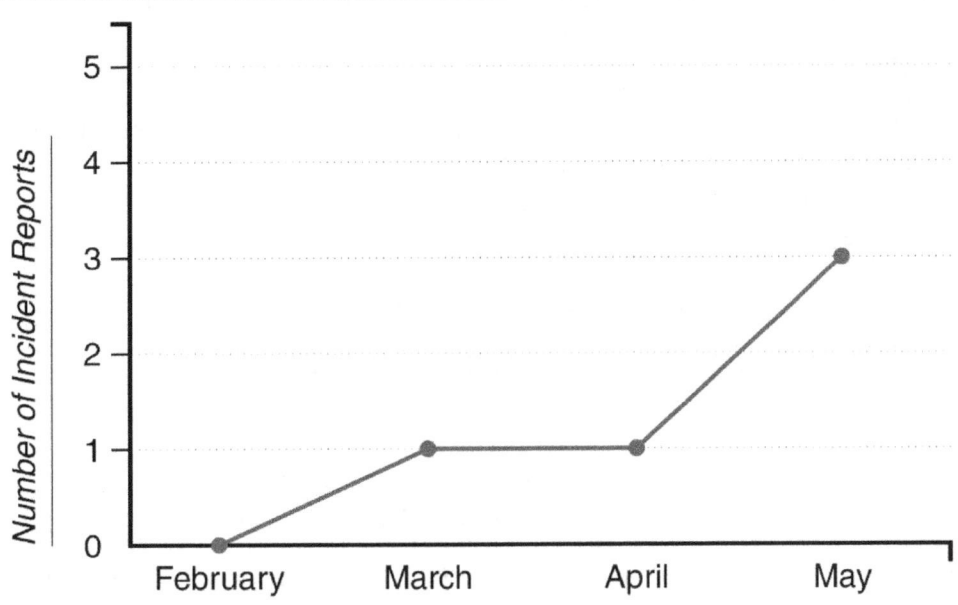

Incident Report

   a. The number of incidents is decreasing.
   b. The number of incidents is increasing.
   c. The number of incidents is constant.
   d. The average number of incidents is one per month.

7. What intervention can be used to help teach an appropriate alternative behavior to replace a challenging one?
   a. Cognitive behavioral therapy
   b. Functional communication training
   c. Neuropsychological evaluation
   d. Narrative therapy

8. An RBT is providing services in a school setting. They are meeting with a client in a room at the school during school hours. During the session, the client becomes upset by an intervention and starts to yell loudly, drawing the attention of their peers in a classroom across the hallway. What should the RBT do?
   a. Continue with the intervention according to the behavior reduction plan because the client is not in crisis or at risk of harm.
   b. Stop the intervention, calm the client down, and consult with a supervisor about whether a more private setting is needed.
   c. Tell the teacher in the classroom across the hall to close their door to give the client privacy.
   d. Document the session to reflect how upset the client became during the intervention.

9. Which of the following is NOT relevant information to include the clinical note following a client session?
    a. The credentials and name of the RBT
    b. A conversation with the client's parent about an upcoming school change
    c. The interventions that were implemented
    d. A subjective assessment of the client's mood

10. During an individualized skill assessment, a client makes multiple independent attempts to perform a skill when directed. Which should the RBT document?
    a. Only document the first attempt.
    b. Only document the final attempt.
    c. Document any successful attempts.
    d. Document the number of attempts and their results.

11. Which of the following is NOT an example of maintaining client dignity?
    a. Ensuring that client sessions occur in a private space
    b. Asking a client if they are ready to start the intervention
    c. Using a reinforcement technique that involves shaming the client
    d. Rescheduling a session that occurs on a client's religious holiday

12. An RBT is documenting a client's behavior in an incident report. Which of the following statements makes the best use of objective documentation practices?
    a. "Sarah became dysregulated when I removed the toy and she began screaming at me."
    b. "When I removed the toy, Sarah's face turned red, and she made a loud, nonverbal noise."
    c. "After shouting, Sarah got up and tried to forcefully take the toy out of my hands."
    d. "Next, Sarah stood up and started threatening me when I did not return the toy immediately."

13. When is the best time to provide reinforcement for a positive behavior when trying to replace a negative behavior?
    a. Immediately following the positive behavior
    b. First thing in the morning
    c. At varied intervals
    d. When the client is hungry

14. Which of the following statements about preparing reinforcers for use in a therapy session is true?
    a. The RBT should always prepare to have the most desirable reinforcer available for the client.
    b. The RBT should prepare a variety of conditioned and unconditioned reinforcers.
    c. The RBT should consult the client's skill acquisition plan to determine appropriate reinforcers.
    d. The RBT should ask the client which reinforcer they'd like to use at the start of the session.

15. A client's mother reports that her son seems lethargic while taking a new medication. The RBT checks their documentation of the client's behavioral therapy sessions to attempt to correlate measured data with the mother's observation and finds that the therapy session documentation corroborates the mother's observation. Which of the following metrics is most likely increasing?
    a. Frequency
    b. Rate
    c. Inter-response time
    d. Latency

16. An RBT is completing documentation following a session with a client. During the session, the client had four instances of escalated aggressive behavior, including shoving. What is the BEST way for the RBT to document this?
    a. "Client will need to work harder and not shove during future sessions."
    b. "Client engaged in a shoving behavior four times during the session."
    c. "Client was in a bad mood that led to several instances of shoving."
    d. "Client was difficult to work with and showed some aggression."

17. An RBT works with a client who has a behavior plan that often uses food-based rewards. The client practices a religion that has holidays that involve abstaining from food as part of the religious tradition. How should the RBT respond?
    a. Seek supervision and reschedule sessions that fall on a holiday.
    b. Continue with the interventions even on a holiday because the RBT cannot change the behavior reduction plan.
    c. Learn more about the client's religious beliefs to better understand the client.
    d. Document the client's refusal to participate in the intervention.

18. An RBT is conducting a discrimination exercise with the goal that the client will be able to discern different types of brightly colored food. While doing the exercise using an orange and a piece of candy in an orange wrapper, the RBT moves the orange so that it is closer to the child than the piece of candy is. This exemplifies which type of prompt?
    a. Positional
    b. Motion
    c. Gesture
    d. Physical

19. Which of the following is the best example of documenting qualitative data?
    a. Recording a behavior's intensity as mild, moderate, or severe
    b. Measuring a behavior's duration with a stopwatch
    c. Charting a client's grades to identify changes during treatment
    d. Reviewing a client's documentation and analyzing long-term trends

20. Which of the following factors should be considered when creating a crisis intervention protocol in a behavior reduction plan?
    a. Client history and triggers
    b. Parental consent to include a crisis plan
    c. Whether a crisis plan is necessary
    d. Effective positive reinforcement

21. Which of the following statements about documentation is NOT true?
    a. Documentation should be submitted as soon as possible following the session.
    b. Most organizations have policies surrounding documentation.
    c. Documentation should only include information obtained directly from the client.
    d. Documentation is an important part of the billing and insurance reimbursement process.

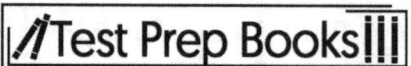

22. An RBT is talking to a parent in the waiting room as they are bringing their child to the session. The parent begins to talk about the child in front of the other families in the waiting room, and tells the RBT that the child has been having a lot of bad behavior at home. What is the best response?
    a. Tell the parent to stop talking about their child in a negative manner.
    b. Empathize and listen to the parent because stakeholder input is important.
    c. Seek supervision to determine how to better support the client in future situations like this.
    d. Ask the parent to come to a private session room to check in further.

23. How are functional assessments of a client's behavior used to design effective treatments?
    a. During a functional assessment, a client's disruptive behaviors are studied in a structured and controlled environment.
    b. Functional assessments identify variables that can be altered during therapy to shape undesirable behaviors.
    c. Analyzing a client's ability to use day-to-day living skills helps the behavior analyst determine any deficiencies in the client's skills.
    d. A functional assessment is more precise than other assessments because it uses both direct and indirect methods.

24. Which of the following is a risk of overreliance on discontinuous methods for recording a client's behaviors?
    a. Discontinuous recording is best used only in functional behavior assessments.
    b. Discontinuous recording may result in overestimating the frequency of a behavior.
    c. Discontinuous recording requires short intervals and is mostly used in clinical settings.
    d. Discontinuous recording cannot be used to document a behavior's duration.

25. At the beginning of a therapy session, the client's parents report that the client is succeeding more frequently at accepting loss when playing games with other children, resulting in fewer angry outbursts. They also report observing that the other children now invite the client to play games more frequently than they used to. Which of the following statements describes the effect of negative reinforcement in this situation?
    a. The client's ability to accept loss is reinforced by getting to play more often with others.
    b. The parents' attentiveness to their child is reinforced by pride in the client's improved social skills.
    c. The other children's willingness to play with the client is reinforced by the client's improved social skills.
    d. The client's ability to win a game is reinforced by praise from the other children.

26. An RBT takes a client on an outing to a nearby convenience store. Which of the following statements best describes the environment during this activity?
    a. Five people were shopping and two cashiers were working at the store when we arrived.
    b. The store was well-organized with no obvious messes or shelf-stocking observed.
    c. We arrived at the store at about 3:15 p.m. to avoid large numbers of shoppers.
    d. James activated the handicap assist button and navigated the door independently.

27. A child has a favorite toy that they want to play with every day. They have started yelling and kicking when they do not have it, and the parent often ends up giving the child the toy. What is the function of the behavior in this example?
   a. Attention
   b. Escape
   c. Tangible
   d. Automatic

28. An RBT is working with an adolescent client. The client states that they feel embarrassed by needing to engage in behavioral support services because "it's for little kids." The client tells the RBT that they do not want to work on their behavior plan because having to work towards a reward is childish and makes them feel embarrassed. What should the RBT do?
   a. Talk to their supervisor about the situation to determine how to alter the plan to support the client.
   b. Proceed with the intervention because the RBT cannot change the behavior reduction plan.
   c. Invite the client and their guardian to a meeting to discuss the concerns.
   d. Change the intervention to something that the client is not embarrassed by and document the change.

29. A behavior technician is working with an adolescent client on reducing behaviors that disrupt the classroom. At the start of the session, they are engaging in some warm-up activities, and the client is sharing about their day. The client tells the technician that they are interested in another student in their class, and might ask them to a school dance. How should the technician document this information?
   a. They should document the conversation objectively because everything shared must be included in the note.
   b. They should document the session in the note and state that the client was in a good mood because of their crush on a schoolmate.
   c. They do not need to document this information because it is not relevant to the services being provided.
   d. They should discuss relationship safety with the client and document that intervention.

30. An RBT should NOT use which of the following groups to practice discerning differences during discrimination training?
   a. A happy smile, a sad frown, and an angry snarl
   b. A human's arm, a cat's paw, and a dog's paw
   c. An orange, a cherry, and an apple
   d. A marble statue, a classical song, and a silk dress

31. Which of the following is an example of showing empathy to a client who is struggling during their session and saying that the work is really hard?
   a. Listening to the client's concerns and offering support
   b. Telling the client that they will be happy once they put in the effort to make the changes
   c. Having the client reflect on the problems that their challenging behavior causes in their life
   d. Changing the behavior plan to not be so challenging for the client

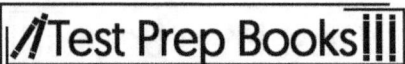

32. An RBT is working with an elementary-school-aged client who was referred by their pediatrician. They have no releases of information signed. Which of the following parties would NOT be able to access the session notes?
    a. The client's guardian
    b. The client's teachers
    c. The insurance provider
    d. The supervisor

33. An RBT interviews a client's stakeholders as part of an indirect assessment, but forgets to bring a notepad. Which of the following is the best example of documentation of client data collected during one of these discussions and later written from memory?
    a. "I called Mrs. Johnson at about 9:00 a.m. and spoke with her for about 20 minutes."
    b. "According to the teacher, Larry no longer struggles with being tardy to class."
    c. "His mother said, 'Larry rarely becomes dysregulated when at home with me and his father.'"
    d. "Mr. Harris reported that Larry begins to get a 'squinty look' when feeling frustrated."

34. An RBT is conducting a preference assessment for a 5-year-old diagnosed with autism spectrum disorder. The client's parent is present during the assessment. Which of the following assessment methods is best targeted at the parent rather than the child?
    a. Single stimulus
    b. Free operant observation
    c. Paired stimulus
    d. Open-ended questions

35. Which of the following is NOT true about behavior reduction?
    a. Behaviors should be replaced, not just eliminated.
    b. Positive and negative behaviors all have functions.
    c. Behavior reduction is linear.
    d. Behavior reduction requires consistency.

36. An RBT is arrested and faces legal charges. What is their professional obligation?
    a. They need to report the situation within 30 days.
    b. They should notify their supervisor of the outcome of the charges once they go to court.
    c. They must immediately resign from active client work until the legal issue is addressed.
    d. They are only required to report the issue if the arrest was for a crime involving harming another person.

37. A client is capable of sharing pencils with other children during schoolwork, but struggles to share a toy doll during recess. The RBT wants to use stimulus control transfer to help the client improve their sharing skills. In this situation, which of the following should be the controlled element?
    a. Using a pencil to write
    b. Playing with the toy doll
    c. Handing an object to someone
    d. Being praised for sharing

38. Which of the following questions is likely to be asked during an indirect functional assessment with a client's parents?
    a. "At what time of day does your child engage in this particular behavior?"
    b. "Does your child already have an Individualized Education Program (IEP) established?"
    c. "What developmental milestones has your child achieved?"
    d. "How frequently throughout the day do you prompt your child to alter their behavior?"

39. An RBT is working with their supervisor to identify stakeholders for a particular client to ensure that the necessary releases and communication methods are in place. Who should be included in this list?
    a. Any party who is a part of the client's life and invested in their care
    b. Insurance payors or whichever party is responsible for payment of services
    c. Any individual who provides supervisory services for other providers
    d. Any parties who are listed in the behavior reduction plan as having a responsibility to provide services

40. At the beginning of treatment, the client identifies an objective of making new friends at school. Which of the following best exemplifies a skill goal that contributes to the client's objective?
    a. "Initiate a conversation with a classmate during recess once per day."
    b. "Practice greetings by addressing the teacher 50% of the times that the client enters the classroom."
    c. "Utilize appropriate hygiene practices (wear clean clothes, wash and comb hair, etc.) 8 out of 10 times that the client comes to school."
    d. "Visit a friend for over an hour during the weekend once per month."

41. An RBT travels between several school sites to meet with their clients. They work with a client in the morning and fill out some data sheets as part of the session, then travel to the next location in their car. What is the best way to handle the data sheets?
    a. They should keep the data sheets in the back seat of the locked car.
    b. They should store the data sheets in a lockbox in the locked trunk of the car.
    c. They should bring the data sheets home and put them on their desk before going to their next session.
    d. RBTs are not allowed to use paper documentation.

42. Which of the following best describes a benefit of preparing a tidy and organized environment prior to a session of behavior therapy?
    a. Increased client engagement with the RBT's exercises
    b. Reduced sources of distraction for the client
    c. Reduced risk of accident or injury from floor hazards
    d. Increased opportunities to reinforce the client's behavior

43. Which of the following permanent products is best suited for assessing a client's money management skills?
    a. The amount of money in their wallet
    b. Paystubs of their income from employment
    c. Receipts of their expenditures
    d. Weekly records of money in their bank account

44. Under what circumstances should an RBT tell their supervisor about a health condition they are experiencing?
   a. If it is impacting their ability to provide services
   b. If they are on a new medication
   c. Never; this is protected health information.
   d. If they need to miss a day of work for doctor's appointment

45. During an outing to a nearby park, the client is climbing on a playground when they slip and fall off a ladder, scraping their knee on the ground. The client then begins to cry, and the RBT hurries over and provides first aid while comforting the client. Which of the following best describes the antecedent to the client's behavior?
   a. Going out to the park
   b. Scraping their knee
   c. Crying on the ground
   d. Receiving verbal concern

46. A behavior technician is working with a 5-year-old client on a behavior reduction plan. The guardian states that they aren't comfortable with the plan and feel that it is too difficult for the child. What should the technician do next?
   a. Discuss the guardian's concerns, provide education on the intervention, and ensure that there is informed consent.
   b. Continue with services because the child's school made the referral for assistance, not the guardian.
   c. Revise the plan to reflect interventions designed for a lower developmental level.
   d. Tell the guardian that this is the only way for their child to improve their behavior.

47. A student persistently refuses to do their homework even after being offered desirable privileges if they complete it. Eventually, the RBT and the student's parents agree to let the student not do their homework and receive the natural consequence for this decision. The student does not do their homework, and their grades are poor enough that they must attend summer courses. Which reinforcement method does this exemplify?
   a. Negative reinforcement
   b. Positive punishment
   c. Negative punishment
   d. No reinforcement method was used

48. Which piece of legislation requires protected health information to be kept confidential?
   a. Health Insurance Portability and Accountability Act
   b. Family Educational Rights and Privacy Act
   c. Children's Online Privacy Protection Act
   d. Federal Information Security Modernization Act

49. An RBT is working with an 11-year-old client diagnosed with autism spectrum disorder. Their goal is to improve the client's ability to pay attention to the teacher during class. Is the discrete trial training method suitable for this goal? Why or why not?
   a. Yes, because the RBT can use discrete trial training to improve the client's attention span over time.
   b. Yes, because discrete trial training is an effective way to teach body language that demonstrates attentiveness.
   c. No, because discrete trial training is best used when trying to improve a client's physical skills.
   d. No, because discrete trial training is more effective at teaching physical tasks than abstract, cognitive ones.

50. Which of the following data collection methods is best suited for recording whether a behavior is becoming less frequent outside of the clinical setting?
   a. Partial interval sampling
   b. Event recording
   c. Momentary time sampling
   d. Continuous measurement

51. When should an RBT begin to implement prompt fading?
   a. When the client is able to consistently perform the skill without assistance
   b. When the client is able to perform the skill without assistance 50% of the time
   c. After the first time the client attempts the skill without a prompt from the RBT
   d. When the client attempts to perform the skill without a prompt 50% of the time

52. A behavior technician is using candy as a reinforcement for a young client who is working to avoid engaging in a target negative behavior of interrupting. In past sessions, the child was given candy when they raised their hand instead of interrupting. The technician puts the container that the client knows holds candy on the table in clear view. Which of the following best describes the principle for why putting the candy out will increase the effectiveness of the intervention?
   a. Extinction burst
   b. Motivating operations
   c. Discriminative stimulus
   d. Behavior function

53. Which of the following best describes the relationship between generalization and discrete trial training?
   a. Discrete trial training practices physical behaviors, while generalization is a goal for all types of behavior.
   b. Discrete trial training is used to teach skills that can then be generalized for use in different settings and situations.
   c. Clients learn generalization by conducting discrete trials to identify differences between types of stimuli.
   d. Generalization is a prerequisite for discrete trial training because the client must be able to perform the skill in different environments.

54. Which of the following is a true statement about using reinforcement to implement shaping during behavioral therapy?
   a. The RBT ought to only provide reinforcement when the client performs the final target behavior, not interim behaviors.
   b. Negative reinforcement is more effective than positive reinforcement when shaping behavior.
   c. The intensity of reinforcement should be changed when the client performs the next step in shaping the behavior.
   d. All types of reinforcement are more effective than any type of punishment when shaping behavior.

55. Which of the following is an example of differential reinforcement of other behavior?
   a. The RBT chooses a time when the client is hungry to offer food as a reinforcement.
   b. The RBT allows 30 minutes of screen time as a reinforcement for 30 minutes of no negative behavior.
   c. The RBT chooses multiple reinforcements to use at different times throughout the day.
   d. The client engages in a behavior to obtain a positive sensory outcome.

56. Which of the following best exemplifies using differential reinforcement?
   a. When the client performs a new behavior correctly, the RBT reinforces it with an additional piece of candy.
   b. A client does not implement their skills in the classroom, so the RBT does not reinforce their behavior.
   c. After the client engages in acting-out behavior, the RBT directs them to take a break in the hallway.
   d. The client's skill acquisition plan identifies three types of reinforcement that they prefer over generic reinforcement options.

57. An RBT uses event recording to document how many times a client flaps their hands during each session and produces the following data. What type of graph should the RBT use to represent this data?

Session	Instances of Hand Flapping
1	3
2	5
3	1
4	10
5	7
6	17

   a. Line graph
   b. Pie chart
   c. Bar graph
   d. Scatter plot

58. Which of the following is the primary reason that using an electronic medical record system is considered a best practice in HIPAA compliance?
   a. It is easier to stay organized when using an electronic system.
   b. Keeping paper documentation and data sheets is more likely to lead to a data breach.
   c. Insurance companies can process electronic claims more efficiently.
   d. Electronic information can be shared quickly with providers in different states.

59. A 14-year-old neurotypical client who loves exciting rides is struggling to improve her grades. To provide the client with additional incentives to do her homework and study, the RBT and the client's parents create a token economy with in which the client can earn a monthly reward. The client receives tokens from her parents for completing homework assignments and studying before a test. The largest reinforcing reward in this token economy is taking a trip to an amusement park. Which of the following monthly goals is most reasonable for earning the amusement park trip?
   a. Earn 80% of possible tokens.
   b. Receive an A on 2 tests.
   c. Earn every possible token for homework.
   d. Earn an average of 5 tokens per week.

60. Which of the following best describes the purpose of a curriculum-based individualized assessment?
   a. The assessment provides guidelines for teaching the assessed skills that need improvement.
   b. The assessment focuses on the client's academic performance in the classroom.
   c. The assessment is tailored for use with clients participating in a particular program.
   d. The assessment focuses on the client's social skills when in a school environment.

61. What is a key difference between extinction and punishment?
   a. Extinction is a form of punishment.
   b. Extinction can eliminate behavior and punishment cannot.
   c. Extinction requires knowing the behavior's function but punishment does not.
   d. Extinction is only effective for young children, while punishment is effective for clients of all ages.

62. Which of the following statements about using discrete trial training with individuals diagnosed with autism spectrum disorder is true?
   a. The RBT should always hold each therapy session in a different location to practice generalization.
   b. Discrete trial training is effective at teaching basic knowledge and skills but does not improve a client's real-life skills.
   c. All discrete trials during a therapy session should utilize consistent verbiage to reduce variation in the trials' tasks.
   d. Discrete trial procedures are not effective as maintenance exercises and therefore do not need to be taught to a client's parents.

63. An RBT is taking a client on an outing and must decide where to go. One of the client's goals is to improve their math skills so that they can run their own errands. Which of the following activities is most likely to provide an opportunity for the RBT to incidentally support this goal during the outing?
   a. Hiking at a public park
   b. Listening to music
   c. Visiting a local bookstore
   d. Going to the pool

64. How does a dual relationship create a potential ethical conflict?
   a. It facilitates duplicate payment for services in a manner that benefits the RBT.
   b. It puts the client at risk of legal recourse from the organization they receive services from.
   c. It puts the client at risk of harm because they have a relationship with the RBT outside of the professional one.
   d. It puts the client at risk because the RBT is practicing without the appropriate certifications.

65. A client takes a sip from a glass of water. Which of the following is most likely to have been the antecedent that provoked this behavior?
   a. The glass was near the client.
   b. The client watched the RBT drink water.
   c. One of the client's goals is hydration.
   d. The client felt thirsty.

66. An RBT is preparing their office for their first session with a new client. The client completed their assessments with another provider, and the behavior analyst has written the client's first skill acquisition plan. The client is a 7-year-old child. Which of the following should the RBT prioritize while preparing the environment for this session?
   a. Keep a printed copy of the client's skill acquisition plan readily available for reference.
   b. Organize and tidy up any small objects that the RBT believes may distract a child.
   c. Preemptively select and set out a desirable toy based on information in the skill acquisition plan.
   d. Prepare a bin containing objects to be used in discrimination training to fulfill one of the plan's skill goals.

67. A child spits on peers when they feel overwhelmed in the classroom. The technician teaches the child to say "I need to take a walk" instead of spitting. What intervention is this?
   a. Noncontingent reinforcement
   b. Functional communication training
   c. Motivating operations
   d. Differential reinforcement of other behavior

68. An RBT is working with a 20-year-old client on reducing some negative behaviors. The client is driven to the sessions by their mother because they do not have their own car. The RBT is familiar with the mother and often waves hello at drop-off. The mother calls the RBT and requests a copy of the client's records to give to their medical provider. What is the best response?
   a. Request a release of information for the medical provider and send them the record directly.
   b. Explain that they cannot release information and that the request would need to come from the client.
   c. Inquire as to why the medical provider needs the session records because this request is unusual.
   d. Provide the mother with the client's records so she can give the needed information to the medical provider.

69. A client is able to recite the steps for brushing their teeth during sessions with the RBT. At home, they perform this skill consistently. However, their parents report that while visiting the client's grandparents for a week, the client required assistance to brush their teeth. Which of the following is the client struggling with when performing this skill?
   a. Maintenance
   b. Discrimination
   c. Generalization
   d. Implementation

70. Event recording would NOT be effective for documenting which of the following behaviors?
   a. Using the toilet independently
   b. Following the work schedule
   c. Vocalizing to greet a friend
   d. Reporting sickness to an employer

71. Which of the following is NOT required to conduct an individualized social skills assessment?
   a. Interviews with the client's parents or other stakeholders
   b. Observing the client in their regular day-to-day environment
   c. Asking the client about their personal interests and goals
   d. Instructing the client to perform specific tasks to evaluate their responses

72. Which of the following skills could most effectively be broken down into steps and taught using task analysis?
   a. Riding the bus to work
   b. Studying for an exam
   c. Conversing with a friend
   d. Relaxing on the couch

73. When should the behavior technician identify the functions of a client's challenging behavior?
   a. During data collection, to assess if the intervention was effective
   b. Prior to the creation of a behavior reduction plan
   c. After engaging in functional communication training
   d. Once extinction of the behavior has been achieved

74. A 9-year-old client enjoys race cars. The RBT is designing a token economy to improve the client's behavior at school. Which of the following objects is the most suitable token for this token economy?
   a. Small toy cars
   b. Red star stickers on a sheet
   c. Printed photos of race cars
   d. Race car stickers on a sheet

75. Which of the following is NOT typically included in a client's skill acquisition plan?
   a. The contact information of the behavior analyst and the RBT
   b. The reasons for the client's admission into the therapy program
   c. A list of the client's physical and mental diagnoses
   d. The contact information of the client's teachers and parents

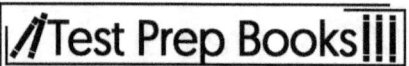

Answer Explanations #3

1. A: Extinction focuses on eliminating a negative behavior by not reinforcing it. An example would be ignoring attempts to get attention that involve aggression, and providing attention at times when the aggressive behavior is not present. Choices *B* and *C* are incorrect because avoidance and compartmentalization are not behavior reduction interventions. Choice *D* is incorrect because positive punishment involves adding a negative stimulus, not taking away a positive one.

2. B: A note should be written following each session. Session notes are part of the client's medical record, and each session should be promptly documented in a note. Choice *A* is incorrect because all sessions require documentation; this is not a decision made by a supervisor or insurance provider. Choice *C* is incorrect because the RBT sees clients weekly, so they will require a note each week, not each month. Choice *D* is incorrect because session notes should be completed following every session, not just when there is a significant change to document.

3. C: A permanent product is the concrete result of behavior. An outcome can be documented with permanent product recording when it is an observable, durable result of a client's behavior (such as improved grades after building a study habit). Choice *A* is incorrect because, while progress can be tracked via documenting the client's output of permanent products, progress itself is not observable data. Choice *B* is incorrect because, while a behavior can be observed and measured and can cause a permanent product, it is not permanent itself. Choice *D* is incorrect because tokens are used as part of a reinforcement plan and are given by a provider, not produced by the client.

4. A: Working with the contractor's child would constitute a dual relationship because the RBT knows the parent outside of the professional setting. It is further complicated because the RBT is paying the parent for a service. Providing services in this situation would constitute an ethical issue of a dual relationship, and is not allowable. The best response is to decline and to offer information to help the contractor get support for their child. Choice *A* is incorrect because, regardless of whether the child feels comfortable with the RBT, this situation constitutes a dual relationship and simply documenting it does not address the ethical concern. Choice *C* is incorrect because there is a dual relationship, and also because the RBT cannot provide services independently of their organization or supervisor. Choice *D* is incorrect because the form of payment for services is not the issue creating the conflict of interest, so it does not matter whether the child has insurance.

5. A: The RBT should ensure that every session of behavioral therapy is related to at least one skill goal in the skill acquisition plan. Choice *B* is incorrect because it is not always necessary to prepare the environment; not all activities benefit from such changes. Choice *C* is incorrect because the RBT should use the principles of incidental teaching to seize such opportunities rather than preparing in advance how to informally practice social skills. Choice *D* is incorrect because the RBT does not need to review a client's individualized assessment prior to every session. While reviewing documentation is important, the RBT should focus on *recent* documentation—such as the client's current skill acquisition plan and notes from recent therapy sessions—rather than an assessment, which is typically documented at the beginning of treatment and may not reflect the skills or challenges that the RBT may work with in an upcoming session.

6. B: Choice *B* is correct because the graph's slope is ascending, rising from the first month to the final month. This visually shows an increase in the number of incident reports. Thus, Choice *A* is incorrect because the number of incidents cannot be both increasing and decreasing. Choice *C* is incorrect

Answer Explanations #3

because the number of incident reports is constant only in March and April, not across all four months. Choice D is incorrect because there are 5 incident reports over a period of 4 months. Thus, the average number of incident reports per month is 1.25.

7. B: Functional communication training is an intervention rooted in differential reinforcement of alternative behavior. It can be used to teach a replacement behavior as a part of behavioral extinction for a negative behavior. Choices A and D are incorrect because cognitive behavioral therapy and narrative therapy are both forms of psychotherapy, not behavior reduction techniques. Choice C is incorrect because a neuropsychological evaluation is a series of diagnostic tests that can provide clarity on neurological diagnoses or disorders.

8. B: The RBT should stop the intervention, calm the client down, and consult with a supervisor about whether a more private setting is needed. Maintaining client dignity is an important part of the RBT's role, and that includes maintaining privacy and ensuring that sessions occur in an appropriate setting. In this case, the best way to maintain client privacy is to stop this situation in which the client's peers have overheard them in a vulnerable situation, and seek supervision to avoid this moving forward. Choice A is incorrect because, while the client may have not reached a level of crisis, continuing without any change is not maintaining their privacy and dignity. Choice C is incorrect because it would be an overstep for the RBT to tell a teacher what to do in their classroom, and the better choice is to change the session location. Choice D is incorrect because, while documentation is always required, this does not address the issue of client privacy and dignity.

9. D: Clinical notes should include objective information, not subjective. For example, "client put their head down on the table and did not answer questions," is an objective statement, whereas "client was in a bad mood and probably upset about school" is subjective. Choices A, B, and C are incorrect because provider credentials, relevant information provided by a parent, and interventions provided during a session are all standard parts of a session note.

10. D: During an individualized assessment, the RBT should always document every attempt a client makes to perform a skill or complete a task because that will ensure that there is comprehensive documentation. Choices A and B are incorrect because only documenting the first or last attempt ignores the other attempts, whether successful or not. Choice C is incorrect because only documenting the client's successful attempts does not provide a full picture of the client's ability to use a skill.

11. C: While certain aspects of behavioral interventions can be challenging for clients, and sometimes negative reinforcement is utilized, there should never be a goal of shaming or embarrassing the client as part of the change process. The RBT should always respect and promote client dignity. Choices A, B, and D are incorrect because they are all examples of maintaining dignity: promoting client privacy, gauging readiness to start the session, and respecting the client's religion and culture.

12. B: Choice B is correct because Sarah's behavior is described in an *objective* manner through the color of her face and the qualification of her shout as *nonverbal*. Choice A is incorrect because *dysregulated* is a subjective conclusion drawn from observations, not an example of objective documentation. For example, a more appropriate version of this account might be a description of Sarah's behaviors followed by the conclusion that the client had become dysregulated. Choice C is incorrect because "tried to forcefully take the toy" does not objectively describe what behavior Sarah used (for example, whether she tried to grab the toy or whether she struck the RBT). Choice D is incorrect for the same reason: the use of *threatening* is a subjective, emotional description rather than an objective description of the client's behavior.

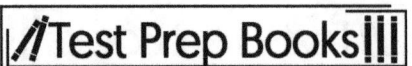

13. A: Behavior that is immediately reinforced will be more likely to continue because the behavior that promoted the reinforcement will be clear. If time has passed and the client has engaged in multiple behaviors, it may not be obvious which one prompted the reward. Choice *B* is incorrect because time of day is not relevant in this instance. Choice *C* is incorrect because reinforcement should happen quickly and predictably, not in a varied or unexpected timeframe. Choice *D* is incorrect because, while certain types of interventions focus on environmental considerations like hunger, that is not generally applicable.

14. C: The methods of reinforcement to be used with a client are usually specified in the client's skill acquisition plan. Choice *A* is incorrect because the most desirable reinforcer may not always be effective or may lose its efficacy if provided too frequently (for example, a child may get bored even of a highly desirable toy). Choice *B* is incorrect because reinforcement methods do not necessarily need to include both conditioned and unconditioned reinforcers. Rather, the RBT should make an individualized decision based on what motivates the client. Choice *D* is incorrect because the most effective reinforcers will already be listed in a client's skill acquisition plan, and all session preparation should be completed before the client arrives.

15. D: The most likely of these metrics to be interpreted as indicative of lethargy is *latency*. Latency is the time between an antecedent and the behavior, so an increased latency indicates that the client is responding to stimuli more slowly. Thus, Choice *D* is correct. Choices *A* and *B* are incorrect because the number of times and how often a client performs a behavior are both likely to decrease if the client is more lethargic. Choice *C* is incorrect because, while the mother's observation might be measured as an increased inter-response time while performing a behavior, it is more likely that she is describing *lethargy* due to a slower response to stimulus (increased latency).

16. B: Session notes should be objective, clear, and specific. The best statement defines the behavior of shoving, specifies the frequency, and does not include judgment or assumptions. Choice *A* is incorrect because it doesn't clearly describe the behavior that occurred and uses a subjective term of *working harder*; even if the note were to include a goal of changing behavior, it should be specific and measurable. Choice *C* is incorrect because *bad mood* is subjective, and the number of times that the behavior occurred should be documented; it is better to be specific about what occurred. Choice *D* is incorrect because it is subjective in the description of being difficult to work with, as well as non-specific. The difficult behavior should be labeled or described rather than using the broad term of *aggression*.

17. A: Respecting a client's culture and religious beliefs is an important part of the RBT's responsibility. In this case, they should work with their supervisor to alter the schedule to avoid causing any tension for the client. Choice *B* is incorrect because, while it is true the RBT does not change the behavioral plan alone, they need to respect their client's religious traditions and work with their supervisor to accommodate the client's needs. Choice *C* is incorrect because, while it may be useful to better understand their client, this does not address the need for the religious tradition of fasting to be respected. Choice *D* is incorrect because documenting a religious tradition as refusal to participate is inaccurate, and it does not reflect the RBT respecting the client's beliefs.

18. A: By moving the object into a different position so that it is more easily noticed by the client, the RBT has used a positional prompt. Choice *B* is incorrect because a motion prompt is not generally recognized as a prompting category—almost all prompts require movement, so the term does not meaningfully identify a particular type of prompt. Choice *C* is incorrect because the RBT has manipulated an object, not made a physical gesture with their hands, body, or face. Choice *D* is incorrect because a physical prompt requires directly assisting a client to perform a skill (for example, using hand-over-hand guidance to move the client's hand up and down to brush their teeth).

19. A: Qualitative data consists of non-numerical and relatively subjective descriptions about a client's behaviors, such as their difficulty or situational appropriateness. Choice A is correct because it describes the behavior's intensity in a non-numerical way. Choice B is incorrect because duration is an objective measurement that provides quantitative data. Choice C is incorrect because the client's grades are a permanent product that other observers can verify, not a subjective description of the client's academic abilities. Choice D is incorrect because analyzing existing data is not a method for documenting new data.

20. A: Understanding the client's history and known triggers will help with crisis planning because it will give insight into how to best maintain safety and avoid a crisis state. This information may also be helpful for safe de-escalation. Choice B is incorrect because, while parental consent is important to obtain when creating a behavior reduction plan for a minor client, it would not be appropriate for the parent to consent to the intervention but not the crisis planning component. Crisis planning is an important part of making the intervention safe. Choice C is incorrect because behavior reduction plans should always include the possibility of crises. Choice D is incorrect because, while information on reinforcement methods would be included elsewhere in the plan, it is not a part of crisis intervention.

21. C: Documentation should not consist entirely of information obtained directly from the client. Relevant information from the parent/guardian or other healthcare providers should also be documented in the notes. For example, if a parent shares at the start of the session that the client is having trouble sleeping due to a medication change, this is relevant and should be documented. Choices A, B, and D are incorrect because they are true about documentation. Notes should be completed promptly and according to agency guidelines, and they are part of the insurance reimbursement process.

22. D: Maintaining client privacy and dignity is a key part of the RBT role. In this situation, the client's privacy is broken because this conversation is happening in a busy waiting room, and it would likely be embarrassing to the client to have their behavior discussed so publicly. Moving the parent to a private space is the best choice. From there, the RBT can determine how to respond and if a supervisor needs to become involved and follow up with the parent about their concerns. Choice A is incorrect because the RBT should not tell the parent what to do, and continuing this conversation in the busy waiting room does not protect client privacy and dignity. Choice B is incorrect because, while it is true that parental input can be important, having this conversation in public is inappropriate even if the parent consents to the setting. Choice C is incorrect because, while supervision would be useful, it does not address the needs of the client in the moment.

23. B: Choice B is correct because the primary benefit of conducting a functional assessment is getting a better understanding of the antecedents and consequences associated with a client's behaviors. These variables can then be altered during behavioral therapy to shape the client's behavior. Choice A is incorrect because, although this statement describes the conditions under which a functional assessment is conducted, it does not describe how that assessment is used to design a treatment plan. Choice C is incorrect because such deficiencies are best identified using an individualized assessment, not a functional assessment. Choice D is incorrect because the combination of direct and indirect assessment methods is not unique to a functional assessment and does not explain how a functional assessment helps the behavior analyst design a treatment plan.

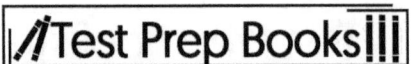

Answer Explanations #3

24. B: Discontinuous recording methods pose the risk of overestimating or underestimating a behavior's frequency. For example, partial interval recording indicates whether the behavior occurred at all during a specific interval. Noting that a behavior occurred even once during an interval can overestimate the behavior because it does not account for the possibility that the intensity or duration was low. If a client claps their hands once during a 1-minute interval, the clapping would be recorded as occurring just as it would if it had lasted the entire interval, an overestimation. Other types of discontinuous recording methods, such as whole interval recording, can underestimate a behavior, as it requires the behavior to occur for the whole interval. Therefore, if a client claps their hands for 50 seconds out of a 1-minute interval, the clapping does not get recorded and therefore the data underestimates the behavior. Choice A is incorrect because both continuous and discontinuous recording methods are used in assessments and during behavioral therapy. Choice C is incorrect because discontinuous recording does not require *short* intervals. Rather, this method simply requires the use of intervals to record behavior (for example, daily attendance at work utilizes partial intervals to record whether the client attended work that day). Choice D is incorrect because discontinuous recording, such as whole interval recording using short intervals, can be used to estimate the duration of a behavior.

25. C: In negative reinforcement, the removal of a stimulus results in a behavior becoming more likely to occur. Choice C is correct because the other children are playing with the client more frequently because an undesired stimulus—the client's angry outbursts—has been removed due to the client's improved social skills. That is, the other children's behavior of playing with the client is reinforced by the absence of the client's outbursts. Choice A is incorrect because the client is receiving positive reinforcement from playing with others. Choice B is incorrect because the parents are also receiving positive reinforcement from being proud of the client. Choice D is incorrect because it is unrelated to negative reinforcement, and does not accurately describe the situation; the parents did not report that the client has been praised by other children after winning a game.

26. A: Choice A is correct because the number of people present in the store is likely relevant as an observable metric about the noise volume and social atmosphere in which the client's behavior took place. Choice B is incorrect because the cleanliness of the store is less relevant to the client's behavior than the number of people in the store. Choice C is incorrect because, although this statement does give an objective description of the time that the RBT and the client arrived, it does not give a description of the environment. Choice D is incorrect because this statement describes James's behavior, not the environment in which he used the behavior (even if information about the environment can reasonably be inferred, such as, "the handicap assist was working").

27. C: Tangible behavior is behavior that gets reinforced because it leads to obtaining a desired object. The kicking and yelling behavior is reinforced by the child getting their favorite toy. Choices A, B, and D are incorrect because they describe different behavior functions. An example of an attention-seeking function would be a child who is kicking and yelling to get their parent to stop spending time with a sibling and provide them with attention. An example of an escape function would be a child who kicks their parent's seat in the car because it results in the parent stopping the car and taking the child out of their car seat. An example of automatic function would be a child who cuts the tags out of their clothes because they are uncomfortable.

28. A: The RBT should talk to their supervisor about the situation and determine how to alter the plan to support the client. The best choice is to pause the intervention and seek supervision input to alter the plan in a way that supports the client's dignity but still helps them reach their goals. Choice B is incorrect because, while it is true that the RBT needs the supervisor to address the plan changes, continuing with the intervention when the client says it is embarrassing them is not appropriate. Choice C is incorrect because the supervisor needs to address the concerns about the plan, not the RBT alone with the client and family. Choice D is incorrect because the supervisor is the one who needs to be consulted to change the plan. The RBT cannot make this change alone even if it is well-documented.

29. C: The RBT does not need to document this information because it is not relevant to the services being provided. A session note has required components that must always be included, but if something occurs in the session that is not relevant to the services, and does not involve the client being at risk of harm or abuse, it does not necessarily need to be included. Notes are a part of a permanent medical record that can be viewed by many parties, and using judgment around what is necessary to include is important. Choice A is incorrect because only relevant content should be included in the notes, not every single statement made by a client. Choice B is incorrect because not only does this content not need to be included in the note, it also describes a subjective account, which is not appropriate in a medical chart. Choice D is incorrect because there is no indicated need for a discussion about relationship safety, nor would this be a typical intervention for behavior analysis services.

30. D: A marble statue, a classical song, and a silk dress are too dissimilar to be useful in a discrimination training exercise and the group is organized conceptually, not based on perceptual differences in the objects (for example, size or color), which also makes it inappropriate for this exercise. Choice A is incorrect because different facial expressions are often used in discrimination training. Choice B is incorrect because this group of body parts is similar enough for a client to recognize similarity (all limbs) yet different enough for the exercise to be used to practice discrimination (different species). Choice C is incorrect because the fruits are similar enough in size, shape, and color to compose an effective group for discrimination training.

31. A: It is important for RBTs to show empathy to their clients. Empathy involves active listening to understand another person's feelings, and is important in building rapport and respecting the client. Listening to the client and why they are struggling and then offering support is a good way to show empathy. Choice B is incorrect because telling the client that they will be happy once they make the changes does not show that the RBT heard or understood what the client is saying about the intervention being difficult. Choice C is incorrect because this is using shame rather than listening, which does not demonstrate empathy. Choice D is incorrect because empathy involves listening to the client and supporting them through hard moments but not necessarily changing the intervention plan if the plan is in their best interest, especially without supervisor support.

32. B: A release of information is a legal form that allows confidential information to be shared between relevant parties if the client or their guardian consents. While medical records (including session notes) are subject to confidentiality and privacy laws, some parties are still able to access session notes as needed. The client's teachers would not be able to view the session note or be updated on progress because there is no release signed. Choice A is incorrect because a legal guardian can request access to medical records if the client is a minor. Choice C is incorrect because insurance providers can access medical records as part of their process to approve payment for services. Choice D is incorrect because it is part of the supervisor's role to oversee the services provided, which includes documentation, and they would have access to the medical record.

33. D: When documenting quotes from a client or stakeholder, it is best to quote short and distinctive phrases because it is most likely that these are recollected accurately. Choice D is correct because the statement documents relevant information with a precise quotation. While a "squinty look" is not necessarily up to the documentation standards expected of an RBT, it is appropriate for use here

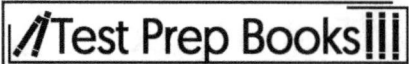

because it is a direct quote from Mr. Harris. Choice A is incorrect because the duration of the indirect assessment is not data about the client. Instead, it is data about the assessment (for example, a short interview may be less relevant). Choice B is incorrect because this paraphrase of the teacher's information does not have adequate precision about the client's reduced tardiness (for example, the length of time since Larry was last tardy). Choice C is incorrect because a full sentence is unlikely to be quoted accurately from memory.

34. D: Of the options given, Choice D—open-ended questions—is the most appropriate when assessing a client's adult caregiver. Choices A and C are incorrect because these methods evaluate the client's preferences by offering a choice of stimuli and so must be applied to the client. Choice B is incorrect because, while it is possible to learn about the client by observing the parent playing with their child, observing the client's independent play is more likely to provide useful information about their preferences.

35. C: Behavior reduction can be a complex process, and sometimes an extinction burst, which is a temporary increase in the negative behavior, occurs before the behavior is reduced or eliminated. Choices A, B, and D are incorrect because these are all true statements; behaviors should be replaced, all behaviors have a function, and change requires consistency.

36. A: RBTs need to report an arrest or legal charge to their licensing and certification board within 30 days. This is an ethical requirement of the profession. Choice B is incorrect because the charges should be reported within 30 days; the RBT cannot wait until the outcome is determined in court. Choice C is incorrect because there is no blanket requirement to resign from all client work because of legal charges; however, RBTs should follow any organizational policies that are stricter than the ethical guidelines. Choice D is incorrect because the obligation to report applies to all legal charges.

37. C: During stimulus control transfer, either the antecedent or the behavior must be controlled to remain the same while the other element is altered. The altered situation is then reinforced by the consequence for the behavior. In this case, the client's ability to share an object should be the control while the antecedent varies. Choices A and B are incorrect because both answers are antecedents. The RBT will use stimulus control transfer to move the client's behavior (handing an object to another child) from one antecedent to another. Choice D is incorrect because praise is a form of reinforcement, which is a consequence and is never a control to remain constant.

38. A: Inquiring about a particular behavior indicates that this question is part of a functional assessment to understand the variables around a behavior, such as the time of day it occurs. Choices B and C are incorrect because these questions are likely part of an individualized assessment providing a broad perspective on the client's abilities. Choice D is incorrect because this question asks about prompting the client in a general sense. It is not part of a functional assessment because the question does not seek information about how prompts are the antecedent to the target behavior.

39. A: RBTs have a responsibility to engage with stakeholders as part of their services provided. A stakeholder is anyone who is engaged with and invested in the client's well-being. The list of stakeholders could include family members, teachers, behavioral health providers, or a pediatrician. Choice B is incorrect because a stakeholder is not necessarily someone responsible for service payment, although it is possible there could be overlap, such as a parent who is paying out of pocket for services. Choice C is incorrect because supervisors would not be considered stakeholders in client care. Choice D is incorrect because, while it is possible for stakeholders to be mentioned in a plan, the term extends far beyond that.

40. A: Initiating a conversation with a classmate during recess once per day is objectively measurable by a teacher and contributes to the client's larger objective of making friends while at school. Choice B is incorrect because, while this skill goal can be used to enhance social skills, it does not encourage the client to engage with other students. Choice C is incorrect because, while improved hygiene is beneficial, as a skill goal it is less directly related to the objective of making new friends as compared to initiating conversations. Choice D is incorrect because this goal does not involve making new friends and happens away from school.

41. B: Storing the data sheets in a lockbox in the trunk of the car is the best option to stay in compliance with privacy and confidentiality requirements when transporting client information. The data sheets contain private client information, and the method of double locking them is the safest choice presented. Choice A is incorrect because, if the car were to be broken into, the sheets would not be secure and could result in a client data breach. Choice C is incorrect because technicians should not store client information in their home. Choice D is incorrect because, although electronic documentation is often more secure, there are instances where using paper data collection is allowed and steps must be taken to protect the information.

42. B: A tidy and organized environment logically has fewer objects available for the client to engage with. This benefits the therapy session by reducing the opportunities for the client to become distracted. Choice A is incorrect because a clean environment on its own does not necessarily increase client engagement. For example, a tidy room has reduced opportunities for distraction but will not necessarily *motivate* a reluctant client to engage with the RBT. Choice C is incorrect because, while reducing tripping hazards is a benefit of cleanliness, it is not common for a room used for behavioral therapy to consistently reach this level of disorganization. Consequently, the RBT does not need to tidy a room prior to the session for the sake of this benefit. Choice D is incorrect because a tidy room does not alter the RBT's opportunities to reinforce client behavior.

43. D: Of the given options, records of a client's bank account would be the most likely to show income and spending behaviors that could be used to assess money management skills. Choice A is incorrect because money management skills cannot be extrapolated from this one piece of information. Choices B and C are incorrect because the client's paystubs and receipts each record only a portion of the client's financial activity. In contrast, the bank account records would demonstrate both income and expenses.

44. A: RBTs need to disclose a physical or mental health problem to their supervisor if it is impairing their ability to provide services. Choice B is incorrect because, while it is possible that a medication could cause impairment that should be disclosed, simply starting a medication is not something that would necessarily have to be shared during supervision. Choice C is incorrect because, while health information is generally private, it does need to be shared if it is impacting the ability to provide services. Choice D is incorrect because a single doctor's appointment would not suggest that the RBT is unable to provide services as usual, and they would therefore not be required to share these health details.

45. B: The antecedent is whatever occurred prior to a behavior. In this situation, the antecedent to the behavior (crying) was the client falling and scraping their knee. Choice A is incorrect because, while going to the park was necessary for this behavior to happen, it did not *cause* the client to cry. Choice C is incorrect because the client's crying best describes their behavior in this situation, not an antecedent to their behavior. Choice D is incorrect because the RBT's concern is the consequence of the client's behavior, which may reinforce their use of crying after injury but did not cause it.

46. A: As with any intervention with a minor child, guardian consent is necessary to implement a behavior reduction plan. It is appropriate to provide education and information on why the plan may be useful, but it is ultimately dependent on guardian consent. Choice B is incorrect because it does not involve obtaining consent. Choice C is incorrect because the focus here should be on working with the guardian, not adapting the plan; there is no indication that the plan is too advanced. Choice D is incorrect because guardian consent is not obtained, and while it may be the right intervention, stating that a behavior reduction plan is the only way to reach improved behavior is not appropriate.

47. B: Positive punishment occurs when a person experiences an undesirable stimulus as a consequence of their behavior. The student's refusal to do their homework resulted in the undesirable stimulus of summer school. Choices A and C are incorrect because a *negative* method of reinforcement consists of the removal of a stimulus. Negative reinforcement removes an undesirable stimulus, while negative punishment removes a desirable stimulus. Choice D is incorrect because this situation's natural consequences do constitute a method of reinforcement—the RBT and the parents decided to intentionally allow the student to experience their choice's consequences.

48. A: The Health Insurance Portability and Accountability Act (HIPAA) is the federal legislation that makes the protection of client privacy a requirement of healthcare providers, which include behavior technicians. Choice B is incorrect because the Family Educational Rights and Privacy Act (FERPA) is focused on school settings and maintaining privacy of educational records. Choice C is incorrect because the Children's Online Privacy Protection Act limits digital collection of information about children who are younger than 13. Choice D is incorrect because, while the Federal Information Security Modernization Act establishes requirements for information security systems, it is not specific to the protection of health information.

49. D: The discrete trial training method breaks a skill down into short, simple tasks as a means of teaching a client to perform a skill. Discrete trial training is not likely to be effective at teaching a client to pay attention for a long period of time (such as a class period) because it is used to teach simple tasks and skills, or more complex tasks and skills that are composed of a series of specific, small tasks that can be chained together. Instead, the RBT should focus on reinforcing attentiveness periodically while increasing the intervals between instances of reinforcement. Thus, Choice A is incorrect. Choice B is incorrect because teaching a client to use attentive body language does not necessarily accomplish the RBT's goal of improving the client's actual ability to pay attention. Choice C is incorrect because discrete trial training is useful for improving social and communication skills—such as practicing social behavior or learning how to respond to someone—as well as physical skills.

50. A: When using partial interval sampling, the RBT simply records whether the behavior occurred during a specified period. Partial intervals are effective because they require little effort on the part of parents, teachers, etc. to document. Choices B and D are incorrect because event recording and continuous measurement entail documenting every instance of a behavior, which often is not realistic outside of the clinical setting. Choice C is incorrect because momentary time sampling assesses whether a behavior is happening at the end of an interval, which is not well suited for recording the overall frequency of a behavior.

51. D: The RBT should implement prompt fading when a client is capable of attempting the skill independently but while prompts are still beneficial for attempting the skill. Choices A and B are incorrect because most prompts are a reminder to implement the skill, not a method of correcting the use of the skill, so the client's independent *attempts* to perform the skill—rather than their ability to *perform* the skill correctly—will guide prompt fading. Choice C is incorrect because a single instance of using the skill without a prompt does not necessarily mean that the client is ready for the RBT to implement prompt fading. More practice is needed before the RBT begins to fade the prompt.

52. C: *Discriminative stimulus* is a concept concerning a reminder of the reinforcement that is available. It can take many different forms, but in this example, seeing the candy container serves as a reminder of the reinforcement that will be provided following the behavior. It helps cue the positive behavior associated with accessing the candy, and makes the intervention more likely to be successful. Choice A is incorrect because an extinction burst is the phenomenon that negative behavior sometimes increases briefly before reducing during this type of intervention. Choice B is incorrect because, while the concept of motivating operations also focuses on the reinforcement, this term refers to environmental changes that can increase or decrease the value of the reinforcement. An example of using motivating operations would be offering candy as a reinforcement when the client is hungry. Choice D is incorrect because it refers to behavior function, which is the reason that a behavior is happening. While there is an example of a tangible function of behavior here, that is not the best answer because the intervention of keeping the candy in view to prompt the positive behavior is a clear example of discriminative stimulus, not behavior function.

53. B: Discrete trial training helps clients become competent in a skill in a specific environment. Generalization is necessary for these skills so the client can use them in other environments. For example, if a client can raise their hand when prompted in the RBT's office, the goal of generalization is for the client to raise their hand independently in their teacher's classroom. Choice A is incorrect because discrete trial training is not used exclusively for teaching physical behaviors. Choice C is incorrect because identifying differences between types of stimuli is the goal of discrimination training, not discrete trial training. Choice D is incorrect because generalization is not a prerequisite for discrete trial training.

54. C: A core principle of shaping is that the client's behavior should be reinforced each time they make further progress toward performing the desired behavior. Providing a more desirable reinforcement after the client achieves a new stage in shaping the behavior increases the client's desire to continue performing the new behavior. Choice A is incorrect because shaping is always conducted by reinforcing the client's use of interim behaviors. Reinforcing interim behaviors is how the client's initial abilities are shaped into performing the target behavior. Choices B and D are incorrect because no single type of reinforcement or punishment (whether positive or negative in either category) is intrinsically more effective when implementing shaping. The efficacy of these types of reinforcement is contingent on what motivates the client, not on the teaching method.

55. B: Differential reinforcement of other behavior is an intervention that provides a reinforcement for avoiding a behavior for a specified amount of time. Choices A, C, and D are incorrect because they discuss reinforcement interventions that are not focused on a specific time interval.

56. A: Differential reinforcement is implemented by providing different intensities of reinforcement depending on the behavior performed by the client. For example, if a client performs a behavior correctly, their behavior is reinforced by time with a desirable toy. If the client instead performs a new, more preferred behavior, the RBT provides a *more desirable* toy. By differentiating the reinforcement, the RBT continues to incentivize the client to use old behavior while providing *increased* incentive to use the new behavior so that they will implement the new behavior more frequently. Thus, Choice A is correct because offering an additional piece of candy for performing a new behavior is an example of differential reinforcement. Choice B is incorrect because withholding reinforcement is not an example of differentiating the intensity of reinforcement. Choice C is incorrect because it is not clear whether *taking*

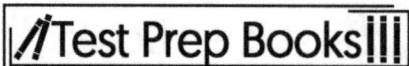

a break is an example of reinforcement or punishment. For example, taking a break may exemplify negative reinforcement of the acting-out behavior because the client wanted to be removed from an undesired stimulus. Choice *D* is incorrect because the skill acquisition plan's individualization of reinforcement methods does not exemplify *using* differential reinforcement. The skill acquisition plan is merely describing three reinforcement methods that have been identified as being preferred by the client.

57. A: A line graph is used to show change over time. In this case, a line graph should be used to show the different values (how many times the client flaps their hands) for each session and demonstrate how this changes as the sessions progress. Choice *B* is incorrect because a pie chart will not provide meaningful information; pie charts show parts of a whole and this data does not include a *whole* to be analyzed. Choice *C* is incorrect because a bar graph is more effective for comparing different categories, not change over time. Using a line graph is a more effective means of representing the data. Choice D is incorrect because a scatter plot represents data with shared x-axis values, not a change over time.

58. B: Paper documentation and data sheets are more likely to lead to a data breach. HIPAA is legislation that requires healthcare providers to maintain privacy of client records and health information and holds providers accountable for data breaches. Paper charts and data collection methods are less secure, and therefore more likely to lead to a breach of client information, which means that an electronic system is more likely to comply with HIPAA requirements. Choices *A*, *C*, and *D* are incorrect because they are not directly related to maintaining patient privacy. Organization, quicker insurance claim processing, and information sharing across a long distance are all useful features of an electronic system, but not relevant to patient privacy.

59. A: This token economy is designed to reinforce the client's performance of academic behaviors (completing homework and studying). Earning 80% of possible tokens is the most reasonable goal because it does not require perfect behavior from the client. This incentivizes her to continue working toward the goal throughout the month even if she misses some opportunities to earn a token. Choice *B* is incorrect because the token economy is meant to reward the client's use of academic behaviors, not her actual grades, which may not accurately reflect her homework and studying. Choice *C* is incorrect because the system would no longer be effective during any given month once the client fails to earn a token for any single homework assignment or study opportunity. Choice *D* is incorrect because it does not account for the number of opportunities the client may be given to earn a token each week, which is not specified in the scenario and may be up to the client's parents' discretion. So if, for example, the client's parents offer a token for both studying and doing homework each of the 5 evenings of the school week, requiring 5 tokens per week would stipulate 100% compliance, which would be unreasonable for the same reason as for choice *C*.

60. A: A curriculum-based assessment is used to analyze the client's current skills and provides relevant educational materials for the behavior analyst and other service providers to use to build an individualized curriculum for the client. Thus, Choice *A* is correct. Choices *B* and *D* are incorrect because individualized assessments in applied behavior analysis typically focus on a client's overall functioning, not their functioning in a single environment (like school). Choice *C* is incorrect because a curriculum-based assessment is used to determine the methods by which education should be provided. The program is built in response to the assessment rather than the assessment being tailored to suit a particular program.

61. C: Extinction requires knowing the behavior's function. Extinction is a method of behavior reduction or replacement that withholds reinforcement of the negative behavior to create change. For this intervention to work, the behavior's function must be known so that reinforcing it can be avoided. Choice A is incorrect because extinction is not a form of punishment. Choice B is incorrect because both extinction and punishment can lead to behavior reduction. Choice D is incorrect because extinction can work for people of any age.

62. C: Giving directions the same way during each task is frequently beneficial when implementing discrete trial training with individuals diagnosed with autism spectrum disorder (ASD). Using the same words, facial expressions, gestures, and so on helps clients with ASD identify the new information in each trial's directions. Consequently, consistent verbiage improves the client's ability to perform the task. Choice A is incorrect. A consistent, controlled environment is key to effective discrete trial training. While it is important to help a client generalize their new skills, this should only be done if the client is ready, based on their current ability level. Choice B is incorrect because discrete trial training is effective for teaching and practicing skills for use in real-life situations. Choice D is incorrect because discrete trial procedures are very effective as maintenance exercises. It is beneficial to teach a client's parents to conduct discrete trials for a few minutes to help practice and maintain skills.

63. C: A bookstore is the location most likely to result in the client wanting to make a purchase, which would allow the RBT to implement incidental teaching to support the client's math skill goal and to help them work toward running errands independently. Choices A, B, and D are incorrect because no details are provided to suggest that the client will want to make a purchase at these outdoor events or while listening to music.

64. C: Dual relationships are an ethical conflict that should be avoided. A dual relationship exists when the RBT has a relationship with their client or a key stakeholder outside of the professional services provided. For example, if an RBT is also the babysitter of a client, or is in a romantic relationship with a client's caregiver, this would be a dual relationship. Choice A is incorrect because a dual relationship is about multiple (professional and personal) relationships existing, not about the RBT being paid twice. Choice B is incorrect because a dual relationship does not create a risk that the client would be in legal trouble. Choice D is incorrect because an RBT can be appropriately certified and still engage in multiple relationships that create ethical issues.

65. D: While all four answer choices could be antecedents to the behavior, it is most likely that feeling thirsty provoked the behavior because thirst is an unconditioned stimulus to seek hydration. Choice A is incorrect because, while the glass's proximity is necessary for the client to perform the behavior, that proximity is less likely to be the stimulus that most immediately provoked the behavior. Choice B is incorrect because, while the client may have sipped water after the RBT's modeling prompt, it is more likely that the client drank due to thirst. Choice C is incorrect because it is less likely that remembering a goal will directly influence behavior than an unconditioned stimulus.

66. B: When preparing for the first session with a new client, the RBT ought to prepare the environment to be neutral and inviting. An organized environment reduces distractions while building therapeutic rapport with the client during the first session. Choice A is incorrect because the RBT should not need a copy of the skill acquisition plan for quick reference—they should have reviewed any relevant information during their session preparation. Choice C is incorrect because the RBT should not offer reinforcement to a client prior to engaging them in conversation or activities. Choice D is incorrect because, during the first session, the RBT's goal should be to build therapeutic rapport; they do not need to prepare for discrimination training exercises for this session.

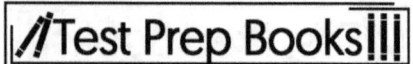

Answer Explanations #3

67. B: Functional communication training is an intervention based on differential reinforcement of alternate behavior. It involves teaching an appropriate behavior, typically a verbal command, to replace the negative behavior while achieving the same function. Both the spitting and the verbal statement of asking to take a walk achieve the escape function. Choice A is incorrect because noncontingent reinforcement is a technique that involves providing the reinforcement often and unrelated to behavior; that is not the case here because the reward of leaving the room happens after the client engages in the target behavior of voicing their request. Choice C is incorrect because the use of motivating operations is not a behavioral intervention on its own, it is a tool that helps support effective interventions by choosing conditions where the reinforcement is more valued. An example would be using food-based rewards when a client is hungry. Choice D is incorrect because differential reinforcement of other behavior is a reduction intervention that focuses on avoiding the negative behavior for a specified time frame, which is not the case in this example.

68. B: The RBT should explain that they cannot release information and that the request would need to come from the client. Once someone is over the age of 18, they are in charge of their own medical records, which their parent cannot access. If the parent has a release of information form, or is the child's guardian, they could have access; however, no indication of these circumstances is given. Choice A is incorrect because the parent cannot sign a release of information on behalf of their adult child in this situation; only the client can. Choice C is incorrect because, regardless of the reason for the request, the parent is not allowed to access the client's medical records without the client's consent. Choice D is incorrect because medical records cannot be disclosed in this situation; it would be a privacy violation.

69. C: The client is struggling to generalize brushing their teeth from their home environment to their grandparents' house. Although the client can recite the skill's steps, it is possible that they have memorized the list without internalizing its meaning. Choices A and D are incorrect because the client's consistent toothbrushing at home indicates that the client is not struggling with maintenance or implementation. Choice B is incorrect because the change of environment is not a task typically requiring discrimination. Rather, *discrimination* typically refers to the ability to discern different objects within an environment.

70. B: Event recording measures how many times a behavior occurs, so it is best suited for behaviors that have a clear and distinct beginning and end. Following a schedule is an ongoing, multi-step behavior, so event recording is not well suited for documenting it. Choice A is incorrect because it is easy to observe and document whether a client required assistance to use the toilet. Choice C is incorrect because the beginning and end of the vocalization make the event easy to identify. Choice D is incorrect because the client's report of illness to an employer is a distinct instance of using their communication skills (even if it is unlikely that the RBT would be asked to record this particular behavior).

71. C: Questions about the client's interests are typically part of a preference assessment, not a social skills assessment. Interviewing stakeholders, observing the client, and directing the client to perform tasks are all common components of social skills assessments. Thus, Choices A, B, and D are incorrect.

72. A: Task analysis can be used to break down riding the bus into small, concrete steps like "look up the bus's pick-up time" and "walk to the bus stop." Choice B is incorrect because the steps used in studying are largely internal, making the task difficult to analyze as a behavior. Choice C is incorrect because a social interaction is open-ended—a conversation could go any direction—and thus not an effective target of task analysis. However, task analysis might be more effective when analyzing *beginning* a conversation. Choice D is incorrect because, while task analysis could be used to break down the steps involved in lying down on the couch, it would not be effective for teaching someone to actually achieve relaxation.

73. B: The function of the behavior should be identified at the start of the process, prior to the creation of a behavior reduction plan. Understanding the behavior's function is essential to making a plan to eliminate it and selecting appropriate alternative behaviors and interventions. Choices A and D are incorrect because both suggest identifying behavior function after engaging in different interventions. Choice C is incorrect because behavior function must be known in order to implement functional communication training.

74. D: Race car stickers engage the client's interest and are a symbolic object that can easily be tracked by the client's teachers and/or parents. Choice A is incorrect because a toy car is an example of a terminal reinforcer of behavior, not a token, which is a generalized conditioned reinforcer that can be exchanged for more desirable, terminal reinforcers. While a token should immediately reinforce behavior, it should not be considered a reward in itself. Because of the client's interest in race cars, the toy itself is desirable, rather than as a token to be exchanged later. Instead, race car stickers can be exchanged for a toy car later on. Choice B is incorrect because, although the color red is often associated with racing, this color association does not necessarily engage the client based on their skill acquisition plan interest in race cars. Choice C is incorrect because, due to the client's age, it is reasonably likely that the client may misplace the photos.

75. D: The parents' contact information is not typically included in the skill acquisition plan, but it is recorded elsewhere in the client's documentation. Choice A is incorrect because the professional contact information of the behavior analyst and the RBT is often listed on the skill acquisition plan for the sake of the parents and other providers. Their personal contact information, however, is not listed. Choice B is incorrect because the reasons for a client's admission are summarized as the client's overall behavior therapy objectives. Choice C is incorrect because both physical and mental medical conditions are included to help provide a full description of the client's abilities and limitations.

Dear RBT Test Taker,

Thank you for purchasing this study guide for your RBT exam. We hope that we exceeded your expectations.

Our goal in creating this study guide was to cover all of the topics that you will see on the test. We also strove to make our practice questions as similar as possible to what you will encounter on test day. With that being said, if you found something that you feel was not up to your standards, please send us an email and let us know.

We would also like to let you know about other books in our catalog that may interest you.

ASWB Bachelors

This can be found on Amazon: amazon.com/dp/1628458836

CPCE

amazon.com/dp/1637759428

NCE

amazon.com/dp/1637757204

NCMHCE

amazon.com/dp/1637759207

We have study guides in a wide variety of fields. If the one you are looking for isn't listed above, then try searching for it on Amazon or send us an email.

Thanks Again and Happy Testing!
Product Development Team
info@studyguideteam.com

Online Resources & Audiobook Access

Included with your purchase are multiple online resources. This includes all three practice tests in interactive format and this study guide in audiobook format. We also have a convenient study timer to help you manage your time.

Scan the QR code or go to this link to access this content:

testprepbooks.com/online378/rbt

The first time you access the tests, you will need to register as a "new user" and verify your email address.

If you have any issues, please email support@testprepbooks.com.

www.ingramcontent.com/pod-product-compliance
Lightning Source LLC
Chambersburg PA
CBHW060327240426
43665CB00047B/2756